Microsoft® Official Academic Course: Implementing and Administering Security in a Microsoft® Windows® Server™ 2003 Network (70-299)

Lab Manual

Craig Zacker

PUBLISHED BY
Microsoft Press
A Division of Microsoft Corporation
One Microsoft Way
Redmond, Washington 98052-6399

Printed and bound in the United States of America.

2 3 4 5 6 7 8 9 QWT 9 8 7 6 5

Distributed in Canada by H.B. Fenn and Company Ltd.

A CIP catalogue record for this book is available from the British Library.

Microsoft Press books are available through booksellers and distributors worldwide. For further information about international editions, contact your local Microsoft Corporation office or contact Microsoft Press International directly at fax (425) 936-7329. Visit our Web site at www.microsoft.com/learning/. Send comments to *moac@microsoft.com*.

Product Planners: Linda Engelman and Lori Oviatt
Project Editor: Kathleen Atkins
Project Manager: Carmen Reid for nSight, Inc.

SubAssy Part No. X11-04147
Body Part No. X11-04148

CONTENTS

LAB 1

PLANNING AN AUTHENTICATION STRATEGY

This lab contains the following exercises and activities:

- Lab Exercise 1-1: Installing Network Monitor
- Lab Exercise 1-2: Capturing Network Traffic
- Lab Exercise 1-3: Capturing Kerberos Traffic
- Lab Exercise 1-4: Modifying Default Domain Policies
- Lab Exercise 1-5: Testing Password Policies
- Lab Review Questions
- Lab Challenge 1-1: Using Kerberos Tools
- Lab Challenge 1-2: Restricting Authentication Protocols

SCENARIO

As the new network administrator for Contoso, Ltd., your primary objective is to tighten up the security of the corporate network. To achieve this end, you decide to install Network Monitor and examine the traffic on the network. After starting work, the first thing you notice is that the password policies imposed on the network users are too severe. As a result, you decide to implement a new set of password policies throughout the company domain.

After completing this lab, you will be able to:

- **Install Network Monitor**
- **Capture and examine network traffic**
- **Modify and test password policies**

Estimated lesson time: 95 minutes

BEFORE YOU BEGIN

The classroom lab for this course is split up into student domains, each of which consists of two computers. The student domains are children of a classroom domain called contoso.com. The names of the student computers in the classroom are numbered consecutively, beginning with Computer01 and Computer02. Each student domain consists of one lower-numbered computer, referred to throughout this manual as Computer*xx*, and one higher-numbered computer, referred to as Computer*yy*. Computer*xx* has been configured as the domain controller for a child domain called domain*xxyy*.contoso.com, where *xx* and *yy* are the numbers your instructor assigned to the two computers in the domain.

To complete this lab, you will need:

- The Windows Server 2003 Resource Kit Tools installation file (Rktools.exe), supplied by your instructor.

EXERCISE 1-1: INSTALLING NETWORK MONITOR

Estimated completion time: 15 minutes
In this exercise, you will install and configure Network Monitor on your Computer*xx* server, so you can capture and analyze network traffic samples throughout this course.

1. Log on to one of your student computers as **Administrator**, using **P@ssw0rd** as the password.
2. Click Start, point to All Programs, point to Accessories, and then click Command Prompt.

   The Command Prompt window appears.
3. In the Command Prompt window, type **ipconfig /all** and then press ENTER.

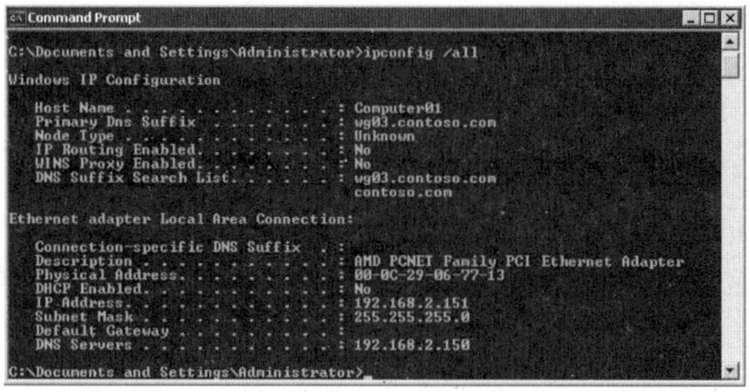

4. Make a copy of the following table and fill in the information for this computer in the First Computer column.

	First Computer	Second Computer
Host Name		
Primary DNS Suffix		
IP Address		
Subnet Mask		
DNS Server		

5. Log on to the other computer, again using the Administrator account and password, and repeat steps 2 and 3.

   Fill in the information for this computer in the Second Computer column.

6. Click Start, point to Control Panel, and select Add or Remove Programs.

   The Add Or Remove Programs dialog box appears.

7. Click Add/Remove Windows Components.

   The Windows Components Wizard launches.

8. Scroll down in the Components list and select Management And Monitoring Tools, and then click Details.

   The Management And Monitoring Tools dialog box appears.

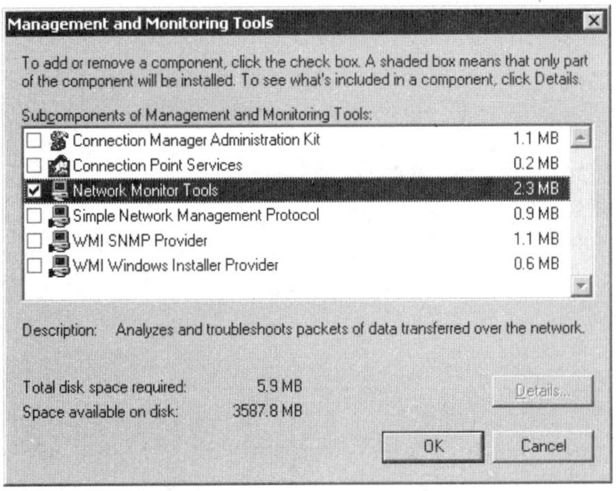

9. Select the Network Monitor Tools check box, and then click OK to close the dialog box.

10. Click Next.

The Configuring Components page appears as the wizard begins to copy the appropriate files. After a short delay, an Insert Disk message box appears and instructs you to insert the Microsoft Windows Server 2003 installation CD-ROM into the drive.

11. Click OK to display the Files Needed dialog box.

12. Type **C:\win2k3\i386** in the Copy Files From text box, and then click OK.

The wizard continues copying files.

> **NOTE Using C:\win2k3\i386** The C:\win2k3\i386 folder on both of the computers in your student domain contains the installation files for Windows Server 2003. At any time during the course, when one of your computers prompts you to insert the Windows Server 2003 installation CD-ROM, you can browse to this folder instead.

13. Click Finish to close the wizard and complete the installation. Then close the Add Or Remove Programs dialog box.

14. Click Start, point to All Programs, point to Administrative Tools, and then click Network Monitor.

A Network Monitor window opens and a message box appears instructing you to specify the network from which you want to capture data. Network Monitor captures all of the frames sent to or from the network interface you choose.

15. Click OK to close the message box.

The Select A Network dialog box appears.

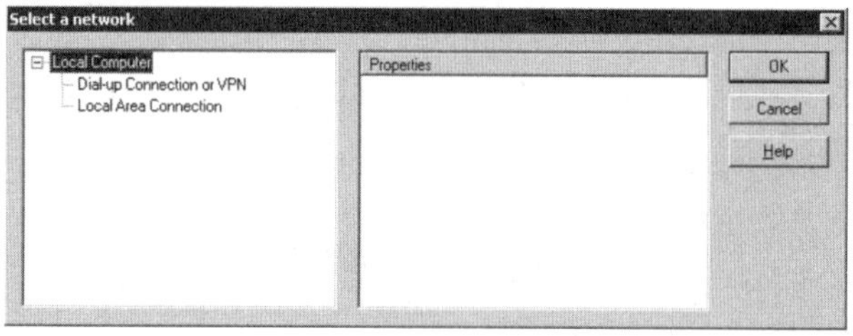

16. Expand the Local Computer heading and select the Local Area Connection interface in the left pane. Then click OK.

A Local Area Connection Capture Window appears.

17. From the Capture menu, select Buffer Settings.

A Capture Buffer Settings dialog box appears.

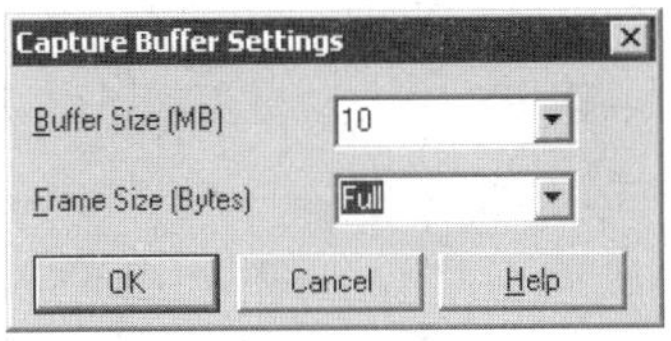

18. Change the Buffer Size (MB) setting from 1 (its default value) to 10, and then click OK.

    The capture buffer is an area of the hard disk where Network Monitor temporarily saves the frames it captures from the network. By default, the capture buffer is only 1 MB in size, but you have just increased its size to 10 MB, enabling you to capture more frames at one time. You can increase the size of the capture buffer further as needed, as long as you have sufficient disk space on the drive.

19. Leave Network Monitor open for the next exercise.

EXERCISE 1-2: CAPTURING NETWORK TRAFFIC

Estimated completion time: 15 minutes

Contoso does not own any protocol analysis software other than the Network Monitor program included with Windows Server 2003. Because you have never used this product before, you begin your analysis of the network's traffic by practicing with the software, capturing traffic samples and examining their contents.

1. On Computer*xx*, in Network Monitor, select Start from the Capture menu.

   Network Monitor begins capturing data.

   > **NOTE Starting a Capture** *To start a capture, you can also click the Start Capture icon on the toolbar or press F10.*

2. Click Start, and then click Windows Explorer.

   A Windows Explorer window appears.

3. Browse to the classroom's Windows Server 2003 computer (Server01) by expanding My Network Places, Entire Network, Microsoft Windows Network, and the Contoso domain.

4. Expand the Server01 icon and select the Win2k3 share. Then copy the Eula.txt file from the I386 folder in the Win2k3 share on Server01 to

the Win2k3\I386 folder on your server's C drive, overwriting the existing copy of the file.

5. Return to Network Monitor and, from the Capture menu, select Stop.

> **NOTE Stopping a Capture** To stop a capture, you can also click the Stop Capture icon on the toolbar or press F11.

6. Based on the information shown in the Capture Window, answer the following questions:

> **QUESTION** How many frames were captured to the buffer?

> **QUESTION** How can you tell how many frames were captured to the buffer?

> **QUESTION** How much space is left in the capture buffer?

> **QUESTION** How can you tell how much space is left in the buffer?

7. In Network Monitor, from the Capture menu, select Display Captured Data.

   A Capture: # (Summary) window appears, where # is the number of the capture in the current Network Monitor session. The window contains the data you just captured.

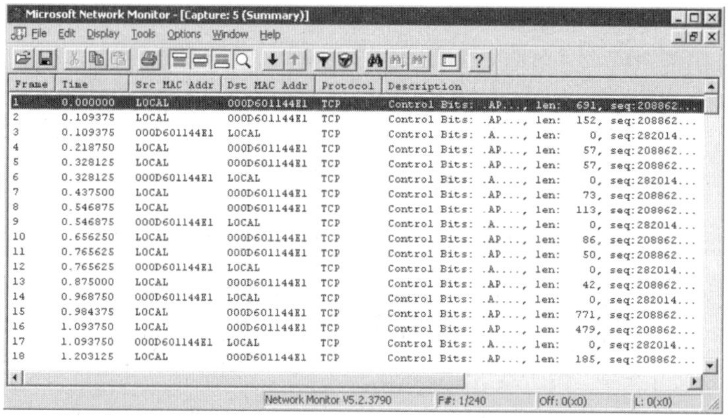

> **NOTE Displaying Captured Data** In addition to selecting Display Captured Data, you can click the Display Captured Data icon on the toolbar or press F12 to display the data you have already captured. When a capture is running, you can also stop the capture process and display the captured data in one step by selecting Stop And View from the Capture menu, clicking the Stop And View Capture button, or pressing SHIFT+F11.

8. Scroll down in the Capture: # (Summary) window until you see frames mentioning the file name Eula.txt in the Description column, and then select the next frame that contains the values shown in the following table:

Dst MAC Addr	Protocol	Description
LOCAL	NBT	SS Session Message Cont.

This frame contains part of the Eula.txt file you copied from Server01 to your server while Network Monitor was capturing frames.

QUESTION *What is the size of the message contained in the frame you selected (as specified in the Description column)?*

9. Double-click the frame you selected.

The window splits into three panes (or segments), as follows:

- ❑ Summary pane—Contains the frame listing you were just viewing.
- ❑ Detail pane—Contains the interpreted contents of the frame.
- ❑ Hex pane—Contains the raw contents of the frame.

Summary Pane

Detail Pane

Hex Pane

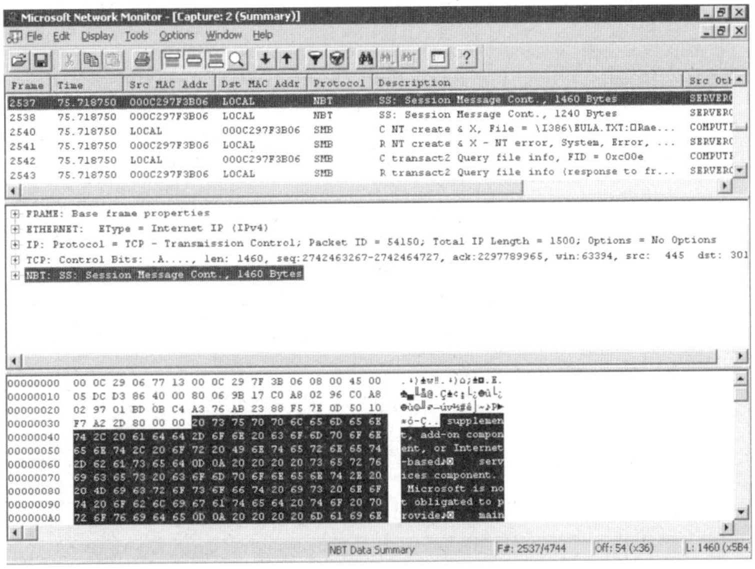

10. Take a screen shot (press ALT+PRINT SCREEN) of the entire Microsoft Network Monitor window. Next paste it into a WordPad document named Domain*xxyy*Lab01-1.rtf (where *xx* and *yy* are the numbers assigned to the computers in your student domain), which you will turn in at the end of the lab.

11. Click the plus sign (+) next to the FRAME: Base Frame Properties entry in the Detail pane.

    The FRAME: Base Frame Properties entry is expanded. This pane contains general information about the captured frame.

    QUESTION What is the total length of the frame you selected?

    QUESTION How many bytes of the frame are added during the data encapsulation process? How can you tell?

12. Select the ETHERNET entry in the Detail pane.

    Notice that selecting the ETHERNET entry in the Detail pane also causes the bytes corresponding to the Ethernet header to be highlighted in the Hex pane.

    QUESTION What are the values of the first six bytes in the currently highlighted area of the Hex pane?

    NOTE Reading Hexadecimal Notation Remember that in hexadecimal notation, each byte is represented by two characters, so six bytes of data are expressed as six two-character strings.

13. Expand the ETHERNET entry in the Detail pane.

    Network Monitor displays the contents of the Ethernet header fields.

    QUESTION What is the value of the Destination Address field in the Ethernet header?

    QUESTION How does this value compare with the first six bytes of raw hexadecimal data you recorded earlier?

14. Select the IP entry in the Detail pane.

    Notice that the Hex pane display changes to highlight the raw data that makes up the IP header fields.

QUESTION As you move down past FRAME in the Detail pane entries, you move higher in the Open Systems Interconnection (OSI) reference model, with each successive entry representing a different protocol. For each of the following OSI model layers, specify what protocol is operating in the frame you are currently analyzing.

1. Data-link
2. Network

3. Transport
4. Application

NOTE ***Protocols and Encapsulation*** Not all frames have only a single protocol operating at a given OSI model layer, as in this example. In some cases, two or more protocols operate at the same layer. The use of multiple protocols at the same layer in one frame most commonly occurs at the application layer, but it can occur at the network layer as well.

QUESTION Which protocol provides the outermost header in the frame you are currently analyzing? How can you tell?

15. Select the NBT entry in the Detail pane.

    The NBT message data is highlighted in the Hex pane.

    QUESTION Why does the NBT message data appear in the Hex pane as clear, readable text, while the data generated by the other protocols does not?

16. From the File menu, click Save As.

    A Save As dialog box appears.

17. Type **Lab1** in the File Name text box, and then click Save.

    Network Monitor copies the contents of the capture buffer to the Lab1.cap file in the C:\Documents and Settings\Administrator\My Documents\My Captures folder.

18. Leave the Network Monitor window open for the next exercise.

EXERCISE 1-3: CAPTURING KERBEROS TRAFFIC

Estimated completion time: 15 minutes

You are in the process of installing a new member server on the Contoso network, and you decide to use Network Monitor to capture the traffic generated by the server as you join it to the domain and log on. By analyzing this traffic, you can ensure that the authentication traffic between the computer and the domain controller is properly encrypted.

1. In Network Monitor on your Computer*xx* server, from the Capture menu, select Start to begin capturing frames.

2. On your Computer*yy* server, click Start, point to Control Panel, and click System.

   The System Properties dialog box appears.

3. Click the Computer Name tab and then click Change.

   The Computer Name Changes dialog box appears.

4. Click the domain option and type **domain*xxyy*** in the accompanying text box, where *xx* and *yy* are the numbers assigned to the computers in your student domain by your instructor. Then click OK.

   Another Computer Name Changes dialog box appears, prompting you for the user name and password of an account with permission to join the domain.

5. In the User Name text box type **Administrator**. In the Password text box, type **P@ssw0rd**. Then click OK.

   A message box appears, welcoming you to the domain.

6. Click OK to close the message box.

   Another message box appears, prompting you to restart the computer.

7. Click OK twice to close the message box and the System Properties dialog box.

8. Click Yes to restart the computer.

9. After Computer*yy* restarts, log on using the domain*xxyy* domain Administrator account and the password P@ssw0rd.

   Make sure you click the Options button and change the value in the Log On To selector to domain*xxyy* when logging on.

10. When the logon process is complete, move back to Network Monitor on the Computer*xx* server and, from the Capture menu, choose Stop And View.

11. From the Display menu, select Filter.

    The Display Filter dialog box appears.

> **NOTE Using Display Filters** A display filter is a Network Monitor feature that enables you to specify which frames in a captured traffic sample the program should display. Using display filters makes it easier to locate specific frames in a large traffic sampling.

12. Click the Expression button, and then click the Property tab.

13. Scroll down the Protocol: Property list and double-click the UDP entry.

14. Select the Destination Port property, click the decimal option, and set the value to 88. Then click OK.

15. Click the OR button, and then click Expression.

16. Set the Source Port property for UDP to a decimal value of 88, and then click OK.

    Port 88 is the well-known port number for the Kerberos authentication protocol, as defined by the Internet Assigned Numbers Authority (IANA).

17. Click OK to close the Display Filter dialog box.

    QUESTION What happens?

18. Take a screen shot (press ALT+PRINT SCREEN) of the entire Microsoft Network Monitor window. Next paste it into a WordPad document named Domain*xxyy*Lab01-2.rtf (where *xx* and *yy* are the numbers assigned to the computers in your student domain), which you will turn in at the end of the lab.

19. Double-click one of the frames to display its contents.

    QUESTION What protocols are displayed in Network Monitor's Hex pane?

    QUESTION Why doesn't the application layer protocol (Kerberos) appear in the display?

20. Close Network Monitor without saving the contents of the capture buffer.

EXERCISE 1-4: MODIFYING DEFAULT DOMAIN POLICIES

Estimated completion time: 15 minutes

After making a general review of Contoso's network policies, you find that the default password policies imposed by Windows Server 2003 are impractical for your organization. In this exercise, you modify the default password policy values for your student domain, relaxing the security level.

1. On your Computer*xx* server, click Start, point to Administrative Tools, and click Domain Security Policy.

   The Default Domain Security Settings console appears.

2. In the console tree, expand the Account Policies icon and select Password Policy.
3. In the following table record the domain's current password policy settings.

Password Policy	Value
Enforce Password History	
Maximum Password Age	
Minimum Password Age	
Minimum Password Length	
Password Must Meet Complexity Requirements	
Store Passwords Using Reversible Encryption	

4. Double-click the Maximum Password Age policy, and change the value to 7. Then click OK.
5. Double-click the Minimum Password Age policy, and change the value to 0. Then click OK.
6. Double-click the Minimum Password Length policy, and change the value to 9. Then click OK.
7. Double-click the Password Must Meet Complexity Requirements policy, and change the value to Disabled. Then click OK.
8. Take a screen shot (press ALT+PRINT SCREEN) of the Default Domain Security Settings console with your new password policy settings displayed. Next paste it into a WordPad document named Domain*xxyy*Lab01-3.rtf (where *xx* and *yy* are the numbers assigned to the computers in your student domain), which you will turn in at the end of the lab.

   QUESTION What are the default Account Lockout Policy settings for the domain?

9. Close the Default Domain Security Settings console.
10. Restart the computer.

EXERCISE 1-5: TESTING PASSWORD POLICIES

Estimated completion time: 20 minutes

Having modified the password policies for the network after hours, you must test them before the users arrive in the morning and attempt to log on.

1. On your Computer*xx* server, click Start, point to Administrative Tools, and click Active Directory Users And Computers.

   The Active Directory Users And Computers console appears.

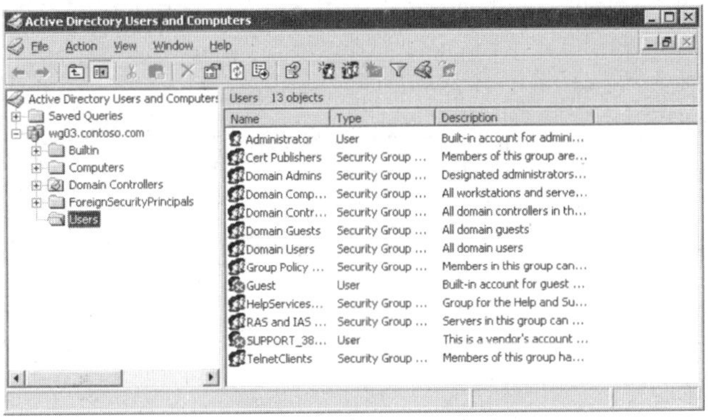

2. In the console tree, expand the icon for your domain (domain*xxyy*.contoso.com, where *xx* is the number assigned to your student domain).
3. Click the Users container and, on the Action menu, point to New and click User.

   The New Object–User Wizard appears.

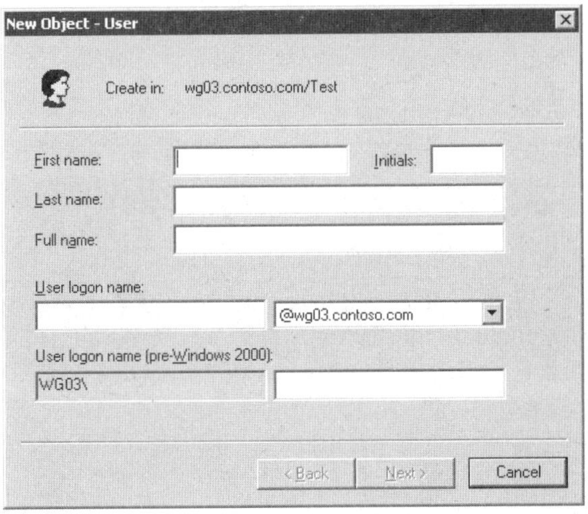

4. Complete the user property fields in the wizard using the values in the following table. Then click Next.

Property	Value
First Name	Mark
Last Name	Lee
Full Name	Mark Lee
User Logon Name	Mlee

5. In the Password and Confirm Password fields, type **markleepass** and click Next, leaving all of the other settings at their default values. Then click Finish.

QUESTION *What happens?*

6. Double-click the Mark Lee object.

   The Mark Lee Properties dialog box appears.

7. Click the Member Of tab, and then click Add.

   The Select Groups dialog box appears.

8. Type **Domain Admins** and click OK.
9. Click OK again to close the Mark Lee Properties dialog box.
10. Create another new user object in the Users container, entering the following values and leaving all other settings at their defaults.

Property	Value
First Name	Don
Last Name	Hall
Full Name	Don Hall
User Logon Name	Dhall
Password	Password

QUESTION *Why were you unable to create the user object?*

11. Click Back and change the password to **donhallpass**, and then click Next and Finish to create the user object.

    QUESTION *What happens?*

12. Open the Domain Security Settings console again, and change the value of the Password Must Meet Complexity Requirements policy to Enabled.
13. Restart the Computer*xx* server.
14. After the Computer*xx* server has restarted, restart the Computer*yy* server.
15. On Computer*yy*, log on to the domain*xxyy* domain using the Mark Lee account you created earlier.

    QUESTION *What happens?*

16. Click OK.

    The Change Password dialog box appears.

17. In the New Password and Confirm New Password dialog boxes, type **markleepass1** and click OK.

    QUESTION *What is the result?*

18. Click OK.
19. In the Change Password dialog box, type **markleepass** in the Old Password text box.
20. In the New Password and Confirm New Password dialog boxes, type **mlpass#111**, then click OK.

    QUESTION *What happens?*

LAB REVIEW QUESTIONS

Estimated completion time: 15 minutes

1. In Exercise 1-5, what would have happened if you had created the new Mark Lee user account without having previously modified the default domain password policies?

2. Assume that the Account Lockout policies for your domain are set to the values shown in the following table. What changes could you make to the policy values that would increase the security of the network? Explain your answer.

Account Lockout Policy	Value
Account Lockout Duration	0
Account Lockout Threshold	3 invalid logon attempts
Reset Account Lockout After	5 minutes

3. In Exercise 1-5, you were unable to change the password for the Mark Lee account to markleepass1. In what ways did this password not conform to the domain password policies?

4. Would lowering the value of the Enforce Password History policy increase or decrease the security of the network? Explain your answer.

LAB CHALLENGE 1-1: USING KERBEROS TOOLS

Estimated completion time: 15 minutes

1. On your Computer*xx* server, install the Windows Server 2003 Resource Kit Tools by executing the Rktools.exe file supplied by your instructor and following the instructions of the Windows Resource Kit Tools Setup Wizard.

2. Run the Kerbtray.exe program and take a screen shot (press ALT+PRINT SCREEN) of the Kerberos Tickets dialog box. Next paste it into a WordPad document named Domain*xxyy*Lab01-4.rtf (where *xx* and *yy* are the numbers assigned to the computers in your student domain), which you will turn in at the end of the lab.

3. Select the entry for the Kerberos ticket-granting ticket (TGT), Krbtgt, for the Administrator user, and click the tabs to examine the ticket's properties.

   QUESTION When is the TGT scheduled to expire?

   QUESTION What flags are set for the TGT?

4. Run the Klist.exe program with each of the available command-line parameters.

   QUESTION What happens when you run Klist with the tickets parameter?

   QUESTION What happens when you run Klist with the tgt parameter?

5. Take a screen shot (press ALT+PRINT SCREEN) of the Command Shell windows with the Klist output displayed. Next paste it into a WordPad document named Domain*xxyy*Lab01-5.rtf (where *xx* and *yy* are the numbers assigned to the computers in your student domain), which you will turn in at the end of the lab.

LAB CHALLENGE 1-2: RESTRICTING AUTHENTICATION PROTOCOLS

Estimated completion time: 10 minutes

Using the Default Domain Security Settings console, configure your domain controller to accept NTLMv2 authentication and to refuse LM authentication. When you are finished, take a screen shot (press ALT+PRINT SCREEN) of the console showing your changes. Next paste it into a WordPad document named Domain*xxyy*Lab01-6.rtf (where *xx* and *yy* are the numbers assigned to the computers in your student domain), which you will turn in at the end of the lab.

LAB 2

AUTHORIZATION STRATEGIES

This lab contains the following exercises and activities:

- Lab Exercise 2-1: Creating User Accounts
- Lab Exercise 2-2: Creating Share Permissions
- Lab Exercise 2-3: Testing Share Permissions
- Lab Exercise 2-4: Examining NTFS Permissions
- Lab Exercise 2-5: Creating Account Groups
- Lab Exercise 2-6: Creating Resource Groups
- Lab Exercise 2-7: Nesting Groups
- Lab Review Questions
- Lab Challenge 2-1: Raising the Domain Functional Level

SCENARIO

In the past, the network administrators at Contoso, Ltd., have used a variety of methods to provide users access to file system resources: some used share permissions, while others assigned NTFS file system (NTFS) permissions directly to user objects. As the new administrator for the company, you plan to standardize authentication with the Account Group/Resource Group permission assignment method, in which account groups contain users as members and resource groups containing the account groups as members have the permissions needed to access the file system resources. By making the account groups members of the resource groups, you can grant users the access they need without assigning permissions to individual user objects.

After completing this lab, you will be able to:

- Create Active Directory users and groups
- Create and manage share permissions
- Create and manage NTFS permissions
- Create account groups and resource groups

Estimated lesson time: 105 minutes

BEFORE YOU BEGIN

To complete this lab, you will need the table of information you gathered in Exercise 1-1 in Lab 1, "Authentication Strategies."

EXERCISE 2-1: CREATING USER ACCOUNTS

Estimated completion time: 15 minutes

Contoso has recently hired some new employees, and you are responsible for providing them with access to the corporate network. The first step of this process is to create a user account for each of the new hires.

1. On Computer*xx*, log on to the domain*xxyy* domain as Administrator, using **P@ssw0rd** as the password.
2. Click Start, point to Administrative Tools, and click Active Directory Users And Computers.

   The Active Directory Users And Computers console appears.
3. Select the Users container and, on the Action menu, point to New and click User.

   The New Object–User Wizard appears.
4. Enter the information for the first user in the following table into the text boxes on the first page of the wizard. Then click Next.

First Name	Last Name	User Logon Name
Max	Benson	maxb
Cynthia	Randall	cynthiar
Judy	Lew	judyl
Deborah	Poe	deborahp
Katie	Jordan	katiej

5. In the Password and Confirm Password text boxes, type **password#1**.
6. Clear the User Must Change Password At Next Logon check box and click Next. Then click Finish.

QUESTION What happens?

7. Repeat steps 3 to 6 to create the other four user accounts listed in the table.

   Use the same password for all five user accounts.

NOTE Supplying Passwords Because this lab is concerned with authorization and not authentication, for the sake of convenience use the same password for all five user objects. On a production network, this practice is not acceptable unless you require users to change their passwords during their first logon.

8. Close the Active Directory Users And Computers console.

EXERCISE 2-2: CREATING SHARE PERMISSIONS

Estimated completion time: 15 minutes

Contoso has a file server that uses the FAT file system, so individual file and folder permissions are not available. Therefore, to control access to the server, you are required to use share permissions. In this exercise, you create a file system share on Computer*xx* and use share permissions to control access to it.

1. On the Computer*xx* server, click Start and then click Windows Explorer.

   The Windows Explorer window opens.

2. Browse to the C drive in My Computer and select the Win2k3 folder.

3. From the File menu, select Properties.

   The Win2k3 Properties dialog box appears.

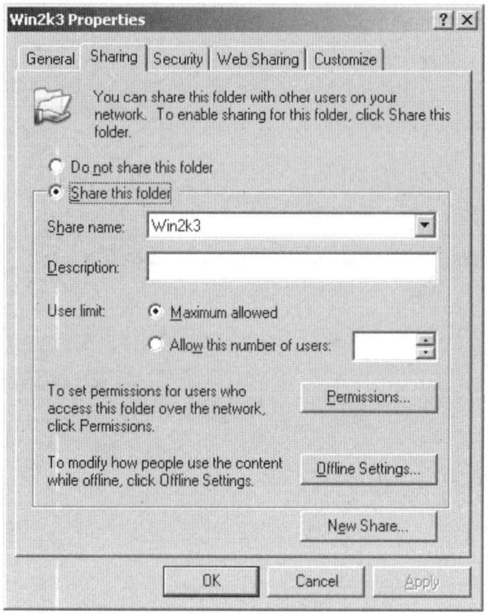

4. Click the Sharing tab and select the Share This Folder option.
5. Leave the default Share Name value (Win2k3) and click Permissions.

   The Permissions For Win2k3 dialog box appears.

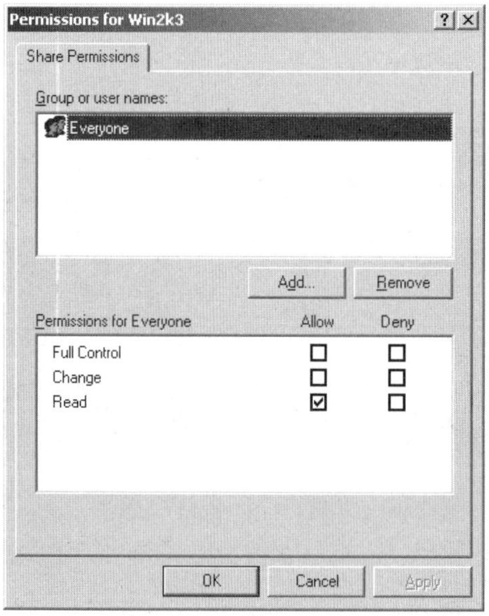

6. Click Remove to delete the Everyone security principal. Then click Add.

   The Select Users, Computers, Or Groups dialog box appears.

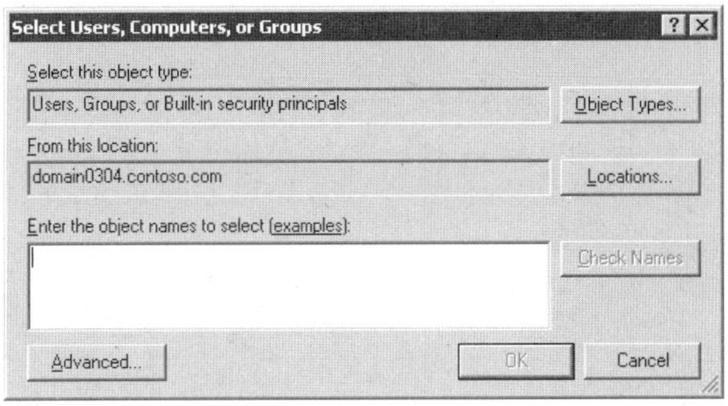

7. In the Enter The Object Names To Select field, type **deborahp** and click Check Names.

   QUESTION *What happens?*

8. Click OK.

   The Deborah Poe security principal is added to the Group Or User Names list.

   QUESTION *What share permissions is Deborah Poe granted by default?*

9. Select the Full Control check box in the Allow column and click Apply.
10. Click Add again and, in the Enter The Object Names To Select field, type **judyl;maxb;katiej** and click Check Names.

    QUESTION *What happens?*

11. Click OK.

    The three users you specified appear as security principals in the Group Or User Names list.

12. Select each of the three new security principals in turn and verify that each one has been granted the Read permission in the Allow column. Then click Apply.

13. Using the same technique, add the Cynthia Randall account as a security principal and assign it the Full Control permission in the Deny column.

14. Take a screen shot (press ALT+PRINT SCREEN) of the Permissions For Win2k3 dialog box containing all of the security principals you just added. Next, paste it into a WordPad document named Domain*xxyy*Lab02-1.rtf (where *xx* and *yy* are the numbers assigned to the computers in your student domain), which you will turn in at the end of the lab.

15. Click OK.

    A Security message box appears, warning you that the deny permissions you are assigning take precedence over allow permissions.

16. Click Yes to continue, then click OK to close the Win2k3 Properties dialog box.

EXERCISE 2-3: TESTING SHARE PERMISSIONS

Estimated completion time: 15 minutes

Contoso has a file server that uses the FAT file system, so individual file and folder permissions are not available. Therefore, to control access to the server, you are required to use share permissions. In this exercise, you examine the functionality provided by the share permissions you assigned to your users in Exercise 2-2.

1. On the Computer*yy* server, log on to the domain*xxyy* domain using the Cynthia Randall account you created in Exercise 2-1.

2. Open Windows Explorer, browse My Network Places, and try to access the Win2k3 share on Computer*xx*.

    QUESTION What happens?

3. Log off Computer*yy* and then log on to the domain again using the Max Benson account.

4. Open Explorer and try to access the Win2k3 share on Computer*xx*.

    QUESTION What happens?

5. Browse to the I386 folder in the Win2k3 share and try to open the Eula.txt file in Notepad.

QUESTION What is the result? Why?

6. Browse to the C:\Win2k3\I386 folder on Computer*yy* and attempt to copy the Eula.txt file to the I386 folder in the Win2k3 share on the Computer*xx* server.

QUESTION What happens? Why?

7. Log off Computer*yy* and then log on to the domain using the Deborah Poe account.
8. Open Windows Explorer, browse to the I386 folder in the Win2k3 share, and try to open the Eula.txt file in Notepad.

QUESTION What happens? Why?

9. Try to copy the Eula.txt file from the C:\Win2k3\I386 folder on Computer*yy* to the I386 folder in the Win2k3 share on Computer*xx*.

QUESTION What is the result? Why?

10. Leave the user Deborah Poe logged on for the next exercise.

EXERCISE 2-4: EXAMINING NTFS PERMISSIONS

Estimated completion time: 15 minutes

Before you can implement your new system of NTFS permissions on the Contoso network, you must determine what permissions are already in place. In this exercise, you examine the permissions for the Deborah Poe user account you created earlier.

1. On the Computer*xx* server, open Windows Explorer and browse to the computer's C drive.

2. Select the C:\Win2k3 folder and, from the File menu, select Properties.

   The Win2k3 Properties dialog box appears.

3. Click the Security tab.

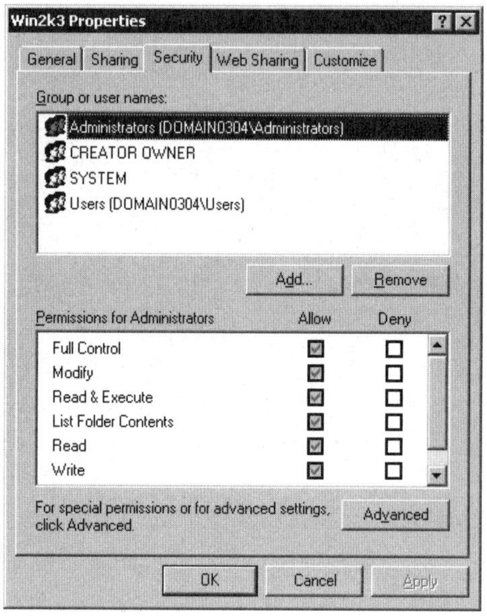

QUESTION Which of the security principals in the Group Or User Names list is responsible for supplying Deborah Poe with her NTFS permissions to the Win2k3 folder?

QUESTION Explain how Deborah Poe receives the permissions she posesses.

QUESTION What standard permissions has the Users group been granted to the Win2k3 folder?

4. Click Advanced.

   The Advanced Security Settings For Win2k3 dialog box appears.

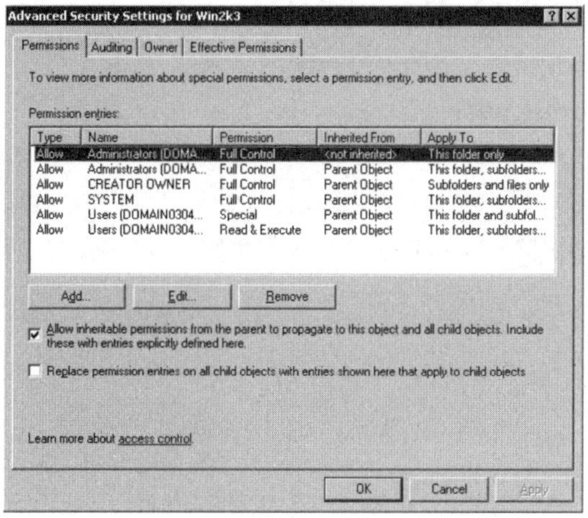

QUESTION What special permissions to the Win2k3 folder does Deborah Poe possess?

QUESTION Explain how you determined Deborah Poe's special permissions.

5. Take a screen shot (press ALT+PRINT SCREEN) of the dialog box displaying the special permissions assigned to the Deborah Poe user. Next, paste it into a WordPad document named Domain*xxyy*Lab02-2.rtf (where *xx* and *yy* are the numbers assigned to the computers in your student domain), which you will turn in at the end of the lab.
6. Close the Advanced Security Settings and Win2k3 Properties dialog boxes.
7. On Computer*yy*, try to copy the Eula.txt file from the C:\Win2k3\I386 folder to the root of the Win2k3 share on Computer*xx*.

QUESTION What is the result?

8. Log off Computer*yy*.

EXERCISE 2-5: CREATING ACCOUNT GROUPS

Estimated completion time: 10 minutes

As part of your plan to implement an Account Group/Resource Group authorization strategy on the Contoso network, you first must create global security groups that gather together users with similar network resource requirements.

1. On Computer*xx*, open the Active Directory Users And Computers console.
2. Select the Users container and, on the Action menu, point to New and click Group.

   The New Object–Group dialog box appears.

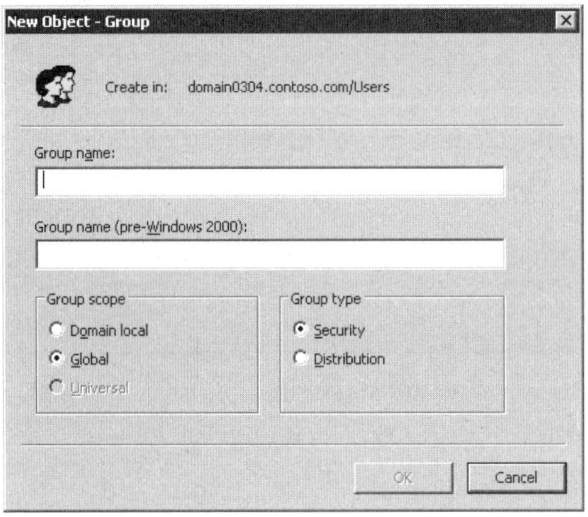

3. In the Group Name text box, type **Trainees**.
4. Click OK, leaving the default Group Scope and Group Type settings in place.

   The Trainees group appears in the Users container.

5. Select the Trainees group you just created and, from the Action menu, choose Properties.

   The Trainees Properties dialog box appears.

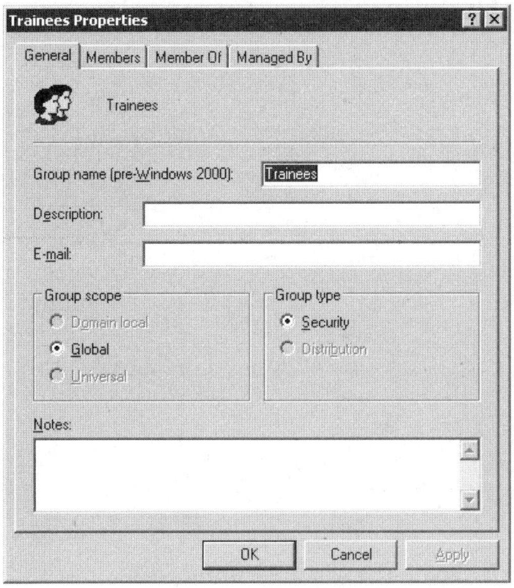

6. Click the Members tab, and then click Add.

   The Select Users, Contacts, Or Computers dialog box appears.

7. Type **judyl;maxb;katiej** in the Enter The Object Names To Select field and click OK.

   QUESTION What happens?

8. Click Add again and attempt to add the Domain Users group as a member of the Trainees group.

   QUESTION Why can't you add the Domain Users group to the Trainees group?

9. Click OK to close the Trainees Properties dialog box.

10. Using the same technique, create another global security group called **Trainee Mgrs** with Deborah Poe as the group's only member.

EXERCISE 2-6: CREATING RESOURCE GROUPS

Estimated completion time: 10 minutes

As the next step in your plan to implement an Account Group/Resource Group authorization strategy on the Contoso network, you must create the domain local groups that you will use to provide varying degrees of access to network resources, and assign NTFS standard permissions to those groups.

1. In the Active Directory Users And Computers console on Computer*xx*, create two domain local security groups in the Users container with the following names:
   - Win2k3 Users
   - Win2k3 Admins
2. In Windows Explorer, open the Properties dialog box for the C:\Win2k3 folder and click the Sharing tab.
3. Click Permissions and, in the Permissions For Win2k3 dialog box, remove the five user objects you added as security principals in Exercise 2-2.
4. Click Add and add the Win2k3 Users and Win2k3 Admins groups as security principals.
5. Grant both groups the Full Control permission to the share and click OK.

> **QUESTION** *Why is it prudent to grant all users the Full Control share permission to the Win2k3 folder?*

6. In the Win2k3 Properties dialog box, click the Security tab.
7. Add the Win2k3 Users and Win2k3 Admins groups to the list of security principals.
8. Select the Win2k3 Admins security principal in the Group Or User Names list and then select the Full Control checkbox in the Allow column.
9. Select the Win2k3 Users security principal in the Group Or User Names list.
10. Ensure that only the checkboxes listed in the following table are selected, and then click OK.

Allow	Deny
Read & Execute	Write
List Folder Contents	
Read	

A message box appears, warning you of the ramifications of using Deny permissions.

11. Click Yes to assign the permissions.

> **NOTE Applying Permissions** There will be a delay as Microsoft Windows Server 2003 applies the permissions you have specified to all of the files and subfolders in the Win2k3 folder.

EXERCISE 2-7: NESTING GROUPS

Estimated completion time: 10 minutes

Once you've created the required account and resource groups, the next steps in implementing an Account Group/Resource Group authorization strategy on the Contoso network are to use group memberships to provide your users with access to the network resources they need, and then to test that access.

1. On Computer*xx*, in the Active Directory Users And Computers console, open the Properties dialog box for the Win2k3 Users domain local group and add the Trainees global group as a member.
2. In the same way, open the Properties dialog box for the Win2k3 Admins domain local group and add the Trainee Mgrs group as a member.
3. On Computer*yy*, log on to the domain*xxyy* domain using the Deborah Poe account you created in Exercise 2-1 and attempt to access the Win2k3 share.

> **QUESTION** Can you read files in the Win2k3 share?

> **QUESTION** Can you delete the Eula.txt file you copied to the root of the Win2k3 share earlier?

> **QUESTION** Can you copy a new Eula.txt file to the Win2k3 share?

4. Log off Computer*yy* and log on again using the Judy Lew account you created in Exercise 2-1.

5. Try to access the Win2k3 share just as you did with the Deborah Poe account.

QUESTION *Can you read files in the Win2k3 share?*

QUESTION *Can you delete the Eula.txt file from the root of the Win2k3 share?*

QUESTION *Can you copy a new file to the Win2k3 share?*

6. Log off Computer*yy*.

LAB REVIEW QUESTIONS

Estimated completion time: 15 minutes

1. After setting up the account groups and resource groups as detailed in this lab, suppose that the current trainee manager, Deborah Poe, decides to leave the company and Max Benson is promoted to her position. What must you do to grant Max the permissions previously assigned to Deborah?
2. In Exercise 2-7, why can't you make the domain local groups members of the global groups, instead of the other way around?
3. In Exercise 2-3, using the Deborah Poe account, you attempted to copy the Eula.txt file from the C:\Win2k3\I386 folder on Computer*yy* to the I386 folder in the Win2k3 share on the Computer*xx* server, and this attempt failed. However, in Exercise 2-4, Deborah was able to copy a file to the root of the Win2k3 share. Which special permissions account for the difference between these two results?
4. When creating resource groups, why is it preferable to use domain local groups instead of machine local groups?
5. What would happen if you added Deborah Poe to the Trainees group as well as the Trainee Mgrs group?

LAB CHALLENGE 2-1: RAISING THE DOMAIN FUNCTIONAL LEVEL

Estimated completion time: 30 minutes

To expand the functionality of the account groups and resource groups you created in this lab, you want to be able to grant groups of trainees from multiple domains access to the Win2k3 folder on the Computer*xx* server. To do this, you plan to create a universal group that contains the global groups from the various domains and make the universal group a member of the Win2k3 Users resource group. However, before you can do this, you must raise the functional level of the domain, so that domain local groups can have universal groups as members.

To complete this challenge, follow these steps:

1. Raise the functional level of your student domain to Windows Server 2003.
2. Create a Universal group called All Trainees and make the Trainees group a member.
3. Remove the Trainees group from the Win2k3 Users group.
4. Make the All Trainees group a member of the Win2k3 Users group.
5. Test the configuration by logging on to the domain using one of the trainee accounts and attempting to access the Win2k3 folder.
6. Draw a diagram illustrating the relationships of all of the groups, users, and resources involved in this configuration.

LAB 3

DEPLOYING AND TROUBLESHOOTING SECURITY TEMPLATES

This lab contains the following exercises and activities:

- Lab Exercise 3-1: Creating a Security Templates Console
- Lab Exercise 3-2: Creating an RSoP Console
- Lab Exercise 3-3: Copying a Security Template
- Lab Exercise 3-4: Deploying a Template Using Group Policies
- Lab Exercise 3-5: Copying a System Configuration Using Secedit.exe
- Lab Review Questions
- Lab Challenge 3-1: Deploying the Workstation Template Using Group Policies

SCENARIO

As the new network administrator for Contoso, Ltd., one of your primary objectives is to increase the level of security throughout the company network. Toward this end, you have decided to create a series of security templates for the various roles that the company's computers perform. The security configurations are to be based on existing settings and predefined templates. Before implementing your plan on the production computers, you set up a test network on which you can experiment with various methods of creating, modifying, and deploying the security templates.

After completing this lab, you will be able to:

- Create and modify security templates using the Security Templates snap-in
- Deploy a security template using group policies
- Copy a system configuration and deploy a security template using Secedit.exe

Estimated lesson time: 110 minutes

BEFORE YOU BEGIN

To complete this lab, you will need the table of information you gathered in Exercise 1-1 in Lab 1, "Authentication Strategies."

EXERCISE 3-1: CREATING A SECURITY TEMPLATES CONSOLE

Estimated completion time: 15 minutes

To create and manage security templates, you must use the Security Templates snap-in for Microsoft Management Console (MMC). However, Windows Server does not include a predefined console containing this snap-in. In this exercise, you create a Security Templates console that you will use throughout this lab to work with security templates and their settings.

1. On Computer*xx*, log on to the domain*xxyy* domain as Administrator and, when prompted, type **P@ssw0rd** as the password.
2. Click Start and point to Administrative Tools.

   QUESTION How many entries are there in the Administrative Tools program group?

3. Click Start, then click Run.

   The Run dialog box appears.

4. Type **mmc** in the Open text box and click OK.

   An empty Console1 window appears.

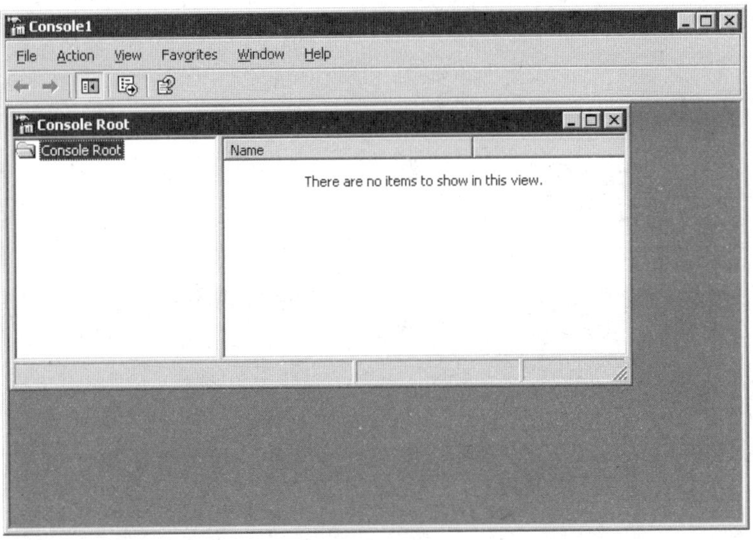

5. From the File menu, select Add/Remove Snap-In.

   The Add/Remove Snap-In dialog box appears.

6. Click Add.

   The Add Standalone Snap-In dialog box appears.

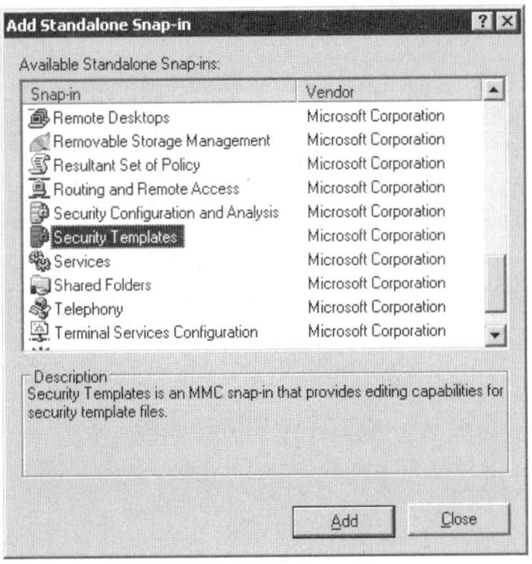

7. Scroll down the Available Standalone Snap-Ins list, and select Security Templates. Then click Add.

8. Click Close to close the Add Standalone Snap-In dialog box.

9. Click OK to close the Add/Remove Snap-In dialog box.

   The Security Templates snap-in appears in the Console1 window.

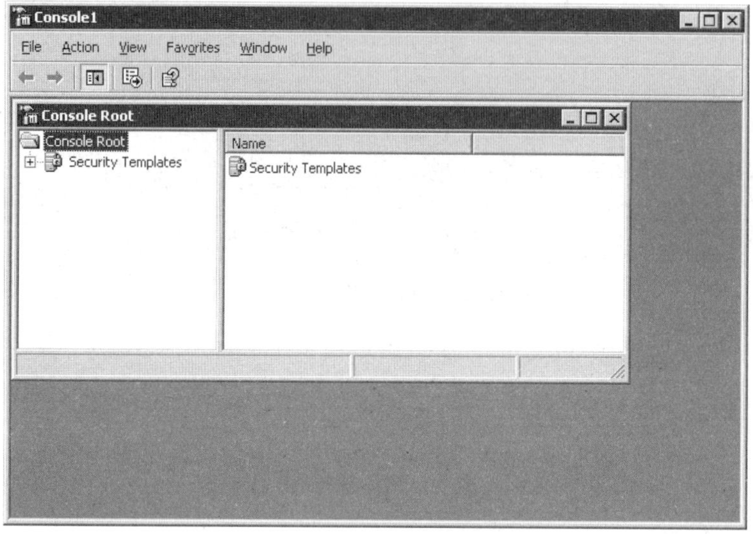

10. Take a screen shot (press ALT+PRINT SCREEN) of the console window, and then paste it into a WordPad document named Domain*xxyy*Lab03-1.rtf (where *xx* and *yy* are the numbers assigned to the computers in your student domain), which you will turn in at the end of the lab.

11. From the File menu, select Save As.

    A Save As dialog box appears.

12. In the File Name text box, type **Security Templates.msc** and click Save.

13. Click Start and point to Administrative Tools again.

> **QUESTION** How many entries are there in the Administrative Tools program group now?

14. Click Start, point to All Programs, and then point to Administrative Tools.

QUESTION How many entries are there in this program group?

QUESTION How do you account for the discrepancy?

15. Leave the Security Templates console open for the next exercise.

EXERCISE 3-2: CREATING AN RSOP CONSOLE

Estimated completion time: 10 minutes

In this exercise, you create another MMC console containing the Resultant Set Of Policy (RSoP) snap-in, so that you can see current policy settings for your lab network's domain controller.

1. On the Computer*xx* server, open a blank MMC console and add the RSoP snap-in, using the same procedure as in Exercise 3-1.
2. Save the new console using the name RSoP.msc.

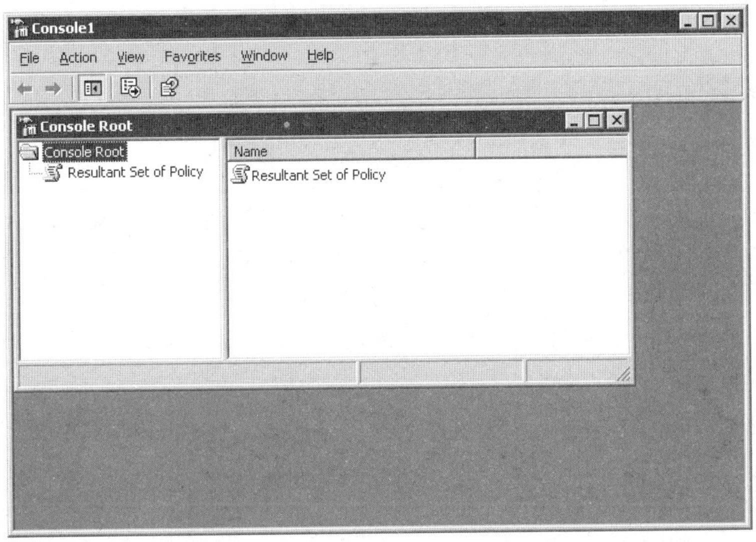

3. Select the Resultant Set Of Policy node in the Scope pane and, from the Action menu, select Generate RSoP Data.

   The Resultant Set Of Policy Wizard appears.

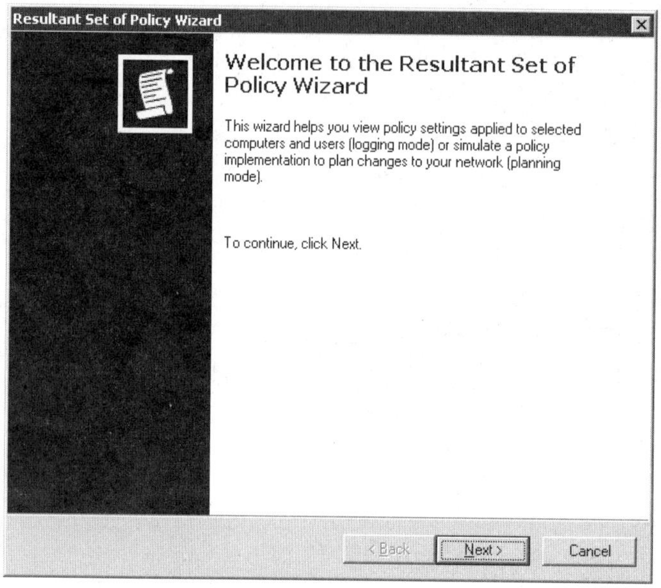

4. Click Next to bypass the Welcome page.

   The Mode Selection page appears.

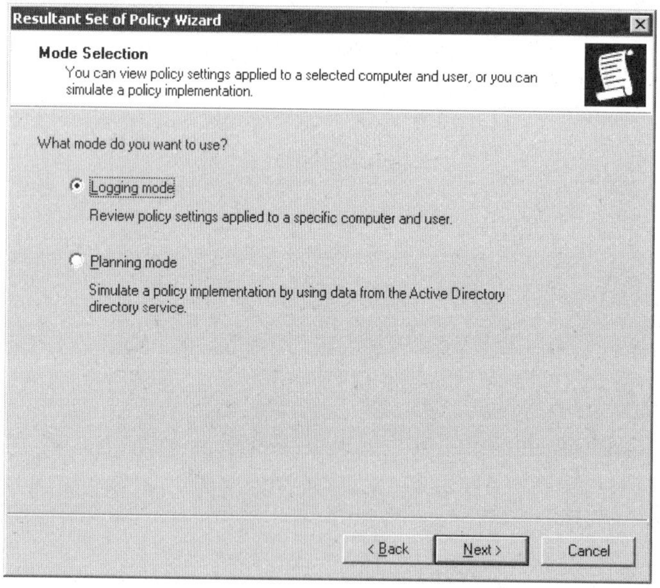

5. Click Next to accept the default option, Logging Mode.

   The Computer Selection page appears.

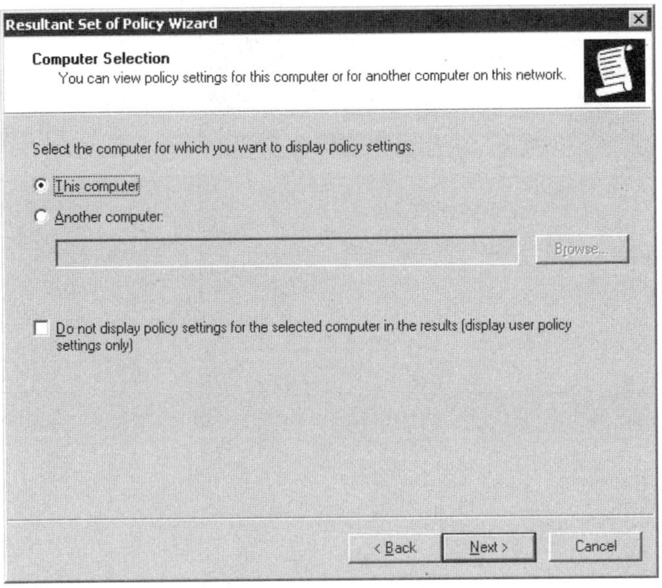

6. Click Next to accept the default option, This Computer.

   The User Selection page appears.

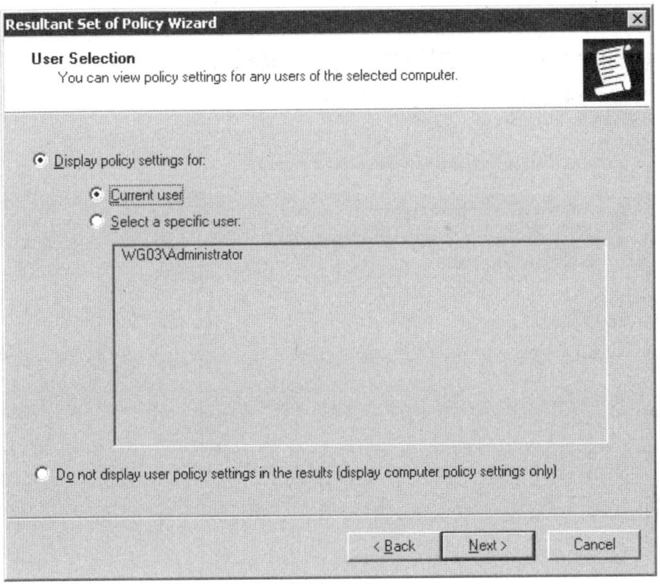

7. Click Next to accept the default option, Current User.

   The Summary Of Selections page appears.

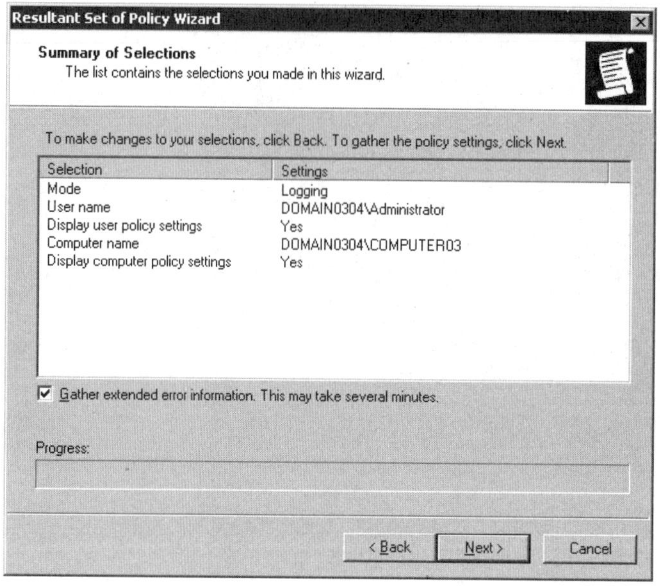

8. Click Next to accept your selections.

   The wizard gathers information, and then the Completing The Resultant Set Of Policy Wizard page appears.

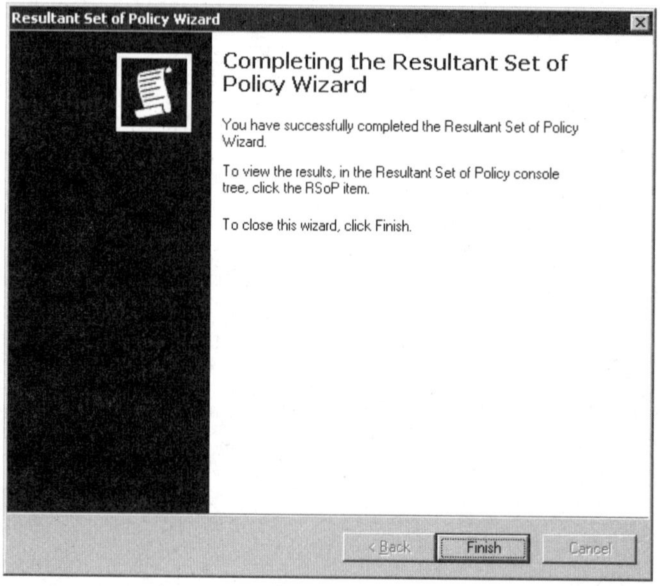

9. Click Finish to display the RSoP data in the console.

10. Take a screen shot (press ALT+PRINT SCREEN) of the RSoP window, with the Computer Configuration/Windows Settings/Security Settings node selected, and then paste it into a WordPad document named Domain*xxyy*Lab03-2.rtf (where *xx* and *yy* are the numbers assigned to the computers in your student domain), which you will turn in at the end of the lab.

EXERCISE 3-3: COPYING A SECURITY TEMPLATE

Estimated completion time: 30 minutes

To increase the security on the Contoso, Ltd., network, you decide to create a new security template based on the DC Security template supplied with Windows Server 2003. You have decided that, in the new template, you will modify the account lockout policy settings, enable auditing, and make other changes to the event log and security option settings.

1. On the Computer*xx* server, in the Security Templates console you created in Exercise 3-1, expand the Security Templates node and the C:\Windows Security Templates folder.

2. Select the DC Security template and, from the Action menu, select Save As.

   A Save As dialog box appears.

3. In the File Name text box, type **Maximum DC Security** and click Save.

   The new Maximum DC Security template appears in the console's Scope (left) pane.

4. Expand the Maximum DC Security template in the console's Scope pane. Then, expand the Account Policies node and select Account Lockout Policy.

   QUESTION What are the current values of the account lockout policies in your template?

   QUESTION What are the current operative account lockout policy settings on your domain controller, as displayed in the RSoP console you created in Exercise 3-2, and how were the settings applied?

5. Enable each of the template's account lockout policy settings and configure them using the settings in the following table:

Account Lockout Policy	Value
Account Lockout Duration	0 minutes
Account Lockout Threshold	3 invalid logon attempts
Reset Account Lockout Counter After	60 minutes

QUESTION *How do these account policy settings increase the security of your domain controller?*

6. Expand the Local Policies node and select Audit Policy.
7. Double-click the Audit Account Logon Events policy.

   The Audit Account Logon Events Properties dialog box appears.

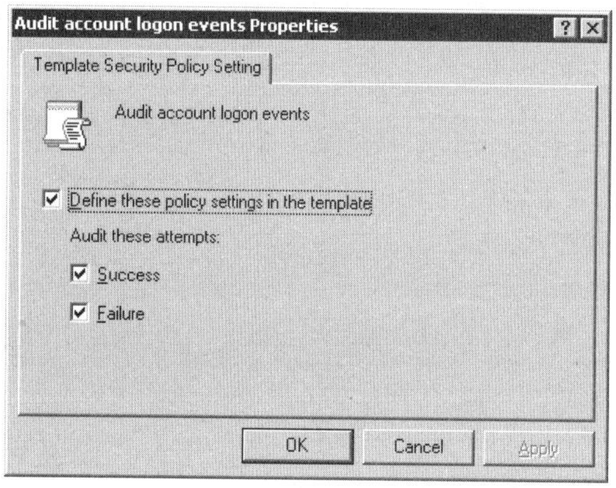

8. Select the Define These Policy Settings In The Template check box and both the Success and Failure check boxes. Then click OK.
9. Configure the following additional policies to audit successes and failures in the same way:
   - ❑ Audit Account Management
   - ❑ Audit Directory Services Access
   - ❑ Audit Logon Events
   - ❑ Audit Object Access
   - ❑ Audit Policy Change
   - ❑ Audit Privilege Use
   - ❑ Audit System Events

10. Take a screen shot (press ALT+PRINT SCREEN) of the Security Templates console showing the Audit Policy settings you just configured, and then paste it into a WordPad document named Domain*xxyy*Lab03-3.rtf (where *xx* and *yy* are the numbers assigned to the computers in your student domain), which you will turn in at the end of the lab.

> **QUESTION** *How do these audit policy settings compare with those that are currently operative on the computer?*

11. Select the Security Options node, and configure the policies in the following table with the settings provided:

Security Option	Value
Accounts: Guest Account Status	Disabled
Accounts: Limit Local Use Of Blank Passwords To Console Logon Only	Enabled
Audit: Audit The Access Of Global System Objects	Disabled
Audit: Shut Down System Immediately If Unable To Log Security Audits	Disabled
Devices: Allowed To Format And Eject Removable Media	Administrators
Devices: Prevent Users From Installing Printer Drivers	Enabled
Devices: Restrict CD-ROM Access To Locally Logged-On User Only	Enabled
Devices: Restrict Floppy Access To Locally Logged-On User Only	Enabled
Devices: Unsigned Driver Installation Behavior	Do Not Allow Installation
Domain Controller: Allow Server Operators To Schedule Tasks	Disabled
Domain Controller: LDAP Server Signing Requirements	Require Signing
Domain Member: Digitally Encrypt Or Sign Secure Channel Data (Always)	Enabled
Domain Member: Digitally Encrypt Secure Channel Data (When Possible)	Enabled
Domain Member: Digitally Sign Secure Channel Data (When Possible)	Enabled

Security Option	Value
Domain Member: Disable Machine Account Password Changes	Disabled
Domain Member: Maximum Machine Account Password Age	7 Days
Domain Member: Require Strong (Windows 2000 Or Later) Session Key	Enabled
Interactive Logon: Do Not Require CTRL+ALT+DELETE	Disabled
Interactive Logon: Number of Previous Logons To Cache	0 Logons
Interactive Logon: Require Domain Controller Authentication To Unlock Workstation	Enabled

12. Select the Event Log node, and configure the policies in the following table with the values provided:

Event Log Policy	Value
Maximum Application Log Size	32,768 kilobytes
Maximum Security Log Size	512,000 kilobytes
Maximum System Log Size	32,768 kilobytes
Retention Method For Application Log	Overwrite Events As Needed
Retention Method For Security Log	Overwrite Events As Needed
Retention Method For System Log	Overwrite Events As Needed

13. Select the Registry node.

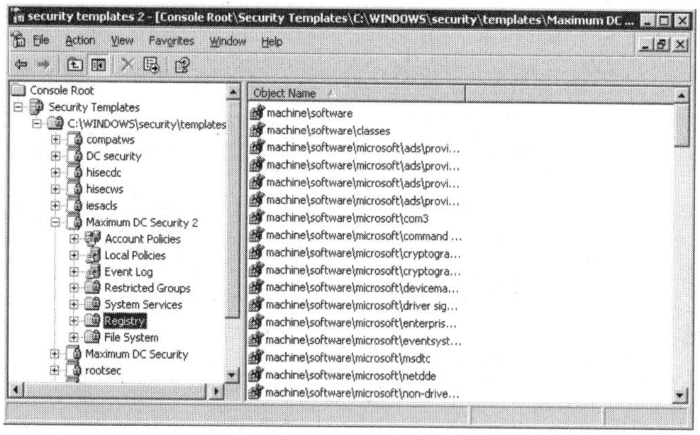

14. Use a bounding outline to select all of the entries in the Registry node and delete them.
15. In the same way, delete all of the entries in the File System node.
16. Select the Maximum DC Security node in the Scope pane and, from the Action menu, select Save.

EXERCISE 3-4: DEPLOYING A TEMPLATE USING GROUP POLICIES

Estimated completion time: 15 minutes

Having created and configured your new Maximum DC Security template for the Contoso, Ltd. network, you must now test the template by deploying it on your lab network. To do this, you will create a new Group Policy object and apply it to the Domain Controllers organizational unit.

1. On the Computer*xx* server, open the Active Directory Users And Computers console.
2. Expand the domain*xxyy*.contoso.com node (where *xx* and *yy* are the numbers assigned to the computers in your student domain), and select the Domain Controllers organizational unit (OU).
3. From the Action menu, select Properties.

   The Domain Controllers Properties dialog box appears.
4. Click the Group Policy tab.

   QUESTION What GPOs are already linked to the Domain Controllers OU?
5. Click New.

   A GPO called New Group Policy Object appears in the list.

6. Type **Maximum DC Security** to rename the GPO and press ENTER.

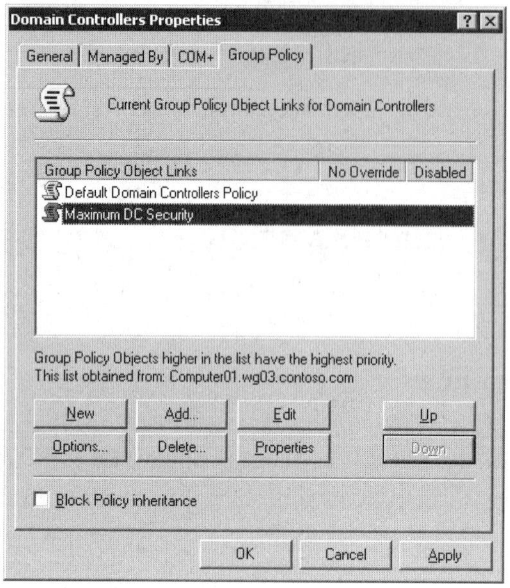

7. Click Edit.

   The Group Policy Object Editor console appears, with Maximum DC Security Policy as its top node.

8. Expand the Windows Settings node and select Security Settings.

9. From the Action menu, select Import Policy.

   The Import Policy From dialog box appears.

10. Select the Maximum DC Security.inf file you created in Exercise 3-3, and click Open.

    QUESTION *What happens?*

11. Close the Group Policy Object Editor console.

12. In the Domain Controllers Properties dialog box, select the Maximum DC Security GPO you just created, and click Up.

    The Maximum DC Security GPO moves to the top of the list.

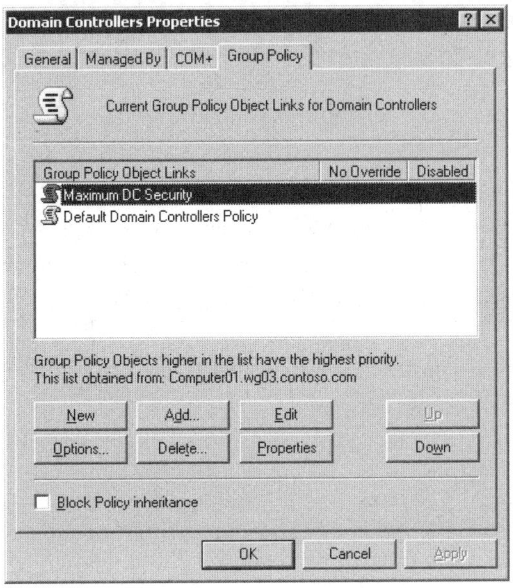

13. Click Close to close the Domain Controllers Properties dialog box.
14. Close the Active Directory Users And Computers console.
15. Open a Command Prompt window. At the prompt, type **gpupdate / force** and press ENTER.

> **QUESTION** What happens?

16. Return to the RSoP console you created in Exercise 3-2.
17. Select the Administrator On Computer*xx*–RSoP node and, from the Action menu, select Refresh Query.
18. Examine the currently operative group policy settings in the console.

> **QUESTION** What has happened since you last used the console?

19. Take a screen shot (press ALT+PRINT SCREEN) of the RSoP console showing some of the policies applied from the security template you created. Then paste the screen shot into a WordPad document named Domain*xxyy*Lab03-4.rtf (where *xx* and *yy* are the numbers assigned to the computers in your student domain), which you will turn in at the end of the lab.

EXERCISE 3-5: COPYING A SYSTEM CONFIGURATION USING SECEDIT.EXE

Estimated completion time: 15 minutes

You have been experimenting with some security setting changes on one of the lab network computers, and now you want to save those settings to a new security template and perform a test deployment on another computer. For both of these tasks, you decide to use the Secedit.exe command line utility.

1. On Computeryy, log on to the local machine as Administrator, by typing **P@ssw0rd** as the password when prompted.

   NOTE **Logging On Locally** Make sure that you log on to the local system for this exercise; do not log on to the domain. In the Log On To Windows dialog box, the value in the Log On To drop-down list should be Computeryy, where yy is the number assigned to your computer, not domainxxyy.

2. Open a Command Prompt window.
3. At the command prompt, type **cd\windows\security\templates** and press ENTER.
4. The default directory changes to C:\Windows\Security\Templates.
5. At the command prompt, type **secedit /export /cfg Workstation.inf** and press ENTER.
6. Create a Security Templates console and save it as Security Templates.msc, as you did in Exercise 3-1.
7. In the Security Templates console, open the Workstation template you created and configure the account lockout policies with the values in the following table:

Account Lockout Policy	Value
Account Lockout Duration	30 minutes
Account Lockout Threshold	5 invalid logon attempts
Reset Account Lockout Counter After	10 minutes

8. When prompted, click Yes to save Security Templates.msc and then close the console.
9. In the Command Prompt window, apply the revised template to the computer by typing **secedit /configure /db workstation.sdb /cfg workstation.inf /log workstation.log** and pressing ENTER.

   QUESTION What is the result?

10. Close the Command Prompt window.

LAB REVIEW QUESTIONS

Estimated completion time: 15 minutes

1. In light of the modifications you made to the default domain policy settings in Lab 1, what would be the result if, in Exercise 3-3, you modified the Password Policy settings in the Maximum DC Security template and then proceeded to deploy the template in the manner described in Exercise 3-4?
2. In Exercise 3-3, why was it necessary to delete all of the entries in the Registry and File System nodes of the Maximum DC Security template?
3. What would be the result if, in Exercise 3-4, you imported the Maximum DC Security template into the Default Domain Controllers Policy GPO instead of creating a new GPO (assuming that you left the Clear This Database Before Importing check box unselected)?
4. What Secedit.exe command would you use in Exercise 3-5 to apply only the Account Lockout Policy settings from the Workstation.inf template to the computer?
5. What would be the result if, in Exercise 3-4, you imported the Maximum DC Security template into the Default Domain Policy GPO instead of the Default Domain Controllers Policy GPO?

LAB CHALLENGE 3-1: DEPLOYING THE WORKSTATION TEMPLATE USING GROUP POLICIES

Estimated completion time: 30 minutes

In Exercise 3-5, you created a security template called Workstation.inf, modified its settings, and then deployed it on Computer*yy* using the Secedit.exe program. The object of this challenge is to deploy that same template to the same computer, and only that computer, using a GPO called Domain*xxyy* Workstations (where *xx* and *yy* are the numbers assigned to the computers in your lab group), instead of Secedit.exe. This way, you would be able to deploy the template to an entire fleet of workstations without running Secedit on each computer and without interfering with the domain controller configuration you already completed in Exercises 3-3 and 3-4.

Write out the steps you must take to complete the challenge, and then execute them on your workstation computers. When you are finished, create an RSoP console on Computer*yy* and use it to display the values of Account Lockout Policy settings and their source. Take a screen shot (press ALT+PRINT SCREEN) of the RSoP console and paste it into a WordPad document named Domain*xxyy*Lab03-5.rtf (where *xx* and *yy* are the numbers assigned to the computers in your student domain), which you will turn in at the end of the lab.

1. Copy the Workstation.inf security template from Computer*yy* to the C:\Windows\Security\Templates folder on Computer*xx*.
2. On Computer*xx*, open the Active Directory Users And Computers console.
3. Create a new OU object.
4. Move the Computer*yy* object from the Computers container to the OU you created.
5. Open the Properties dialog box for the new OU and click the Group Policy tab.
6. Click New and create a GPO called Domain*xxyy* Workstations.
7. Edit the GPO in the Group Policy Object Editor console and import the Workstation.inf template into the Security Settings node.
8. On Computer*yy*, run **gpupdate** in a Command Prompt window.

LAB 4

HARDENING COMPUTERS FOR SPECIFIC ROLES

This lab contains the following exercises and activities:

- Lab Exercise 4-1: Configuring Software Restriction Policies
- Lab Exercise 4-2: Testing Software Restriction Policies
- Lab Exercise 4-3: Configuring Packet Filtering
- Lab Exercise 4-4: Installing IIS
- Lab Exercise 4-5: Securing an IIS Server
- Lab Cleanup
- Lab Review Questions
- Lab Challenge 4-1: Creating a Packet Filtering Configuration for Exchange Server
- Lab Challenge 4-2: Performing a Trace on a SQL Server Computer

SCENARIO

You are a new network administrator for Contoso, Ltd., a company with a medium-sized network consisting of servers running Microsoft Windows Server 2003 and Microsoft Windows 2000 Server and workstations running Microsoft Windows XP and Microsoft Windows 2000 Professional. You have been assigned to a team of administrators whose task is to increase the security of computers performing specific roles on the network.

After completing this lab, you will be able to:

- Configure and deploy software restriction policies
- Configure ICF packet filtering on a Windows Server 2003 computer
- Control access to an IIS Web server

Estimated lesson time: 95 minutes

BEFORE YOU BEGIN

To complete this lab, you will need the following information:

- The names of the computers in your student domain (Computer*xx* and Computer*yy*)
- The name of your student domain (domain*xxyy*.contoso.com)

EXERCISE 4-1: CONFIGURING SOFTWARE RESTRICTION POLICIES

Estimated completion time: 20 minutes

Recently, the management at Contoso has become concerned that employees spend too much paid time running unauthorized software such as games. In addition, the IT director has noticed a dramatic rise in the amount of time spent troubleshooting computer problems that should be resolved easily, due to users' installation of unauthorized software on their computers. As a result, you have been assigned the task of developing a plan that uses software restriction policies to limit the software users can run on their workstations to programs on a list of approved applications.

Toward this end, you have created a platform for testing software restriction policies. In this exercise, you'll create a new Group Policy Object (GPO) containing samples of software restriction policies.

1. On your Computer*xx* server, log on to the domain*xxyy* domain (where *xx* and *yy* are the number assigned to the computers in your student domain) as Administrator, using the password **P@ssw0rd**.

2. Open the Active Directory Users And Computers console.
3. In the console tree, select the domain*xxyy*.contoso.com domain object. On the Action menu, point to New and select Organizational Unit.

   The New Object–Organizational Unit dialog box appears.

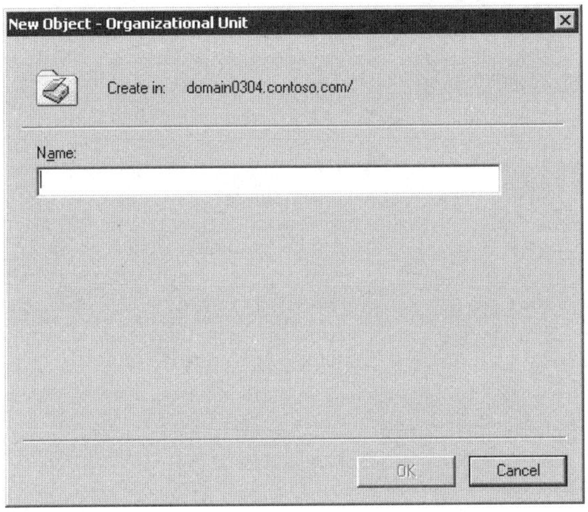

4. In the Name text box, type **Workstations** and click OK.

   The New Workstations organizational unit (OU) appears in the console tree.

5. Locate the Computer*yy* object in your Active Directory tree, and move it to the Workstations OU you just created.

> **NOTE Finding the Computer*yy* Object** By default, the Computer*yy* object was created in the Computers container when you joined the computer to the domain in Exercise 1-1. However, if you completed Lab Challenge 3-1 in Lab 3, you moved the Computer*yy* object to another OU.

6. Open the Properties dialog box for the Workstations OU, and click the Group Policy tab.

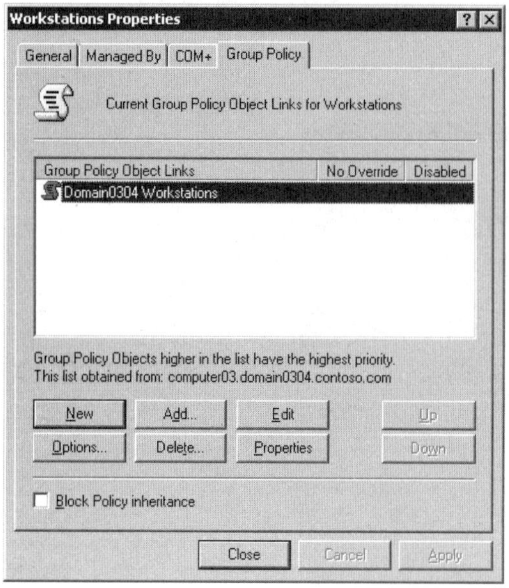

7. Click New to create a new GPO, and call it Software Restriction Policies Test.

8. Click Edit to load the new GPO into the Group Policy Object Editor.

9. In the console tree under Computer Configuration, expand the Windows Settings folder and the Security Settings node, then click the Software Restriction Policies node.

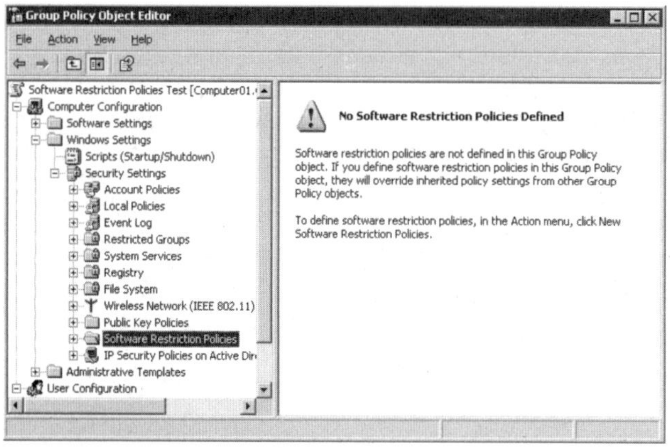

10. From the Action menu, select New Software Restriction Policies.

    Two folders and three policies appear in the console.

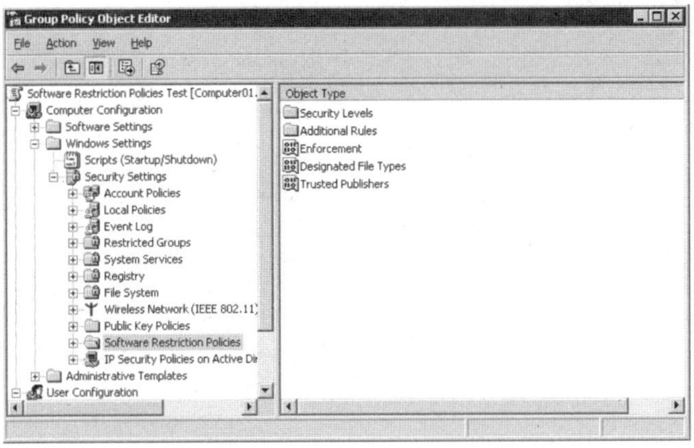

11. Select the Enforcement policy and, on the Action menu, click Properties.

    The Enforcement Properties dialog box appears.

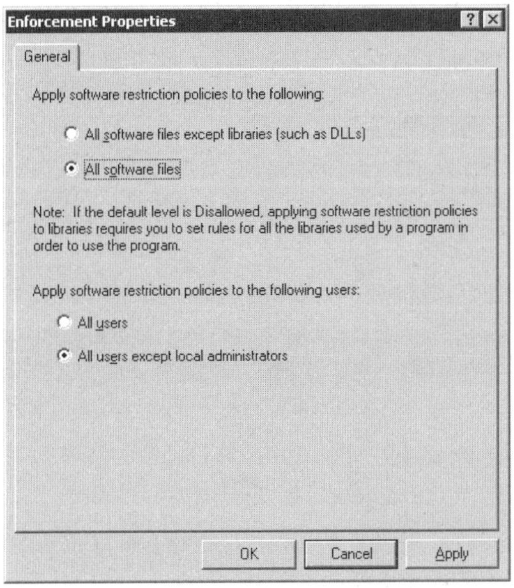

12. Select the All Software Files option and click OK.
13. In the console tree, expand the Software Restriction Policies folder and click Security Levels.

14. Two policies appear in the Security Levels folder: Disallowed and Unrestricted.

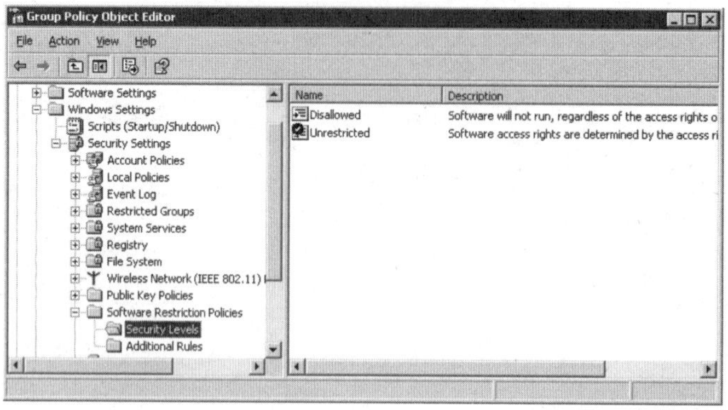

QUESTION *Which of the two policies is currently the default?*

15. In the console tree, select the Additional Rules folder and, from the Action menu, select New Hash Rule.

16. The New Hash Rule dialog box appears.

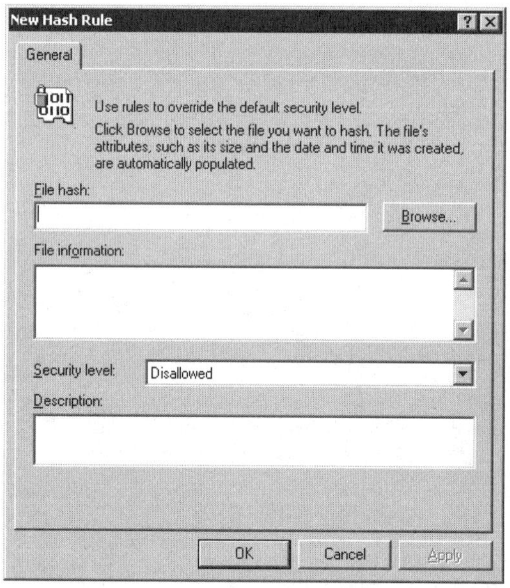

17. Click Browse. In the Open dialog box that appears, browse to the C:\Windows\Notepad.exe file. Then click OK.

    A hash of the Notepad.exe file appears in the File Hash text box.

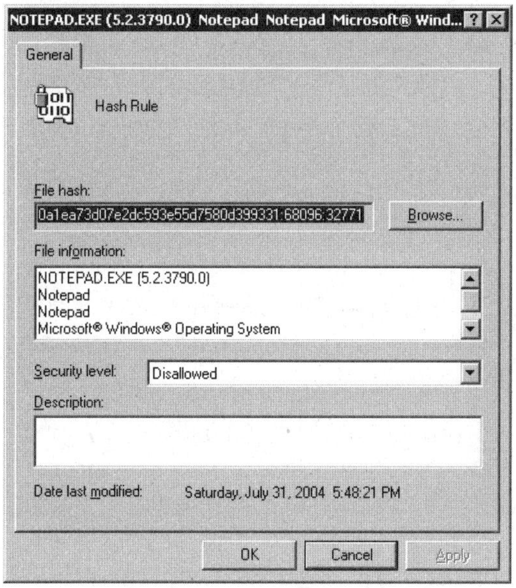

18. In the Security Level drop-down list, leave the default Disallowed value in place and then click OK.

    The new hash rule appears in the Additional Rules folder.

19. Select the Additional Rules folder and, from the Action menu, select New Path Rule.

    The New Path Rule dialog box appears.

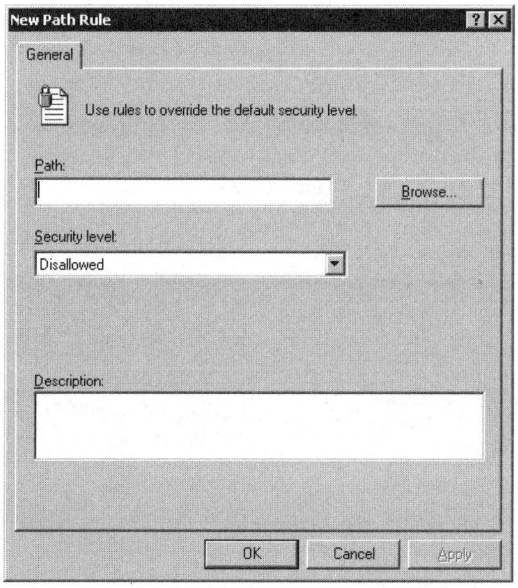

20. Click Browse. In the Browse For File Or Folder dialog box that appears, browse to the C:\Windows\PcHealth\Helpctr\Binaries folder and click OK.

    The path you selected appears in the Path text box.

21. In the Security Level drop-down list, leave the default Disallowed value in place and then click OK.

    The new path rule appears in the Additional Rules folder.

22. Close the Group Policy Object Editor console.
23. Click Close to close the Workstations Properties dialog box.
24. Leave the computer logged on for later exercises.

EXERCISE 4-2: TESTING SOFTWARE RESTRICTION POLICIES

Estimated completion time: 10 minutes

In Exercise 4-1, you created a GPO containing test rules for software restriction policies. In this exercise, you will apply the GPO to your Computer*yy* server and examine the effect of the policies on the computer.

1. Restart (or turn on) your Computer*yy* server.
2. On Computer*yy*, log on to the domain*xxyy* domain using the Administrator account by typing the password **P@ssw0rd**.
3. Click Start, and then click Run. Type **Notepad**, and then click OK.

   QUESTION What happens?

4. Take a screen shot (press ALT+PRINT SCREEN) of the dialog box that appears when you run Notepad and paste it into a WordPad document named Domain*xxyy*Lab04-1.rtf (where *xx* and *yy* are the numbers assigned to the computers in your student domain), which you will turn in at the end of the lab.

5. Click Start, and then click Run. Type **Msconfig**, and then click OK.

QUESTION What happens?

6. Open Windows Explorer and browse to the C:\Windows folder.
7. Right-click Notepad.exe, and then click Copy.
8. Right-click the C:\Windows folder, and then click Paste.

   A file called Copy Of Notepad.exe appears at the bottom of the list of files in the C:\Windows folder.

9. Double-click the Copy Of Notepad.exe file.

QUESTION What happens? Why?

10. In Windows Explorer, browse to the C:\Windows\PcHealth\Helpctr\Binaries folder.
11. Right-click Msconfig.exe, and then click Copy.
12. Right-click the C:\Windows folder, and then click Paste.

    A copy of the Msconfig.exe file appears in the C:\Windows folder.

13. Double-click the Msconfig.exe file in the C:\Windows folder.

QUESTION What happens? Why?

14. Close Windows Explorer and leave the computer logged on for the next exercise.

EXERCISE 4-3: CONFIGURING PACKET FILTERING

Estimated completion time: 20 minutes

You have been assigned the task of increasing the level of security on the Contoso network's domain controllers. You have decided that the best way to do this is to use packet filtering to prevent unauthorized network traffic from reaching the computers functioning as domain controllers. In this exercise, you configure the Internet Connection Firewall (ICF) on Windows Server 2003 to permit only legitimate domain controller traffic to reach the computer.

1. On Computer*yy*, open a Command Prompt window.
2. At the command prompt, type **ping computer*xx*** (where *xx* is the number assigned to the domain controller in your student domain) and press ENTER.

   QUESTION What is the result?

3. On Computer*xx*, click Start, click Control Panel, click Network Connections, right-click Local Area Connection, and then click Properties.

   The Local Area Connection Properties dialog box appears.

4. Click the Advanced tab.

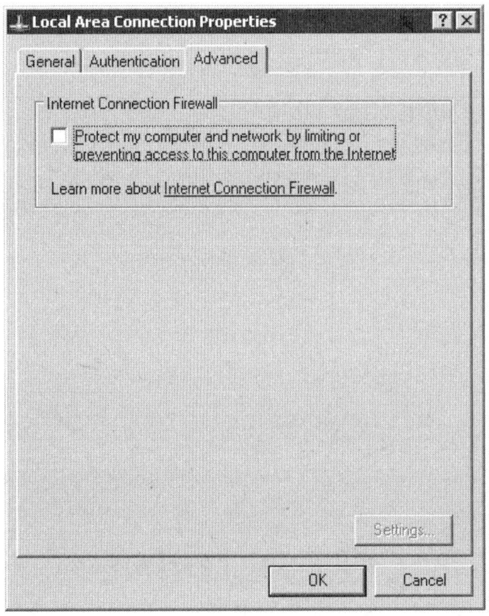

5. Select the Protect My Computer And Network By Limiting Or Preventing Access To This Computer From The Internet check box.
6. Click the Settings button.

   The Advanced Settings dialog box appears.

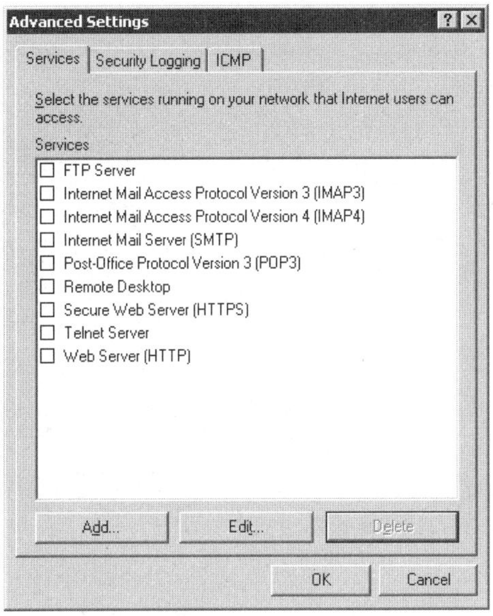

7. Click Add.

   The Service Settings dialog box appears.

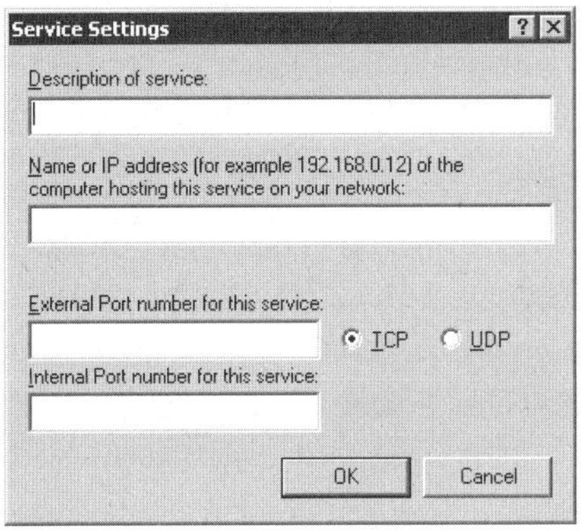

8. Fill in the fields of the dialog box with the values in the first row of the following table, and then click OK.

Description of Service	Name or IP Address	External and Internal Port Number	TCP/UDP
DNS-TCP	127.0.0.1	53	TCP
DNS-UDP	127.0.0.1	53	UDP
Kerberos-TCP	127.0.0.1	88	TCP
Kerberos-UDP	127.0.0.1	88	UDP
LDAP-TCP	127.0.0.1	389	TCP
LDAP-UDP	127.0.0.1	389	UDP

Description of Service	Name or IP Address	External and Internal Port Number	TCP/UDP
Microsoft-DS-TCP	127.0.0.1	445	TCP
Microsoft-DS-UDP	127.0.0.1	445	UDP
LDAP-SSL-TCP	127.0.0.1	686	TCP

> **NOTE** **Using the Loopback Address** *Remember, 127.0.0.1 is the standard loopback address, meaning that it refers to the local computer.*

9. Repeat steps 7 and 8 for each row in the table.
10. Take a screen shot (press ALT+PRINT SCREEN) of the Advanced Settings dialog box and paste it into a WordPad document named Domain*xxyy*Lab04-2.rtf (where *xx* and *yy* are the numbers assigned to the computers in your student domain), which you will turn in at the end of the lab.
11. Click OK twice to close the Advanced Settings dialog box and to finalize the changes to the firewall configuration.
12. On Computer*yy*, repeat the ping test you performed in step 2.

> **QUESTION** *What is the result? Why?*

13. To ensure that future exercises work correctly on Computer*xx*, disable the firewall by returning to the Local Area Connection Properties dialog box and clicking the Advanced tab. Then, clear the Protect My Computer And Network By Limiting Or Preventing Access To This Computer From The Internet check box and click OK.
14. Repeat the ping test you performed in step 2 to ensure that the firewall is disabled. The test should succeed.
15. Leave the computers logged on for later exercises.

EXERCISE 4-4: INSTALLING IIS

Estimated completion time: 15 minutes

As your next assignment, you are instructed to configure the security settings on an Internet Information Services (IIS) intranet Web server, so that only specific people are permitted to access it. First, however, you must install IIS on your test server and configure it with a default Web page.

1. On Computer*xx*, click Start, point to Control Panel, and click Add Or Remove Programs.

   The Add Or Remove Programs window appears.

2. Click Add/Remove Windows Components.

   The Windows Components Wizard appears.

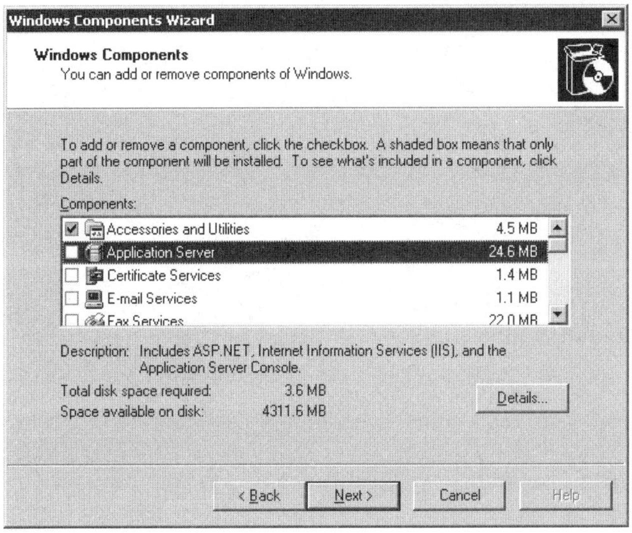

3. In the Components list, clear the Internet Explorer Enhanced Security Configuration.

4. In the Components list, click the Application Server entry (but do not select its check box), and then click Details.

   The Application Server dialog box appears.

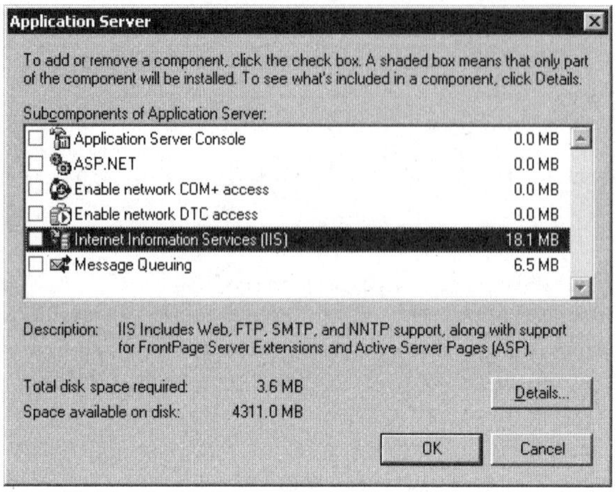

5. Select the Internet Information Services (IIS) check box, and then click OK.

6. Click Next.

   The Configuring Components page appears as the wizard installs the new software.

> **NOTE** ***Locating Installation Files*** *If the wizard prompts you for the location of your Windows Server 2003 distribution files, browse to the C:\Win2k3 folder on your system.*

7. When the Completing The Windows Components Wizard page appears, click Finish.

8. Close the Add Or Remove Programs window.

9. Click Start, point to All Programs, point to Accessories, and click Notepad.

   The Notepad window appears.

10. In the Notepad window, type the following:

```
<HTML>
<TITLE>W A R N I N G !</TITLE>
<BODY BGCOLOR="FF0000">
<H1>WARNING!</H1>
<H2>You have accessed a secured page on a server belonging to
Domainxxyy. Terminate this connection immediately or be prepared to
face departmental sanctions including loss of pay and termination of
employment.</H2>
</BODY>
</HTML>
```

11. Replace the *xxyy* in the code listing with the number assigned to the computers in your student domain by your administrator.
12. From the File menu, select Save As and save the file in the C:\Inetpub\Wwwroot folder with the name **Default.htm**.
13. Close Notepad.
14. Click Start, point to Programs, and click Internet Explorer.

    The Internet Explorer window appears.
15. In the Address text box, type **http://localhost** and press ENTER.

    QUESTION What is the result?

16. On Computer*yy*, open Microsoft Internet Explorer. In the Address box, type **http://computerxx**, where *xx* is the number assigned to the computer by your instructor, and press ENTER.

    QUESTION What is the result?

EXERCISE 4-5: SECURING AN IIS SERVER

Estimated completion time: 15 minutes

To limit access to the intranet Web server, you have decided to configure IIS by specifying the IP addresses of the computers that are to be permitted access to the server and denying access to all other addresses. In this exercise, you use the

Internet Information Services (IIS) Manager to configure the properties of the default Web site hosted by IIS.

1. On Computer*xx*, click Start, point to Administrative Tools, and click Internet Information Services (IIS) Manager.

   The Internet Information Services (IIS) Manager console appears.

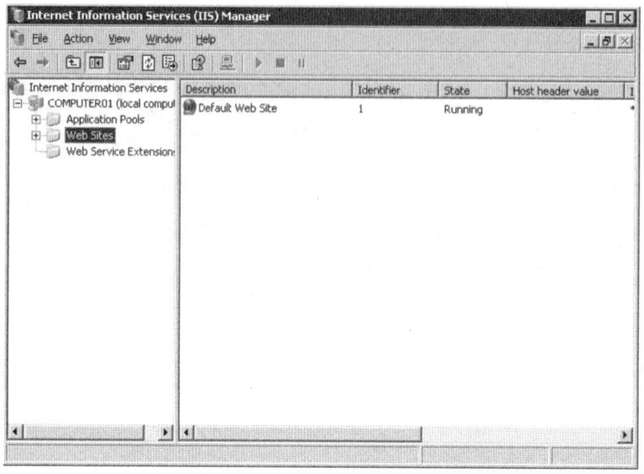

2. In the console tree, expand the Web Sites folder and click Default Web Site.

3. From the Action menu, select Properties.

   The Default Web Site Properties dialog box appears.

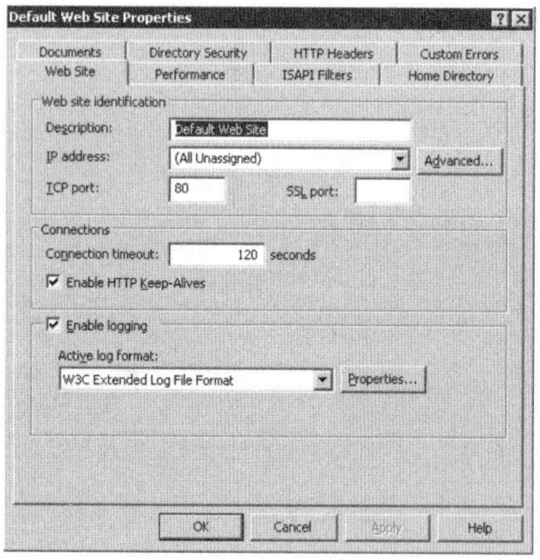

4. Click the Directory Security tab.
5. Under IP Address And Domain Name Restrictions, click Edit.

   The IP Address And Domain Name Restrictions dialog box appears.

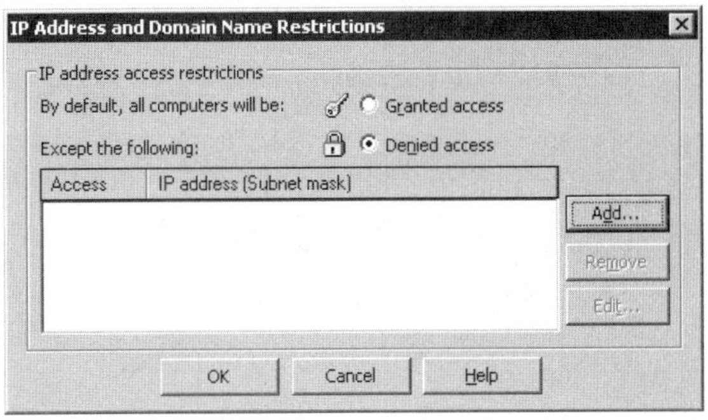

6. Select the Denied Access option and click Add.

   The Grant Access dialog box appears.

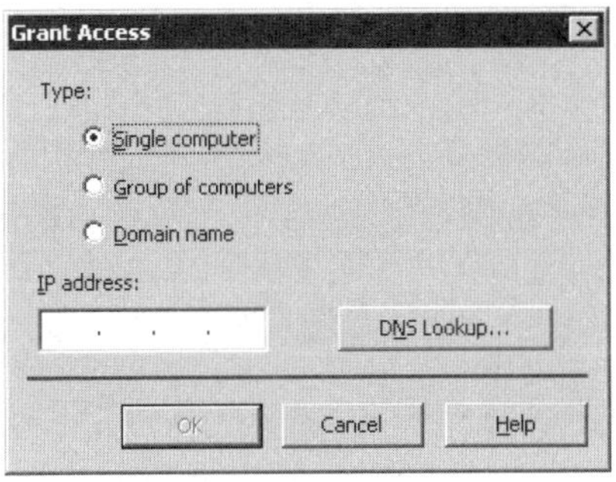

7. Click DNS Lookup.

   The DNS Lookup dialog box appears.

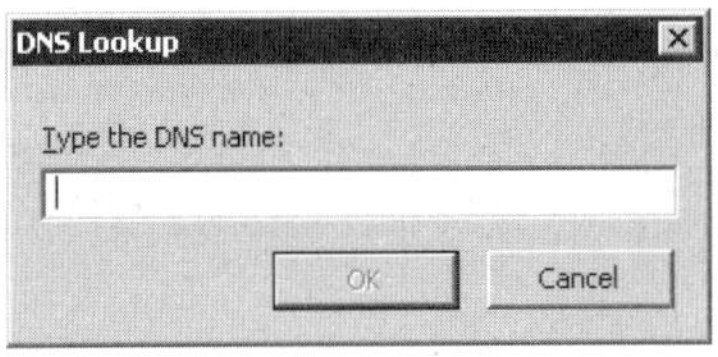

8. In the Type The DNS Name text box, type Computer*yy* and click OK.

   In the Grant Access dialog box, the IP address of Computer*yy* appears in the IP address text box.

9. Click OK.

   In the IP Address And Domain Name Restrictions dialog box, the IP address appears in the Except The Following box, with an access value of Granted.

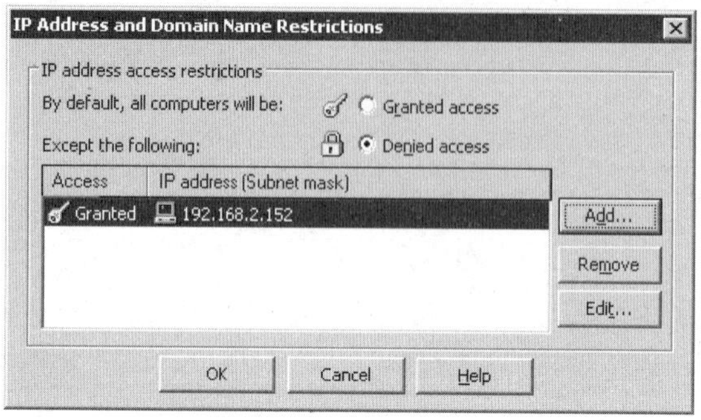

10. Click OK to close the IP Address And Domain Name Restrictions dialog box.
11. Click OK to close the Default Web Site Properties dialog box.
12. On Computer*xx*, in Internet Explorer, type **http://localhost** in the Address box and press ENTER.

QUESTION What is the result?

13. On Computer*yy*, in Internet Explorer, type **http://computer*xx*** in the Address box, where *xx* is the number assigned to the computer by your instructor, and press ENTER.

QUESTION What is the result? Why?

14. Open the IP Address And Domain Name Restrictions dialog box again and select the Grant Access option to disable the IP address restriction.

LAB CLEANUP

1. Open the Active Directory Users And Computers console.
2. Locate the Computer*yy* computer object in the Workstations OU and drag it to the Computers container.
3. Close the Active Directory Users And Computers console.

LAB REVIEW QUESTIONS

Estimated completion time: 15 minutes

1. In Exercise 4-1, why was it necessary to move the Computer*yy* object to an OU before you could apply software restriction policies to it?
2. Assuming that you do not have the permissions needed to create a new OU and move the Computer*yy* object, what other method could you use to test your software restriction policies on Computer*yy*?
3. In Exercise 4-3, you were unable to ping the domain controller after you enabled and configured ICF. Specify a way to modify the ICF configuration that would permit the ping test to succeed with the firewall enabled.
4. In Exercise 4-3, why would it not be possible to add another service in the ICF Advanced Settings dialog box that would enable the ping test to succeed with the firewall enabled?
5. In Exercise 4-5, why was Computer*xx* unable to connect to the Web server running on the local computer?

LAB CHALLENGE 4-1: CREATING A PACKET FILTERING CONFIGURATION FOR EXCHANGE SERVER

Estimated completion time: 20 minutes

For the purposes of this challenge, assume that you plan to deploy your Computer*yy* server as a Microsoft Exchange Server computer on your network, and you want to make sure you protect it against unauthorized traffic. To complete the challenge, configure the ICF firewall in the server to permit only the traffic required by Exchange Server, assuming that some of the server's clients will be using Secure Sockets Layer (SSL) and Transport Layer Security (TLS), but that none will be using instant messaging or chat. Refer to Table 4-3 in Chapter 4 of the textbook, "Ports Used by Exchange Server," for information on the ports you must leave open in the firewall.

> **QUESTION** *How many new services did you have to add to the Advanced Settings dialog box?*

When you have completed configuring the firewall, take a screen shot (press ALT+PRINT SCREEN) of the Advanced Settings dialog box and paste it into a WordPad document named Domain*xxyy*Lab04-3.rtf (where *xx* and *yy* are the numbers assigned to the computers in your student domain), which you will turn in at the end of the lab.

After you have completed the challenge, be sure to clear the Protect My Computer And Network By Limiting Or Preventing Access To This Computer From The Internet check box to disable the firewall, and then click OK.

LAB CHALLENGE 4-2: PERFORMING A TRACE ON A SQL SERVER COMPUTER

Estimated completion time: 20 minutes

To complete this challenge, you must perform a trace on a Microsoft SQL Server computer to view the exact queries being submitted by database clients. To perform this exercise, you must have access to a Windows Server 2003 computer with SQL Server 2000 installed, as well as active database clients.

> **CAUTION** **Using a Lab Computer** *Do not perform this exercise on a production system, because performing a trace has a negative performance impact.*

1. Log on to the SQL Server computer using an account that has administrative access to the database.
2. Start the SQL Profiler by clicking Start, clicking All Programs, clicking Microsoft SQL Server, and then clicking Profiler.
3. Click the File menu, click New, and then click Trace.
4. In the Connect To SQL Server dialog box, select your authentication method. If your account has administrator access to the database, click Windows Authentication, and then click OK. If you must connect using a SQL Server account, click SQL Server Authentication, provide your logon name and password, and then click OK.
5. In the Trace Properties dialog box, type Security Audit in the Trace Name box. Click Run.
6. Wait for a query to execute. Then, on the File menu, click Pause Trace.
7. Click each event, and examine the event details in the lower pane.
8. After you have familiarized yourself with the level of detail provided by the SQL Profiler tool, close it.

LAB 5

DEPLOYING UPDATES

This lab contains the following exercises and activities:

- Lab Exercise 5-1: Using Security Configuration And Analysis
- Lab Exercise 5-2: Using MBSA
- Lab Exercise 5-3: Deploying a Service Pack Using Group Policy
- Lab Review Questions
- Lab Challenge 5-1: Command-Line Scanning with Mbsacli.exe
- Lab Challenge 5-2: Uninstalling a Service Pack Using Group Policies

> **NOTE** **When to Perform This Lab** Chapters 5 and 6 of the course textbook cover the planning of an update management infrastructure and the deployment of that infrastructure respectively. Because Labs 5 and 6 both cover the deployment process, you should begin Lab 5 only after you have read and your instructor has presented Chapter 6, and then proceed immediately to Lab 6.

SCENARIO

You are a network administrator for Contoso, Ltd., a company with a medium-sized network consisting of servers running Microsoft Windows Server 2003 and Microsoft Windows 2000 Server and workstations running Microsoft Windows XP and Microsoft Windows 2000 Professional. You are part of a team of administrators assigned the task of implementing and maintaining an update management infrastructure.

After completing this lab, you will be able to:

- Use the Security Configuration And Analysis snap-in to analyze a computer.
- Use Microsoft Baseline Security Analyzer to scan computers for missing updates and security vulnerabilities.
- Deploy a service pack using group policies.

Estimated lesson time: 80 minutes

BEFORE YOU BEGIN

To complete this lab, you will need the following:

- The names of the computers in your student domain (Computer*xx* and Computer*yy*)
- The name of your student domain (domain*xxyy*.contoso.com)
- The Microsoft Baseline Security Analyzer (MBSA) installation file (MBSASetup-en.msi), supplied by your instructor
- The network installation file for the latest Windows XP Service Pack, supplied by your instructor

EXERCISE 5-1: USING SECURITY CONFIGURATION AND ANALYSIS

Estimated completion time: 20 minutes

You are a network administrator for Contoso and your supervisor has instructed you to prepare a report detailing the compliance of the network's member servers with the Hisecws.inf security template included with Windows Server 2003. You intend to use the Security Configuration And Analysis snap-in to compare the configuration of each computer with the settings in the template. In this exercise, you create a Security Configuration And Analysis console and run a test analysis on the local computer.

1. On Computer*yy*, log on using the local Administrator account with the password **P@ssw0rd**.
2. Create a new Microsoft Management Console (MMC) console, and add the Security Configuration And Analysis snap-in.

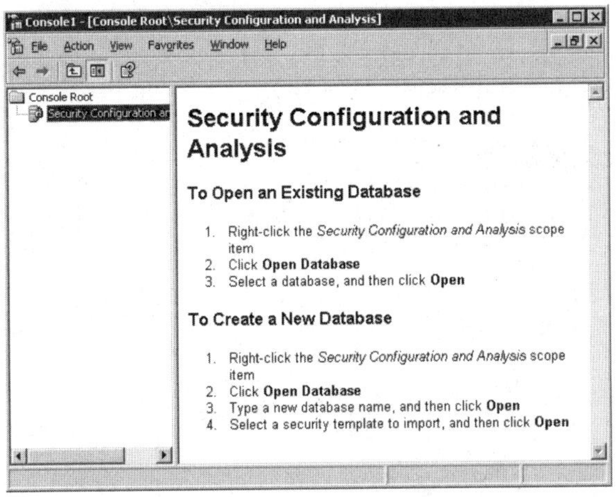

MORE INFO ***Creating an MMC Console*** *See Exercise 3-1 in Lab 3, "Creating a Security Templates Console," to review the process of creating an MMC console and adding an MMC snap-in.*

3. Click Security Configuration And Analysis in the console tree and, from the Action menu, select Open Database.

   The Open Database dialog box appears.

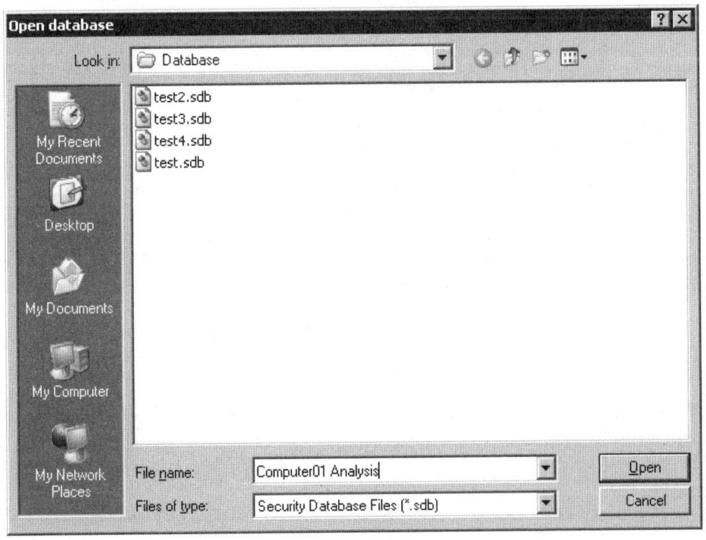

4. In the File Name text box, type **Computeryy Analysis** and click Open.

   The Import Template dialog box appears.

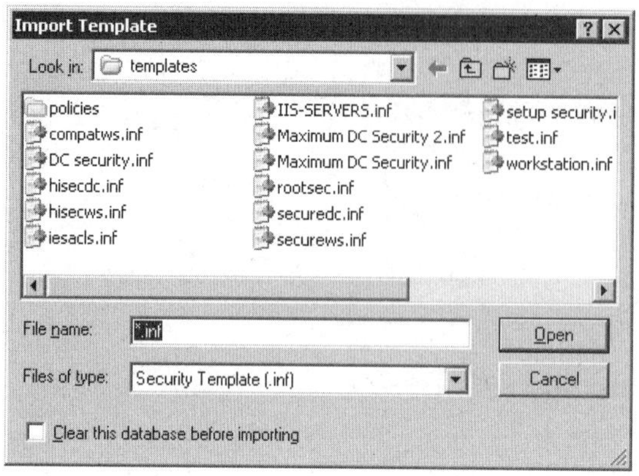

5. Select the Hisecws.inf template and click Open.
6. From the Action menu, select Analyze Computer Now.

   The Perform Analysis dialog box appears.

7. Click OK to accept the default error log file path.

   The snap-in performs the analysis and displays the results in the console.

8. In the console tree, expand the Security Configuration And Analysis and Account Policies nodes and select the Password Policy node.

QUESTION Which of the password policy settings currently active on the computer are identical to those in the security template?

9. Double-click the Password Must Meet Complexity Requirements policy.

   The Password Must Meet Complexity Requirements Properties dialog box appears.

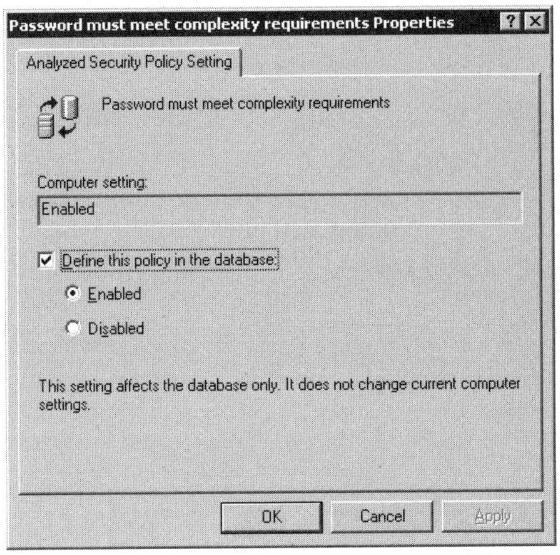

QUESTION What are the settings shown in the dialog box?

10. Click OK.

11. Take a screen shot (press ALT+PRINT SCREEN) of the Security Configuration And Analysis console displaying the Password Policy node. Then, paste it into a WordPad document named Domain*xxyy*Lab05-1.rtf (where *xx* and *yy* are the numbers assigned to the computers in your student domain), which you will turn in at the end of the lab.

12. Close the custom console you created without saving it and leave the computer logged on for the next exercise.

EXERCISE 5-2: USING MBSA

Estimated completion time: 20 minutes

After a recent incident in which the security of dozens of computers was compromised by a failure to install a crucial security update, the IT director at Contoso has ordered all computers to be scanned for missing updates and patched as soon as possible. You have decided to use Microsoft Baseline Security Analyzer (MBSA) to scan the computers. In this exercise, you install MBSA and test it by scanning the local computer for security problems.

1. On Computeryy, open the Run dialog box, click Browse, and navigate to the folder containing the MBSASetup-en.msi file supplied by your instructor.
2. Select the MBSASetup-en.msi file and click OK.

   The Microsoft Baseline Security Analyzer Setup wizard appears.

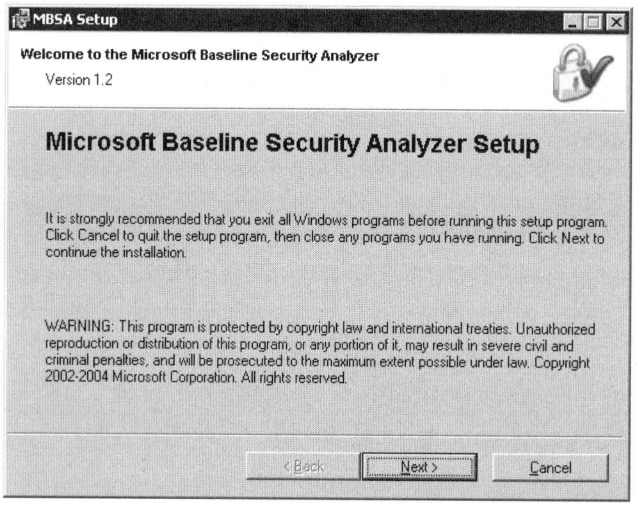

3. Click Next to bypass the Welcome page.

   The License Agreement page appears.

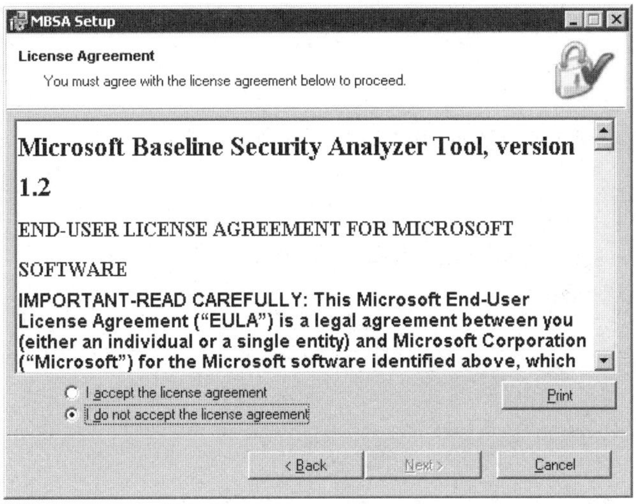

4. Select the I Accept The License Agreement option and click Next.

   The Destination Folder page appears.

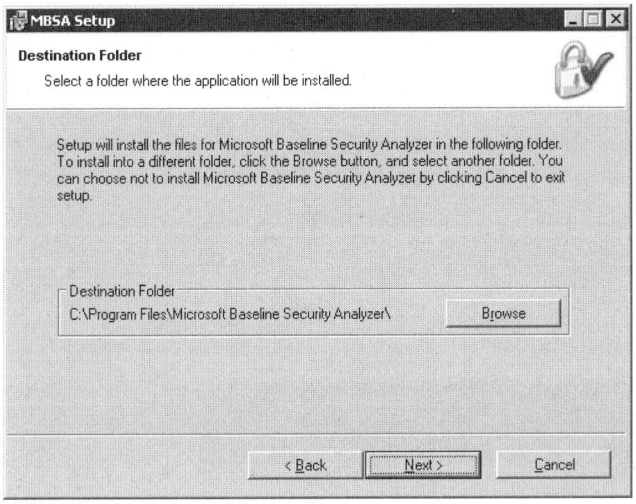

5. Click Next to accept the default destination folder.

   The Start Installation page appears.

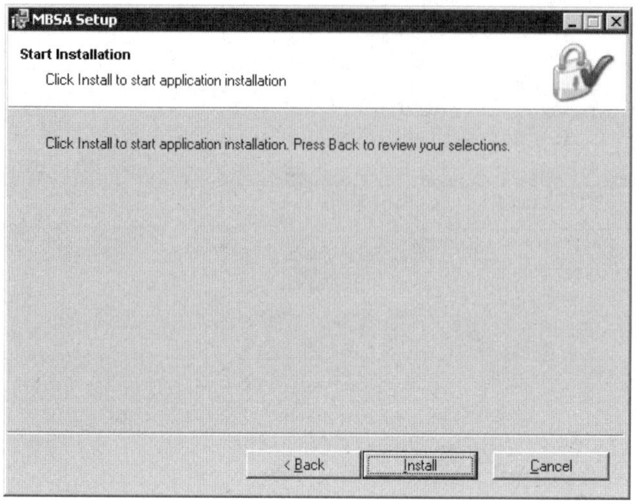

6. Click Install.

   The installation proceeds, and eventually an MBSA Setup message box appears, stating the the installation has completed successfully.

7. Click OK.

8. Click Start, point to All Programs, and click Microsoft Baseline Security Analyzer.

   The Microsoft Baseline Security Analyzer window appears.

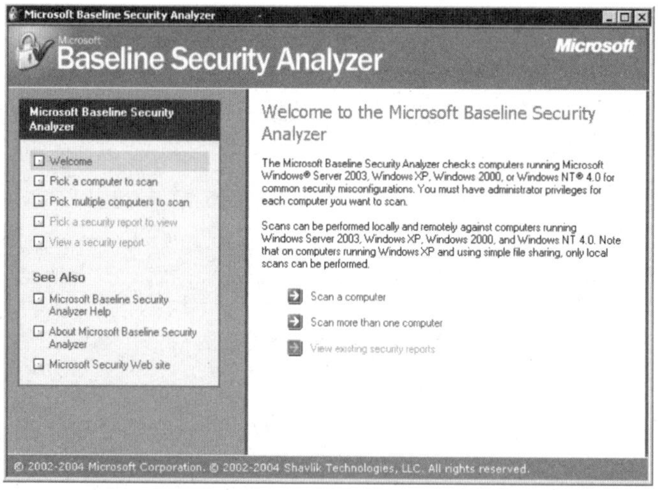

9. Click Scan A Computer.

   The Pick A Computer To Scan page appears.

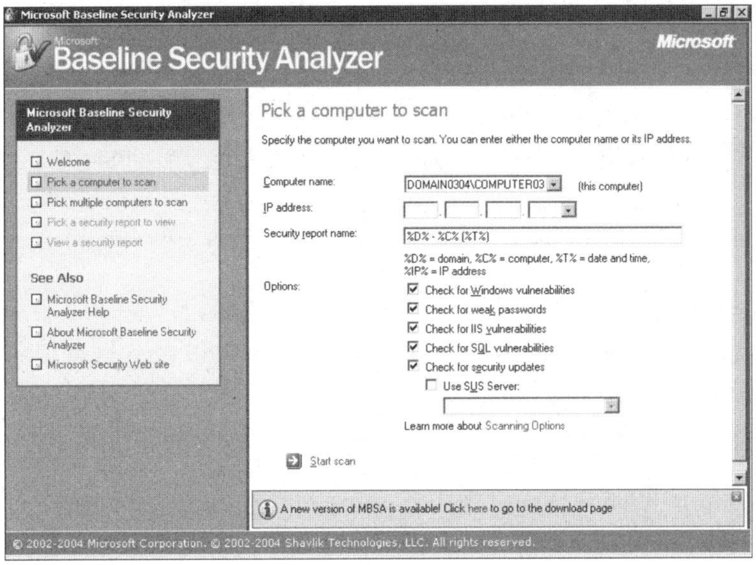

10. Select the Use SUS Server check box and, in the text box, type **http://server01**.

Leave all of the other controls at their default settings.

11. Click Start Scan.

The View Security Report page appears.

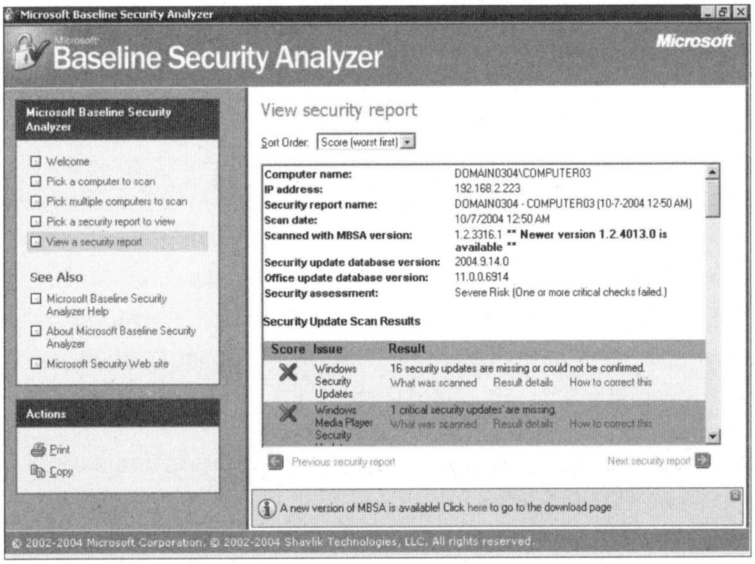

QUESTION *What is the overall Security Assessment for the computer?*

12. In the Windows Security Updates row, click the Result Details link.

    The Result Details page appears.

    QUESTION *How many critical security updates is the computer missing?*

13. Take a screen shot (press ALT+PRINT SCREEN) of the Result Details page, and paste it into a WordPad document named Domain*xxyy*Lab05-2.rtf (where *xx* and *yy* are the numbers assigned to the computers in your student domain), which you will turn in at the end of the lab.

14. Close the Result Details window.

15. Scroll down the View Security Report page and study the information presented there.

    QUESTION *Apart from Windows Security Updates, what other elements on the View Security Report page have red or yellow Xs indicating security problems?*

16. Close the Microsoft Baseline Security Analyzer window.

17. Log off the computer.

EXERCISE 5-3: DEPLOYING A SERVICE PACK USING GROUP POLICY

Estimated completion time: 20 minutes

A new service pack has been released for Windows XP, and you want to deploy it to all of Contoso's Windows XP workstations at once. To do this, you decide to use a software installation package deployed using a Group Policy Object (GPO). In this exercise, you create a new organizational unit (OU) and link a new GPO containing the software installation package to it.

1. On Computer*xx*, log on to the domain*xxyy* domain as Administrator, using the password **P@ssw0rd**.

2. Open Windows Explorer and create a new folder on the C drive called Service Pack.

3. Copy the service pack network installation file supplied by your instructor to the C:\Service Pack folder.

4. Right-click the C:\Service Pack folder, and select Sharing And Security from the context menu.

   The Service Pack Properties dialog box appears, with the Sharing tab selected.

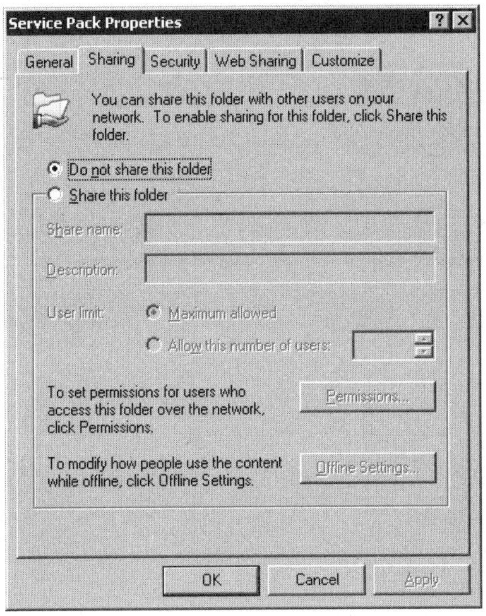

5. Select the Share This Folder option, accepting the default Share Name value, and click OK.
6. Open a Command Prompt window.
7. Switch to the Service Pack folder you just created, using the command **cd\Service Pack**.
8. At the command prompt, type **xpsp1 /x** and press ENTER to extract the files from the Service Pack archive.

   The Choose Directory For Extracted Files dialog box appears.

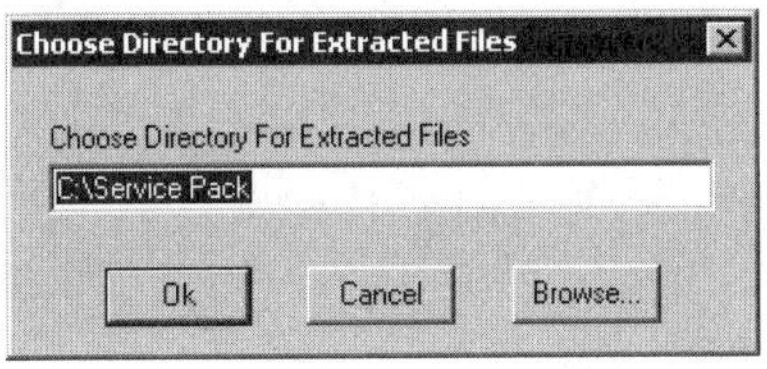

9. Click OK to accept the default C:\Service Pack folder.

   The files in the service pack archive are extracted to the C:\Service Pack folder, after which an Extraction Complete message box appears.

10. Click OK.
11. Open the Active Directory Users And Computers console.
12. Create a new OU in your domain*xxyy* domain called **XP Workstations**.
13. Open the Properties dialog box for the XP Workstations OU and click the Group Policy tab.

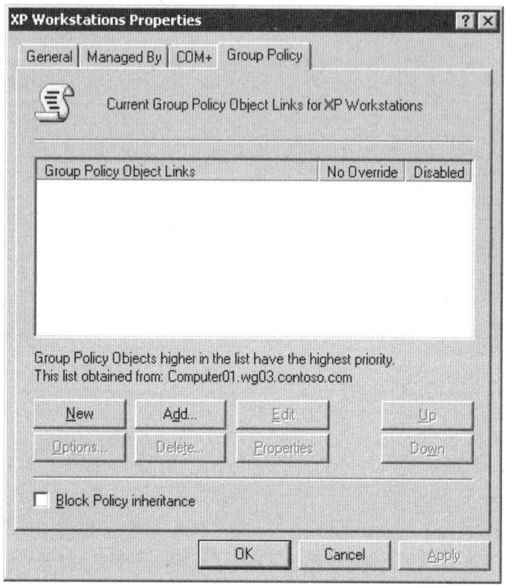

14. Click New to create a new GPO and give it the name **Service Pack**.
15. Click Edit.

    The Group Policy Object Editor console appears.

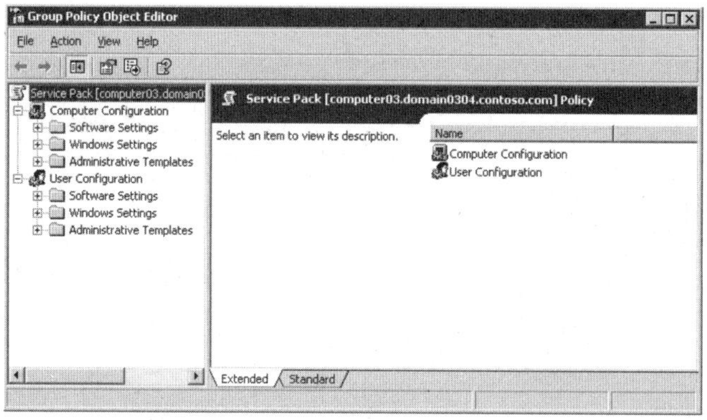

16. In the console tree, expand the Software Settings folder under Computer Configuration and select Software Installation.
17. On the Action menu, point to New and click Package.

    The Open dialog box appears.
18. In the File Name text box, type **\\Computer*xx*\Service Pack\Update\Update.msi**, where *xx* is the number assigned to the computer by your instructor, and click Open.

    The Deploy Software dialog box appears.

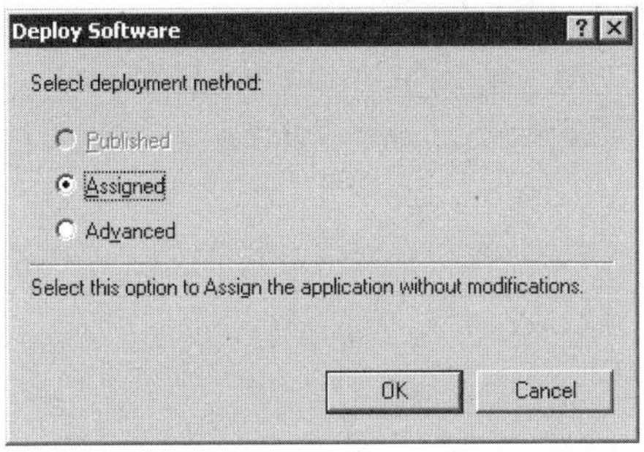

19. Click OK to accept the default Assigned option.
20. The Windows XP Service Pack package appears in the Group Policy Object Editor console.

> **QUESTION** *After you install a new Windows XP workstation on the network, what must you do for it to receive the service pack installation package you just created?*

21. Close the Group Policy Object Editor console.
22. Click OK to close the XP Workstations dialog box.
23. Close the Active Directory Users And Computers console.
24. Log off the computer.

LAB REVIEW QUESTIONS

Estimated completion time: 20 minutes

1. In Exercise 5-1, after you open the Password Must Meet Complexity Requirements Properties dialog box, enable the policy, and click OK, is the policy now enabled on the computer? Explain why or why not.
2. In Exercise 5-2, based on the information on the Result Details page, how did MBSA determine which updates were missing from the computer?
3. For each of the elements with red or yellow Xs that you listed in Exercise 5-2, specify what you must do to rectify each problem.
4. In Exercise 5-3, why was it necessary to supply a Universal Naming Convention (UNC) path, such as \\Computer*xx*\Service Pack\Update\Update.msi, when you created the Software Installation policy, rather than a local drive path, such as C:\Service Pack\Update\Update.msi?

LAB CHALLENGE 5-1: COMMAND-LINE SCANNING WITH MBSACLI.EXE

Estimated completion time: 20 minutes

You want to perform a number of MBSA scans at regular intervals by scheduling them with the Windows Server 2003 Task Scheduler application. To do this, you must use MBSA's command-line interface instead of the graphical interface. To complete this challenge, for each of the following scenarios, specify the command you must use to perform the scan. Use the **mbsacli /h** command for help with the program's syntax.

1. Scan all of the computers on the 10.43.0.0/16 network for missing updates only, using a Software Update Services (SUS) server on the local network called SUS1.
2. Scan a computer with the IP address 192.168.54.199 for all security vulnerabilities, using the Windows Update servers and redirecting output to a file called 192.168.54.199.txt.
3. Scan all of the computers in the contoso.com domain for missing updates, password problems, and operating system vulnerabilities only. Use an SUS server called Intranet1, and save the output to a file called contoso.txt, all without displaying any output on the screen.

LAB CHALLENGE 5-2: UNINSTALLING A SERVICE PACK USING GROUP POLICIES

Estimated completion time: 20 minutes

After deploying the new Windows XP service pack on a number of computers, you have discovered a minor incompatibility with a custom application running on your network. Because this problem only affects a small percentage of your workstations, you are going to proceed with the service pack deployment, but you want to have the option to uninstall the service pack automatically from computers that are affected. To complete this challenge, you must modify the software installation package you created in Exercise 5-3 so that moving a computer out of the XP Workstations OU will cause the service pack to be uninstalled the next time the computer is restarted. Then take a screen shot (press ALT+PRINT SCREEN) of the interface containing the control you modified, and paste it into a WordPad document named Domain*xxyy*Lab05-3.rtf (where *xx* and *yy* are the numbers assigned to the computers in your student domain), which you will turn in at the end of the lab.

LAB 6
DEPLOYING SUS

This lab contains the following exercises and activities:

- Lab Exercise 6-1: Installing SUS
- Lab Exercise 6-2: Configuring SUS
- Lab Exercise 6-3: Configuring the Automatic Updates Client
- Lab Exercise 6-4: Scheduling Automatic Updates
- Lab Review Questions
- Lab Challenge 6-1: Examining SUS Log Entries

SCENARIO

You are a network administrator for Contoso, Ltd., a company with a medium-sized network consisting of servers running Microsoft Windows Server 2003 and Microsoft Windows 2000 Server and workstations running Microsoft Windows XP and Windows 2000 Professional. You have been assigned the task of deploying a Microsoft Software Update Services (SUS) server on the company network and configuring the computers in a domain to download updates from it.

After completing this lab, you will be able to:

- **Install and configure an SUS server**
- **Synchronize and approve updates on an SUS server**
- **Configure the Automatic Updates client**

Estimated lesson time: 100 minutes

BEFORE YOU BEGIN

To complete this lab, you will need the following information:

- The names of the computers in your student domain (Computer*xx* and Computer*yy*)
- The name of your student domain (domain*xxyy*.contoso.com)
- The Microsoft Software Update Services 1.0 with Service Pack 1 installation file (Sus10sp1.exe), supplied by your instructor

EXERCISE 6-1: INSTALLING SUS

Estimated completion time: 20 minutes

SUS is a Web-based server application, so it requires you to install Internet Information Services (IIS) on the Windows Server 2003 computer first. In this exercise, you install IIS and then SUS.

1. On Computer*yy*, click Start, point to Control Panel, and click Add Or Remove Programs.

   The Add Or Remove Programs window appears.

2. Click Add/Remove Windows Components.

   The Windows Components Wizard appears.

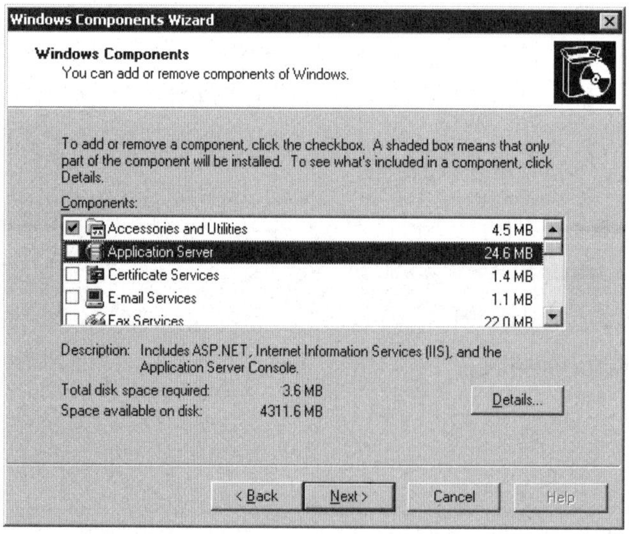

3. In the Components list, clear the Internet Explorer Enhanced Security Configuration check box.

4. In the Components list, click the Application Server entry (but do not select its check box), and then click Details.

   The Application Server dialog box appears.

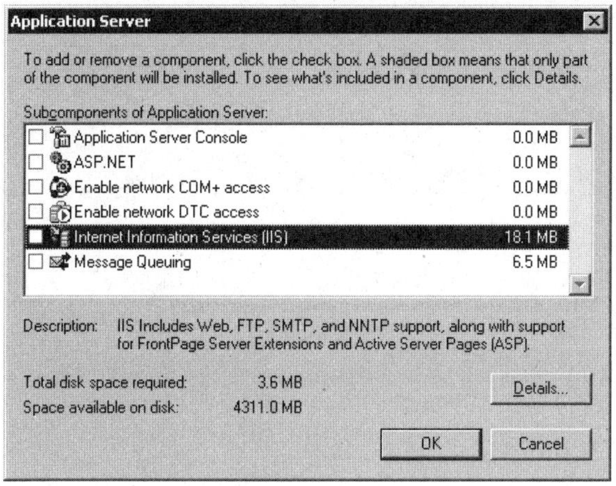

NOTE Disabling Internet Explorer Enhanced Security Configuration Windows Server 2003, by default, implements a high level of protection on Microsoft Internet Explorer because, in most cases, servers are not used for extensive Web browsing and are tempting targets for potential attackers. The Internet Explorer Enhanced Security Configuration feature sets the security levels for the Internet zone to High and implements custom settings for the other zones that prevent the browser from connecting to many sites. For the purposes of this lab, you are disabling this feature to prevent Internet Explorer from blocking access to the SUS administrative Web site. On a production server, you should leave Internet Explorer Enhanced Security Configuration activated or study the browser security settings carefully before you disable them.

5. Select the Internet Information Services (IIS) check box and then click OK.

6. Click Next.

   The Configuring Components page appears as the wizard installs the new software.

7. When the Completing The Windows Components Wizard page appears, click Finish.

NOTE Locating Installation Files If the wizard prompts you for the location of your Windows Server 2003 distribution files, browse to the C:\Win2k3 folder on your system.

8. Close the Add Or Remove Programs window.
9. Click Start and open the Run dialog box.
10. Browse to the Win2k3 share on the Server01 computer and run the Sus10sp1.exe file located in the root of that share.

    Windows Installer extracts the files from the archive, and, eventually, the Microsoft Software Update Services Setup Wizard launches.

11. Click Next to bypass the Welcome page.

    The End-User License Agreement page appears.

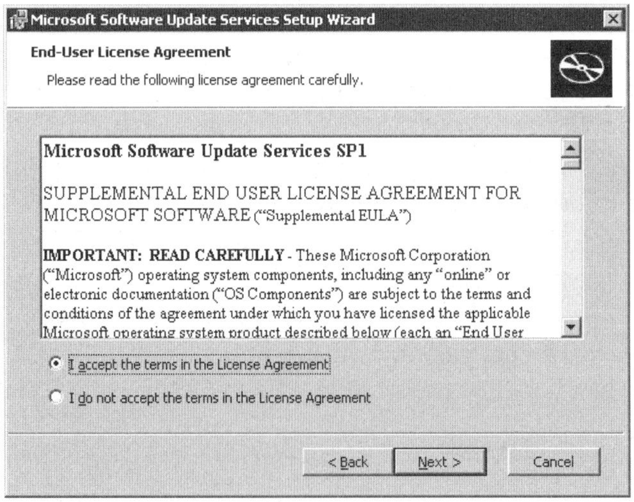

12. Study the license agreement carefully and then select I Accept The Terms In The License Agreement. Click Next.

    The Choose Setup Type page appears.

13. Click Custom.

    The Choose File Locations page appears.

14. Click Next to accept the default file location settings.

The Language Settings page appears.

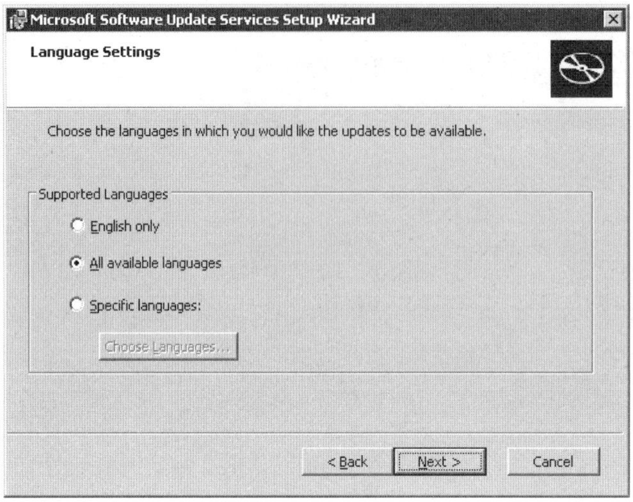

15. Select English Only and click Next.

The Handling New Versions Of Previously Approved Updates page appears.

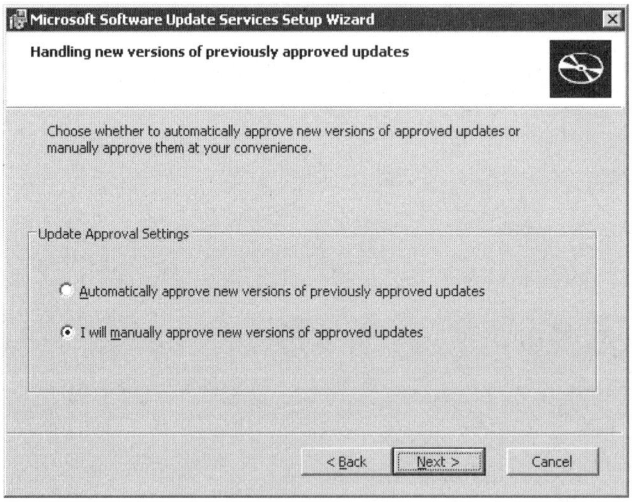

16. Click Next to accept the default I Will Manually Approve New Versions Of Approved Updates option and then click Next.

The Ready To Install page appears.

> **QUESTION** What is the download URL specified by the wizard?

17. Click Install.

The wizard installs SUS. Eventually, the Completing The Microsoft Software Update Services Setup Wizard page appears.

18. Click Finish.

Internet Explorer opens and the SUS administrative Web site appears.

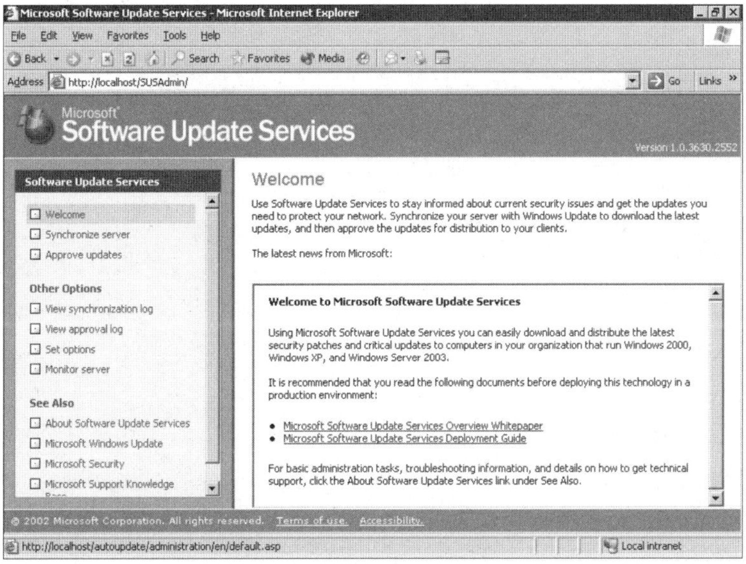

19. Take a screen shot (press ALT+PRINT SCREEN) of the SUS administrative Web site and paste it into a WordPad document named Domain*xxyy*Lab06-1.rtf (where *xx* and *yy* are the numbers assigned to the computers in your student domain), which you will turn in at the end of the lab.

20. Leave Internet Explorer open for the next exercise.

EXERCISE 6-2: CONFIGURING SUS

Estimated completion time: 30 minutes

Before clients can access an SUS server, you must configure its properties, synchronize it with a source providing the latest updates, and then select the updates you want to deploy to your clients. In this exercise, you configure the SUS server you just installed, synchronize with the Server01 classroom server (which is also running SUS), and approve updates for Windows Server 2003.

1. On Computeryy, in Internet Explorer, click the Set Options link on the SUS administration Web page.

   The Set Options page appears.

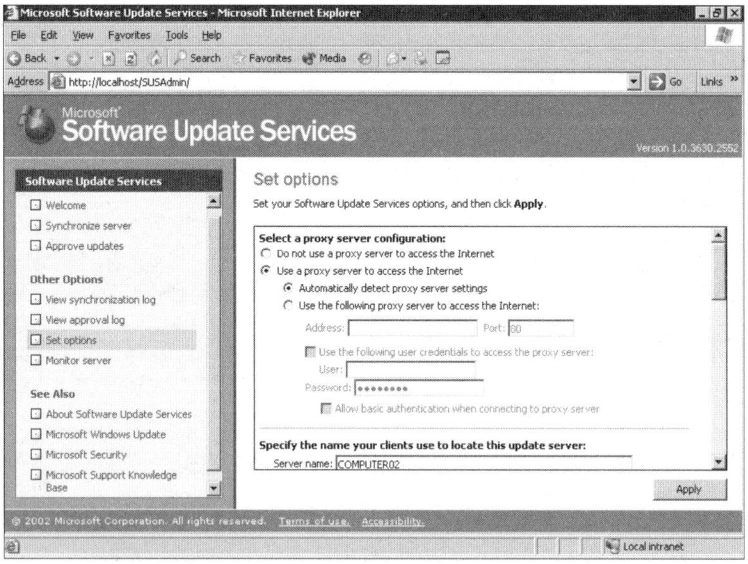

2. In the Select A Proxy Server Configuration area, select the Do Not Use A Proxy Server To Access The Internet option.
3. Scroll down and, in the Select Which Server To Synchronize Content From area, select the Synchronize From A Local Software Update Services Server option. In the accompanying text box, type **server01**.
4. Make sure the Synchronize List Of Approved Items Updated From This Location check box is cleared. Then click Apply.

   A message box appears, stating that your settings have been successfully saved.

5. Click OK.
6. Click the Synchronize Server link.

   The Synchronize Server page appears.

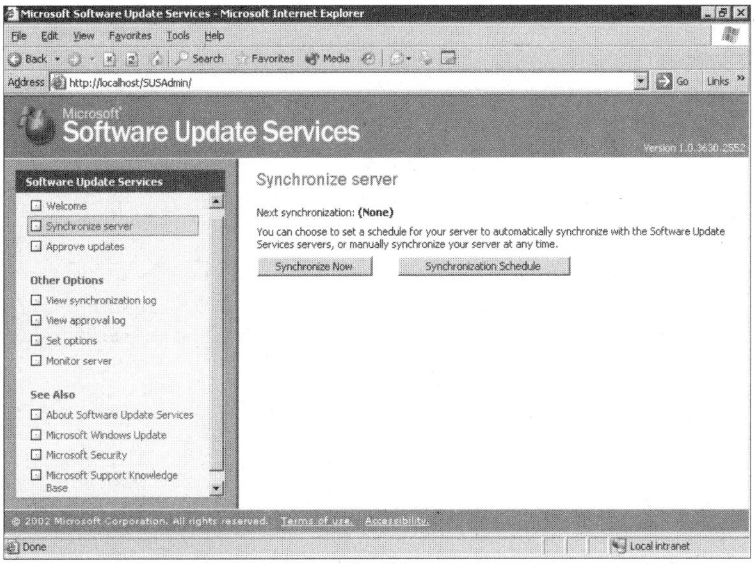

7. Click Synchronization Schedule.

   The Schedule Synchronization dialog box appears.

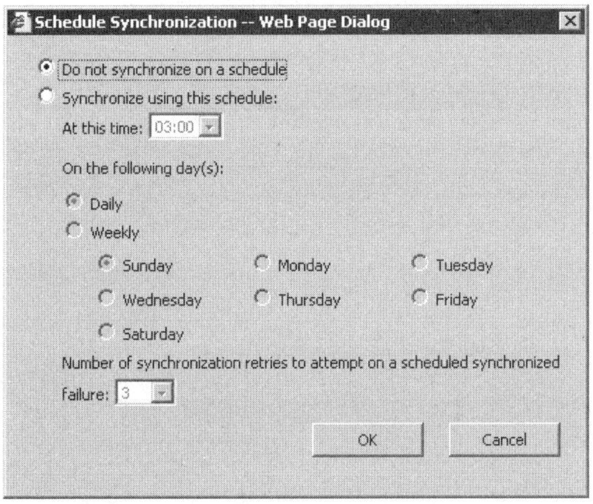

8. Select the Synchronize Using This Schedule option.
9. In the At This Time drop-down list, select 12:00.
10. Select the Weekly option and then click OK.

    The page updates to show the date and time of the next scheduled synchronization.

11. Click Synchronize Now to perform a manual synchronization immediately.

    The synchronization process begins; it will take several minutes to complete.

    QUESTION How many updates does the server synchronize?

12. A VBScript message box appears, indicating that the synchronization is complete.

    NOTE **Understanding Synchronization** The VBScript message box states that your server successfully synchronized with the Microsoft Windows Update servers, even though the server actually synchronized with a local SUS server.

13. Click OK.

    The Approve Updates page appears.

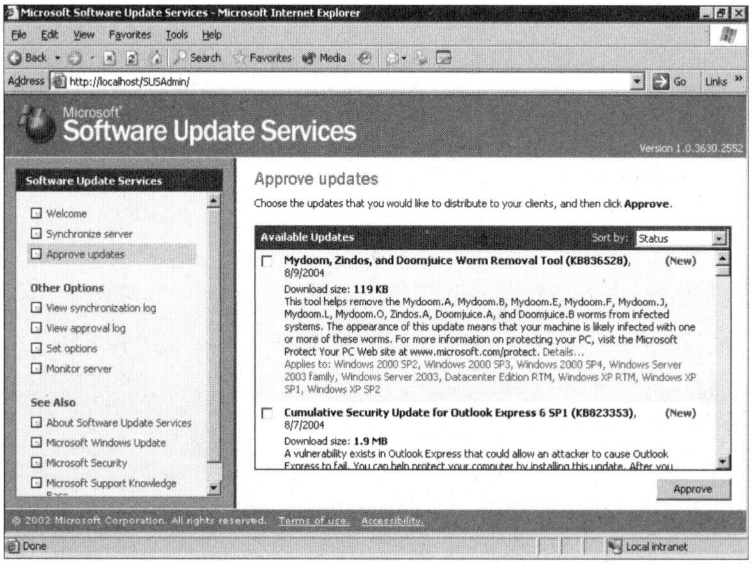

14. Take a screen shot (press ALT+PRINT SCREEN) of the Approve Updates page and paste it into a WordPad document named Domain*xxyy*Lab06-2.rtf (where *xx* and *yy* are the numbers assigned to the computers in your student domain), which you will turn in at the end of the lab.

15. In the Sort By drop-down list, select Platform.

The page reloads and displays the list of updates sorted by operating system.

16. Scroll down in the list and select the check box for each of the Windows Server 2003 updates. Then click Approve.

> **NOTE Avoiding Service Packs** To save lab time, if a Windows Server 2003 Service Pack release appears in the list, do not select it.

A VBScript: Software Update Services message box appears, asking you to confirm your approval of the updates you selected.

17. Click Yes.

> **NOTE Approving Updates** Under normal conditions, you would test each update, or at the very least read its accompanying Knowledge Base article, before approving it for distribution on your network. For the purposes of this lab, however, you can approve all of the available Windows Server 2003 updates immediately.

A Software Update Services dialog box appears, containing the end-user license agreements for all of the updates you selected.

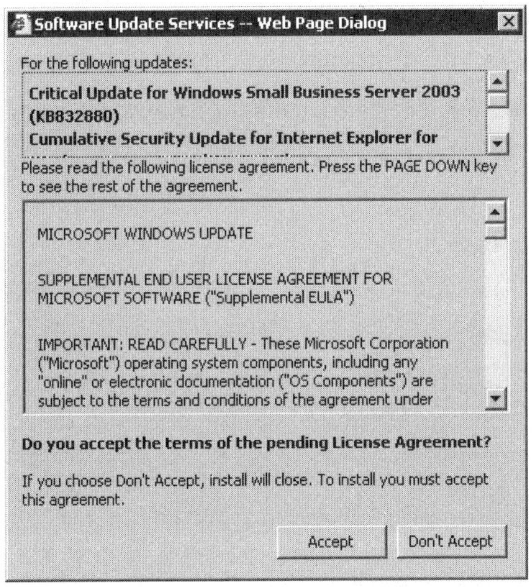

18. Read the license agreement carefully and click Accept.

    A VBScript: Software Update Services message box appears, stating that your selections have been approved and are now available to clients.

19. Click OK.

    The Approved Updates page reloads, showing the updates you selected with the Approved status.

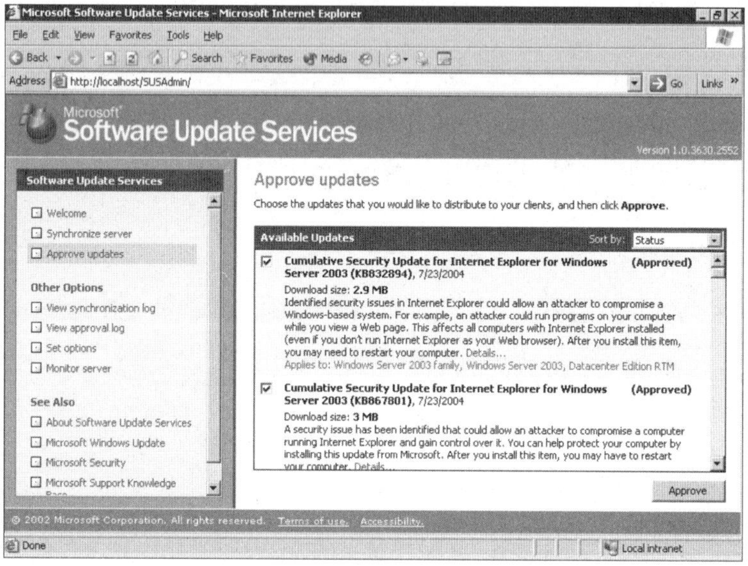

20. Leave the computer logged on for the next exercise.

EXERCISE 6-3: CONFIGURING THE AUTOMATIC UPDATES CLIENT

Estimated completion time: 20 minutes

For the Automatic Updates client to download its updates from an SUS server, rather than the Windows Update servers on the Internet, you must deploy Automatic Updates configuration settings using group policies. In this exercise, you create a new Group Policy Object (GPO) containing the appropriate settings and apply it to your domain.

1. On Computer*xx*, log on to the domain*xxyy* domain using the Administrator account and the password **P@ssw0rd**.
2. Open the Active Directory Users And Computers console.
3. Open the Properties dialog box for the domain*xxyy*.contoso.com domain and click the Group Policy tab.

4. Click New and give the new GPO the name **Automatic Updates**.

5. Click Edit.

   The Group Policy Object Editor console appears.

6. In the console tree under Computer Configuration, expand the Administrative Templates and Windows Components folders and select the Windows Update folder.

   The four Windows Update policies appear in the right pane.

7. Click the Standard tab.

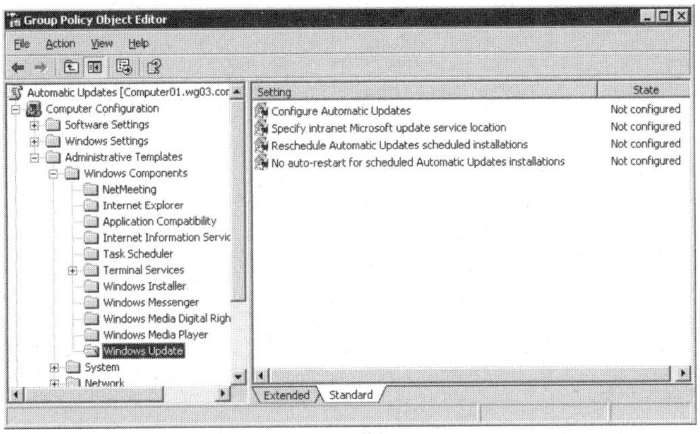

8. Double-click the Configure Automatic Updates policy.

   The Configure Automatic Updates Properties dialog box appears.

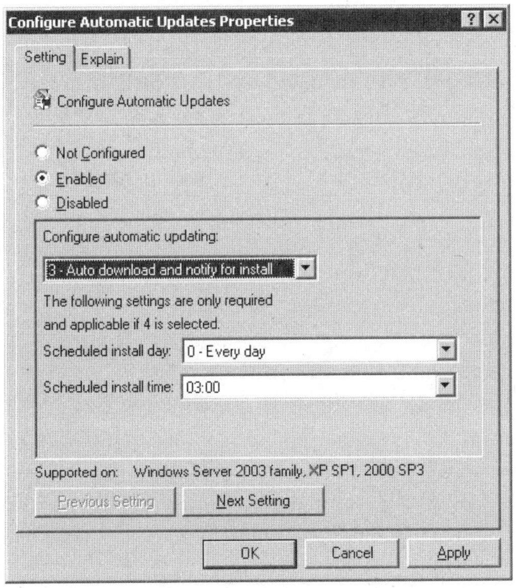

9. Select the Enabled option.
10. In the Configure Automatic Updating drop-down list, select 3–Auto Download And Notify For Install. Then click OK.
11. Double-click the Specify Intranet Microsoft Update Service Location policy.

    The Specify Intranet Microsoft Update Service Location Properties dialog box appears.

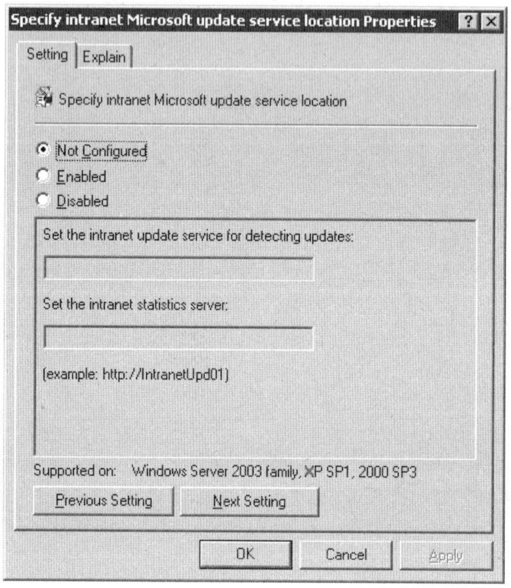

12. Select the Enabled option.
13. In the Set The Intranet Update Service For Detecting Updates text box, type **http://computer*yy***, where *yy* is the number of the computer in your lab group running SUS.
14. Type the same URL in the Set The Intranet Statistics Server text box and click OK.
15. Double-click the Reschedule Automatic Updates Scheduled Installations policy.

The Reschedule Automatic Updates Scheduled Installations Properties dialog box appears.

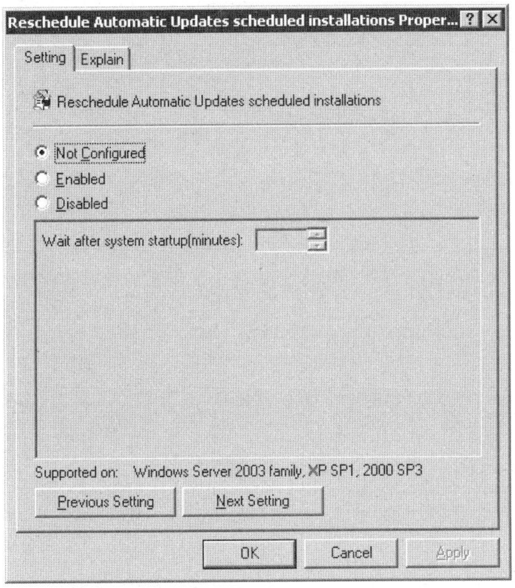

16. Select the Enabled option, and click OK to accept the default value of 5 minutes.

17. Close the Group Policy Object Editor console, and click OK to close the domain*xxyy*.contoso.com Properties dialog box.

18. Close the Active Directory Users And Computers console.

19. Open a Command Prompt window and type the command **gpupdate /force**. Then press ENTER.

    The policies are refreshed on the computer.

    After a few minutes, an Automatic Updates icon appears in the taskbar's notification area, indicating that new updates have been downloaded and are ready to install.

20. Click the Automatic Updates icon in the notification area.

    An Automatic Updates dialog box appears.

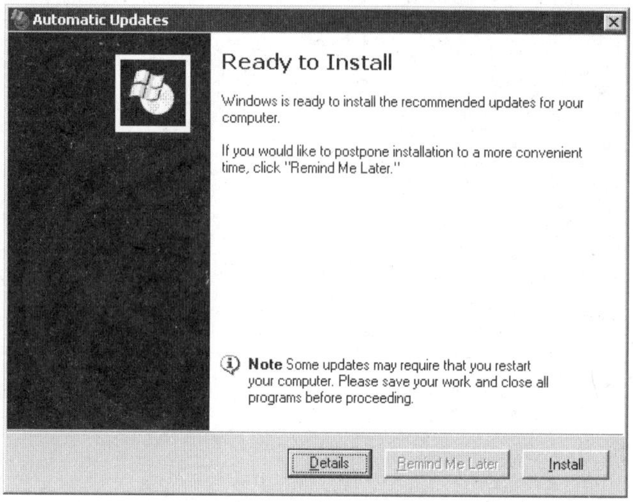

21. Click Install.

    The Automatic Updates client installs the updates it downloaded from the SUS server. After a few minutes, the Restart Your Computer To Finish page appears.

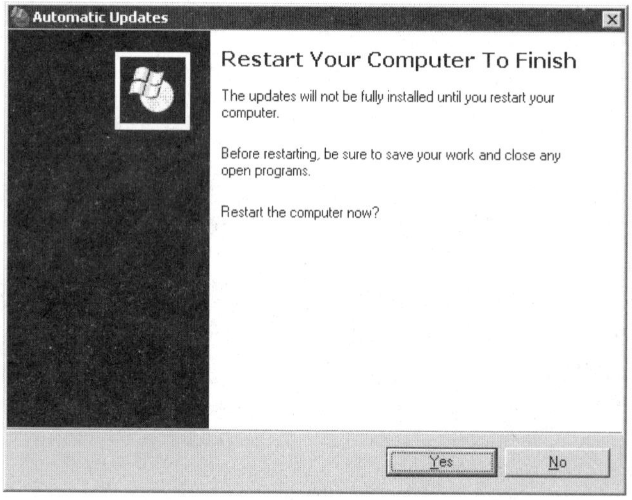

22. Click No to defer the system restart until later.
23. Leave the computer logged on for the next exercise.

EXERCISE 6-4: SCHEDULING AUTOMATIC UPDATES

Estimated completion time: 15 minutes

After you initially test the updates you deployed to the computers on Contoso's network, you decide that you want the Automatic Updates installations to occur after normal working hours, so you plan to create a daily schedule for them. Because automatic updates occur every 17 to 22 hours, testing a scheduled installation can often be a time-consuming process. In this exercise, you reconfigure the GPO you created in Exercise 6-3, and then you manually trigger an automatic update by modifying the registry on a client computer.

1. On Computer*xx*, open the Automatic Updates GPO you created in Exercise 6-3.
2. Open the Configure Automatic Updates Properties dialog box, and set the Configure Automatic Updating value to 4–Auto Download And Schedule The Install.
3. On the Scheduled Install Day drop-down list, select 0–Every Day.
4. On the Scheduled Install Time drop-down list, select the next hour after the current time. Then click OK.
5. Double-click the No Auto-Restart For Scheduled Automatic Updates Installations policy.

   The No Auto-Restart For Scheduled Automatic Updates Installations Properties dialog box appears.

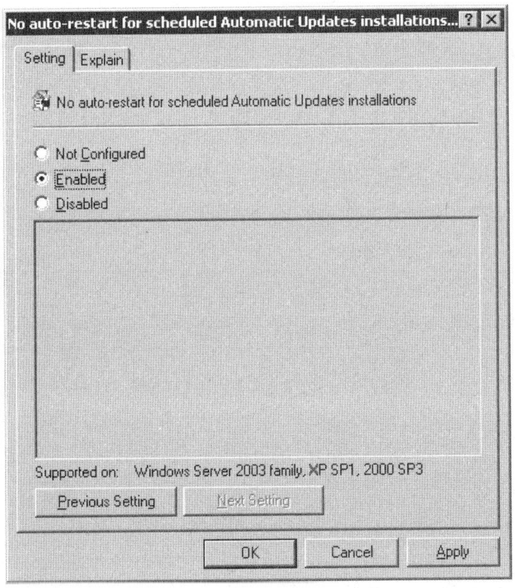

6. Select Enabled and click OK.

7. Close the Group Policy Object Editor console and the Active Directory Users And Computers console.

8. On Computeryy, open a Command Prompt window and type the command **gpupdate /force**. Then press ENTER.

   The policies are refreshed on the computer.

9. Click Start, point to Administrative Tools, and select Services.

   The Services console appears.

10. Click the Standard tab.

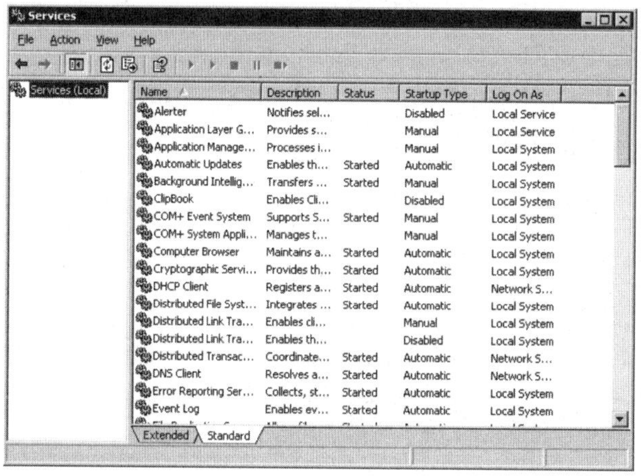

11. Right-click the Automatic Updates service and, from the context menu, select Stop.

    The Automatic Updates Service stops.

12. Click Start and open the Run dialog box. In the Open text box, type **regedit** and click OK.

    The Registry Editor window appears.

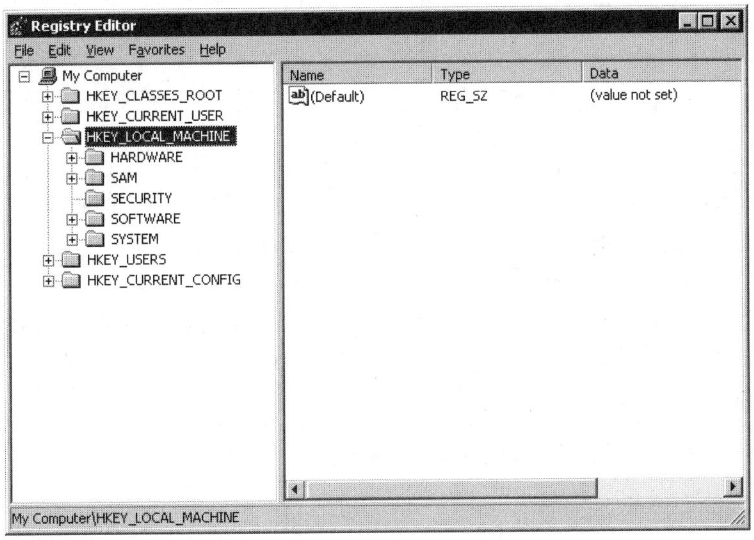

13. Browse to the HKEY_LOCAL_MACHINE\Software\Microsoft\Windows\CurrentVersion\WindowsUpdate\Auto Update registry key.

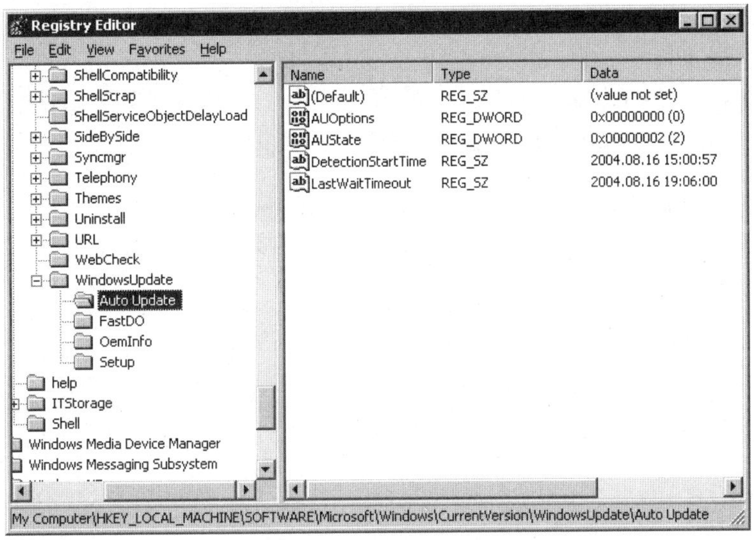

14. Confirm that the value of the AUState registry value is set to 2.
15. Click the LastWaitTimeout registry value and press DELETE.
16. Click Yes to confirm the deletion of the registry value.
17. Switch back to the Services console, and restart the Automatic Updates service.

    In approximately 10 minutes, the update detection process begins. Within a few more minutes, the New Updates Are Ready To Install icon appears in the notification area.

18. Log off both computers.

LAB REVIEW QUESTIONS

Estimated completion time: 15 minutes

1. What would happen if you installed SUS first, and then installed IIS?
2. In Exercise 6-2, you synchronized your newly installed SUS server from another SUS installation running on the classroom Server01 computer. If you were to synchronize to the Windows Update servers on the Internet instead, would the process in most cases take more or less time? Explain why.
3. In Exercise 6-3, why was it not necessary to configure the No Auto-Restart For Scheduled Automatic Updates Installations policy?

LAB CHALLENGE 6-1: EXAMINING SUS LOG ENTRIES

Estimated completion time: 30 minutes

By default, IIS stores logs of its activity in the C:\Windows\System32\Logfiles\W3SVC1 folder, as text files with a .log extension. To complete this challenge, open the log file on Computer*yy* in Notepad and use the information it contains to answer the following questions.

1. How many updates did Computer*xx* receive from the SUS server? How can you tell?
2. What account did Internet Explorer use to access the SUS administrative Web site? How can you tell?
3. What account did the Automatic Updates client on Computer*xx* use to connect to the SUS server? How can you tell?
4. Locate the GET command generated in Exercise 6-2 when you configured the SUS server to use Server01 to synchronize its updates and copy it to a new Notepad file with the name Domain*xxyy*Lab06-3.txt (where *xx* and *yy* are the numbers assigned to the computers in your student domain), which you will turn in at the end of the lab.
5. What is the name of the file containing the list of updates available from the SUS server?
6. Locate one of the commands in the log file generated by a client requesting the list of available updates from the SUS server, copy it, and paste it into the Domain*xxyy*Lab06-3.txt file you created in Step 4.

TROUBLESHOOTING LAB A: DEPLOYING UPDATES

Troubleshooting Lab A is a practical application of the knowledge you have acquired from Labs 1 through 6. Your instructor or lab assistant has changed your computer's configuration, causing it to "break." Your task in this lab will be to apply your acquired skills to troubleshoot and resolve the break. Two scenarios are presented that lay out the parameters of the breaks and the conditions that must be met for the scenarios to be resolved. The first break scenario involves the Microsoft Software Update Services (SUS) server and the second break scenario involves the Automatic Updates client.

> **NOTE** In this lab you see the characters xx and yy. These directions assume that you are working on computers configured in pairs and that each computer has a number. When you see xx, substitute the unique number assigned to the lower-numbered computer of the pair. When you see yy, substitute the unique number assigned to the higher-numbered computer of the pair. For example, if you are using computers named Computer01 and Computer02:
>
> Computerxx = Computer01 = lower-numbered computer
>
> Computeryy = Computer02 = higher-numbered computer

> **CAUTION** **Do not proceed with this lab until you receive guidance from your instructor.** Your instructor will inform you which break scenario you will be performing (Break Scenario 1 or Break Scenario 2) and which computer to use. Your instructor or lab assistant may also have special instructions. Consult with your instructor before proceeding.

Break Scenario 1

You are a senior network administrator at Contoso, Ltd., and you receive a call from a colleague, Bryan, at one of the company's branch offices. Bryan is attempting to deploy Microsoft Software Update Services (SUS) at the branch site, to automatically install updates on all of the computers at that office. However, although Bryan thinks he installed SUS successfully, the server consistently fails to synchronize updates. Bryan explains that he installed the SUS software on a

Microsoft Windows Server 2003 computer called Computer*yy* and configured it to obtain its updates from the master SUS server, called Server01 and located at the company headquarters. You agree to help Bryan by taking a look at his SUS server, to see if you can locate the problem. Because the Microsoft Internet Explorer branch office is located in another city, your only means of accessing Computer*yy* is to connect using on your workstation, Computer*xx*.

> **TIP Hint** *The default URL for an SUS server's administrative interface is http://servername/susadmin.*

As you resolve the problem, fill out the worksheet in the Lab Manual\TroubleshootingLabA folder and include the following information:

- Description of the problem.
- A list of all steps taken to diagnose the problem, even the ones that did not work.
- Description of the exact issue and its solution.
- A list the tools and resources you used to help solve this problem.

Break Scenario 2

Bryan, the network administrator at a branch office of Contoso, Ltd., called you about a problem he has implementing Software Update Services on his network. Bryan seems to have the SUS server, which is called Computer*yy*, running properly, but some of his computers successfully retrieve updates, while others do not. Bryan explains that, to configure the Automatic Updates clients on his computers, he created a new Group Policy object (GPO) called Automatic Updates and applied it to his domain object, which is called domain*xxyy*.contoso.com. In the Automatic Updates GPO, Bryan configured the Windows Update settings using the following values:

- Configure Automatic Updates: Enabled
  - Configure Automatic Updating: 4–Auto Download And Schedule The Install
  - Scheduled Install Day: 0–Every Day
  - Scheduled Install Time: 06:00
- Specify Intranet Microsoft Update Service Location: Enabled

    - Set The Intranet Update Service For Detecting Updates: *http://computeryy*
    - Set The Intranet Statistics Server: *http://computeryy*
- Reschedule Automatic Updates Scheduled Installations: Enabled
    - Wait After System Startup (Minutes): 5
    - No Auto-Restart For Scheduled Automatic Updates Installations: Enabled

After creating and applying this GPO, and then using the Gpupdate.exe utility to force a Group Policy update on his computers, Bryan notices that the computers in the Sales organizational unit (OU) are being updated properly, but none of the computers in any other container are being updated. Bryan asks you to look at his system and see if you can locate the problem.

> **TIP Hint** *Because Computeryy is not located in the Sales OU, you can troubleshoot the problem by determining why Computeryy is not receiving updates from the SUS server.*

As you resolve the problem, fill out the worksheet in the Lab Manual\TroubleshootingLabA folder and include the following information:

- Description of the problem.
- A list of all steps taken to diagnose the problem, even the ones that did not work.
- Description of the exact issue and its solution
- A list the tools and resources you used to help solve this problem.

LAB 7

INSTALLING, CONFIGURING, AND MANAGING CERTIFICATION SERVICES

This lab contains the following exercises and activities:

- Lab Exercise 7-1: Preparing the Lab Environment
- Lab Exercise 7-2: Installing an Enterprise CA
- Lab Exercise 7-3: Using the Certificate Templates Snap-In
- Lab Exercise 7-4: Using the Certificates Snap-In
- Lab Exercise 7-5: Installing a Stand-Alone CA
- Lab Exercise 7-6: Using Web Enrollment
- Lab Review Questions
- Lab Challenge 7-1: Backing Up a CA

SCENARIO

Contoso, Ltd., is in the process of deploying a public key infrastructure (PKI), and you have been assigned the task of installing, configuring, and testing two certification authorities (CAs). One of the CAs is intended for the company's internal users, to provide them with certificates for secure e-mail, digital signing, and the use of the Encrypting File System (EFS). The other CA is for Contoso's clients, who will be able to access the company extranet after requesting and obtaining certificates from a Web site.

After completing this lab, you will be able to:

- Install a CA
- Modify a certificate template
- Request certificates using the Certificates snap-in and the Web enrollment interface

Estimated lesson time: 105 minutes

BEFORE YOU BEGIN

To complete this lab, you will need the following information:

- The names of the computers in your student domain (Computer*xx* and Computer*yy*)
- The name of your student domain (domain*xxyy*.contoso.com)

EXERCISE 7-1: PREPARING THE LAB ENVIRONMENT

Estimated completion time: 5 minutes

1. On Computer*yy*, log on using the local Administrator account and the password **P@ssw0rd**.
2. Click Start, point to Control Panel, and select Add Or Remove Programs.

   The Add Or Remove Programs window appears.
3. Select Software Update Services and click Remove.
4. Follow the instructions to uninstall Software Update Services (SUS).
5. In the Add Or Remove Programs window, click Add/Remove Windows Components.

   The Windows Components Wizard appears.
6. Select Application Server and click Details.

   The Application Server dialog box appears.
7. Clear the Internet Information Server (IIS) check box and click OK.
8. Click Next and follow the instructions to remove IIS from the system.
9. Close the Add Or Remove Programs window.
10. Log off the computer.

EXERCISE 7-2: INSTALLING AN ENTERPRISE CA

Estimated completion time: 15 minutes

The CA that Contoso's internal clients will use to obtain their end-user certificates will run on Computer*xx*, the domain controller for the domain*xxyy* domain. This will be an enterprise CA, but because there is already an enterprise root CA running on Server01, Computer*xx* can be an enterprise subordinate CA. In this exercise, you install the CA and retrieve a certificate from the root CA.

1. On Computer*xx*, log on to the contoso domain using the Administrator account and the password **P@ssw0rd**.

   NOTE Logging On to the Parent Domain In the Log On To Windows dialog box, be sure to select contoso in the Domain drop-down list.

2. Click Start, point to Control Panel, and then click Add Or Remove Programs.

   The Add Or Remove Programs dialog box appears.

3. Click Add/Remove Windows Components.

   The Windows Components Wizard appears.

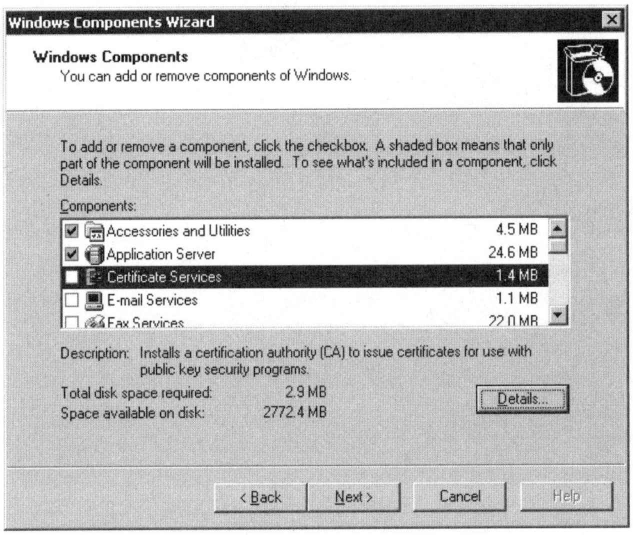

4. Select Application Server and then click Details.

   The Application Server dialog box appears.

5. Select the Internet Information Services (IIS) check box and then click Details.

   The Internet Information Services (IIS) dialog box appears.

6. Select World Wide Web Service and click Details.

   The World Wide Web Service dialog box appears.

7. Select the Active Server Pages check box and click OK.
8. Click OK to close the Internet Information Services (IIS) dialog box.
9. Click OK to close the Application Server dialog box.
10. Select the Certificate Services check box.

    A Microsoft Certificate Services message box appears, warning you that after you install Certificate Services, you cannot change the computer's machine name or domain membership without affecting the function of the CA.

11. Click Yes to continue.
12. In the Windows Components Wizard, click Next.

    The CA Type page appears.

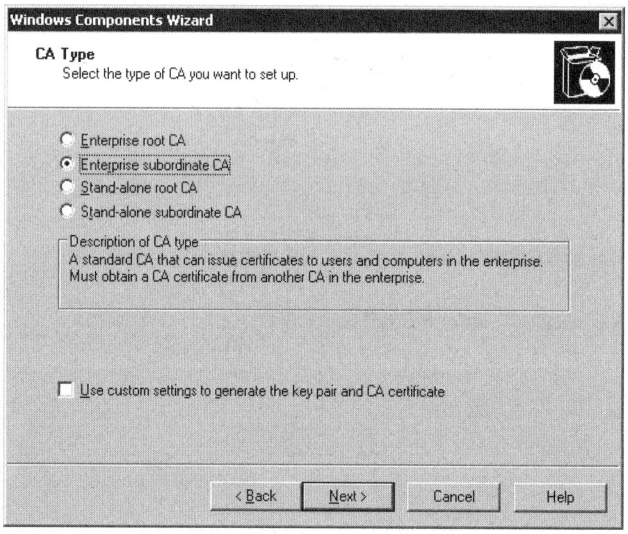

13. Select the Enterprise Subordinate CA option and the Use Custom Settings To Generate The Key Pair And CA Certificate check box, and then click Next.

    The Public And Private Key Pair page appears.

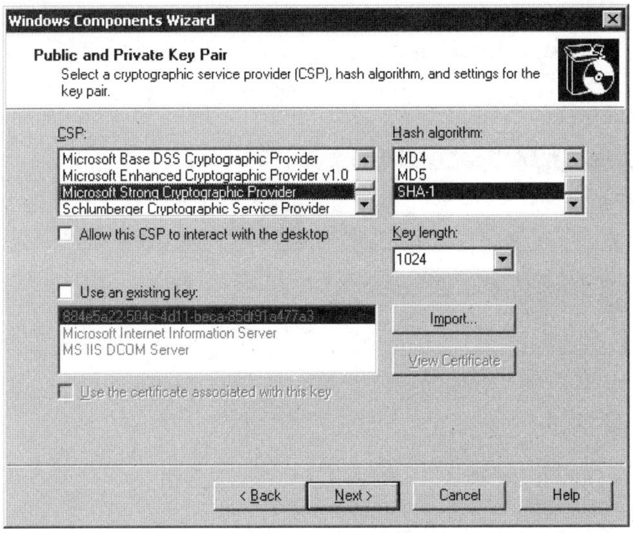

14. Change the Key Length setting to 4096, and click Next.

The CA Identifying Information page appears.

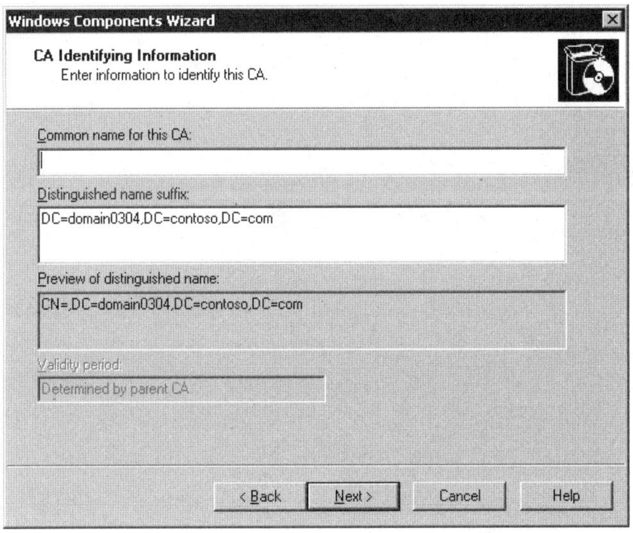

QUESTION What are the advantages and disadvantages of increasing the Key Length setting?

15. In the Common Name For This CA text box, type **EntSub**, and then click Next.

The Cryptographic Key Generation page appears. When the system finishes generating the keys, the Certificate Database Settings page appears.

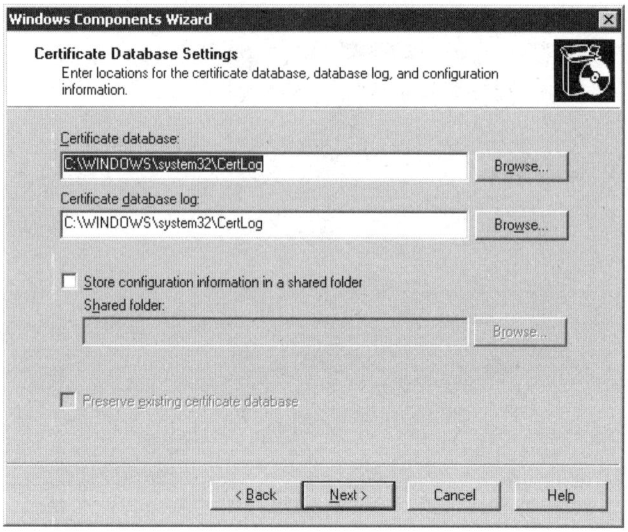

16. Click Next to accept the default database settings.

    The CA Certificate Request page appears.

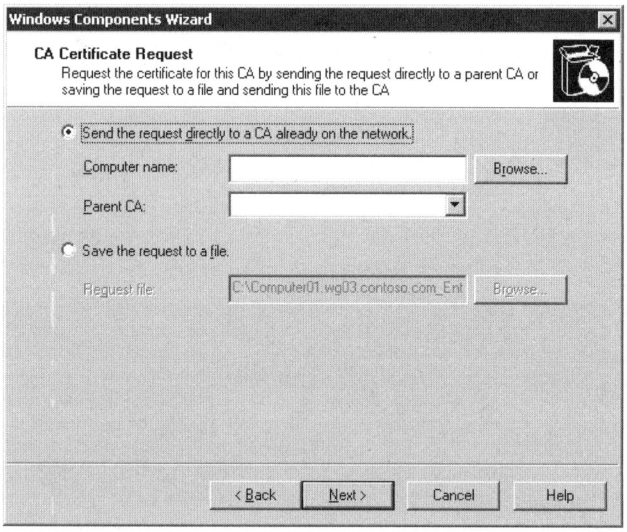

17. In the Computer Name text box, type **server01.contoso.com**.
18. In the Parent CA text box, type **EntRoot**. Then, click Next.

    A Microsoft Certificate Services message box appears, stating that the system must temporarily stop the IIS service to complete the installation.
19. Click Yes to proceed.

    The Configuring Components page appears, displaying a progress indicator as the wizard installs Certificate Services. Eventually, another Microsoft Certificate Services message box appears, stating that the system must activate Active Server Pages (ASP) in IIS.
20. Click Yes to proceed.

    The Configuring Components page finishes showing the progress of the installation.
21. When the Completing The Windows Components Wizard page appears, click Finish.
22. Close the Add Or Remove Programs dialog box.
23. Leave the computer logged on for the next exercise.

EXERCISE 7-3: USING THE CERTIFICATE TEMPLATES SNAP-IN

Estimated completion time: 15 minutes

To minimize the number of certificates issued by the EntSub CA you installed in Exercise 7-1, you plan to create a master certificate template providing all the functions the company's end users need. In this exercise, you use the Certificate Templates snap-in to copy an existing certificate template and modify it to function as the master client certificate template for the internal users.

1. On Computer*xx*, open a blank Microsoft Management Console (MMC) window and add the Certificate Templates snap-in.

2. In the console tree, select the Certificate Templates node.

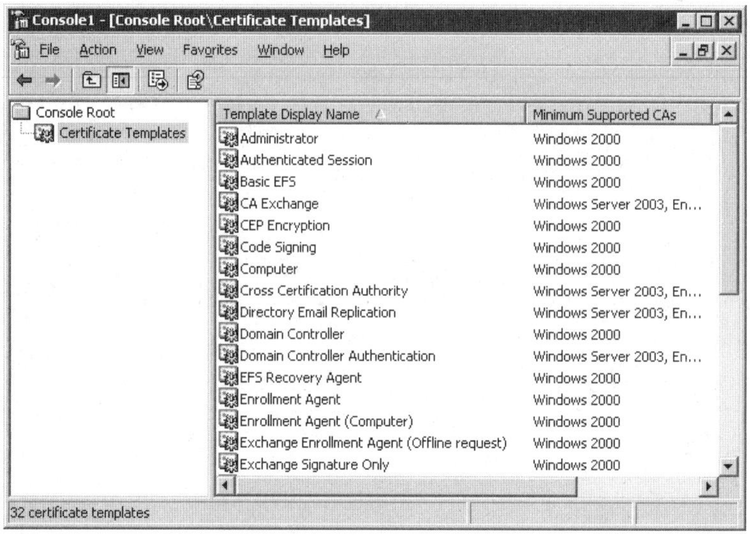

3. In the list of templates, select Basic EFS and, from the Action menu, select Duplicate Template.

   The Properties Of New Template dialog box appears.

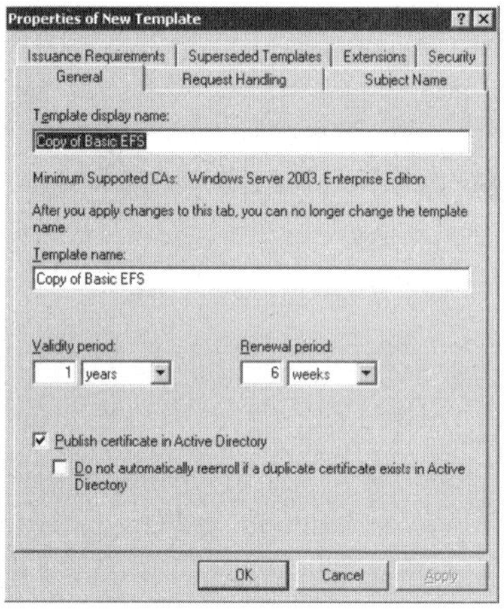

4. On the General tab, in the Template Display Name text box, type **Master Client**.

5. Click the Request Handling tab.

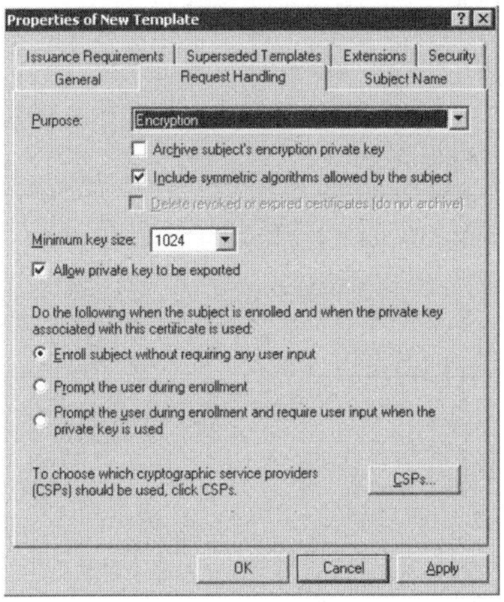

6. In the Purpose drop-down list, select Signature And Encryption.
7. In the Minimum Key Size drop-down list, select 4096.
8. Select the Prompt The User During Enrollment option.
9. Click the Extensions tab.

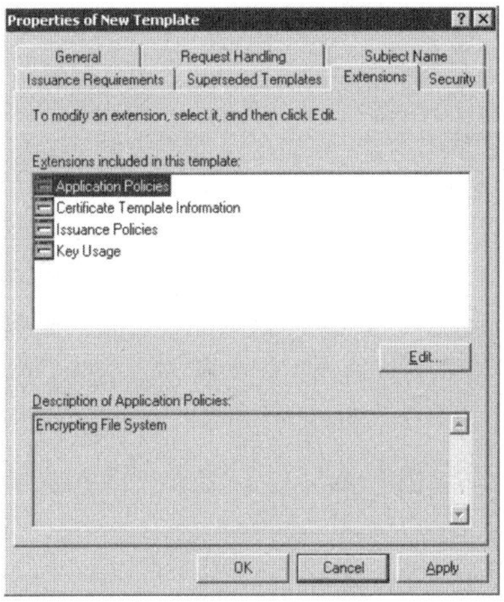

10. With Application Policies selected in the Extensions Included In This Template list, click Edit.

    The Edit Application Policies Extension dialog box appears.

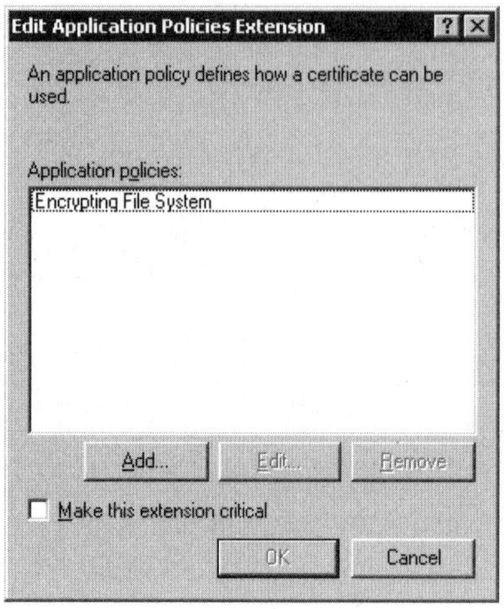

QUESTION *What application policies are currently included in the template?*

11. Click Add.

    The Add Application Policy dialog box appears.

12. Select the Document Signing, IP Security User, and Secure Email policies, and click OK.

    The new policies appear in the Edit Application Policies Extension dialog box.

13. Click OK to close the Edit Application Policies Extension dialog box.

14. Click the Security tab.

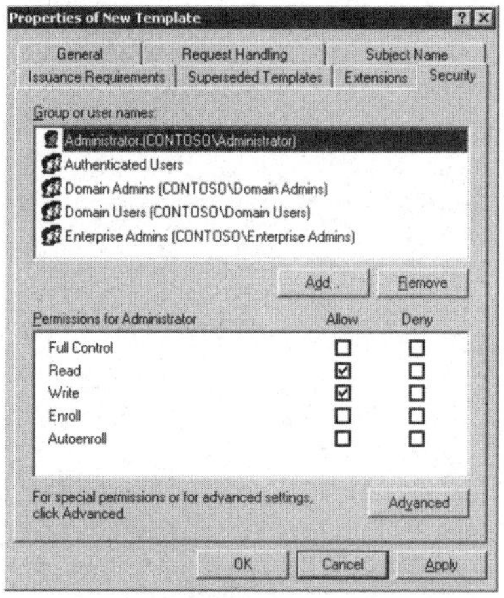

15. Select the Authenticated Users security principal and assign it the Read, Enroll, and Autoenroll permissions in the Allow column.

16. Click OK to close the Properties Of New Template dialog box.

    The Master Client template appears in the console.

17. Take a screen shot (press ALT+PRINT SCREEN) of the Certificate Templates console, showing the Master Client template you created, and paste it into a WordPad document named Domain*xxyy*Lab07-1.rtf (where *xx* and *yy* are the numbers assigned to the computers in your student domain), which you will turn in at the end of the lab.

18. Close the MMC console window.

19. A Microsoft Management Console message box appears, prompting you to save the console settings.

20. Click Yes and save the console with the name Certificate templates.msc.

21. Leave the computer logged on for later exercises.

EXERCISE 7-4: USING THE CERTIFICATES SNAP-IN

Estimated completion time: 15 minutes

Having installed the CA and created the Master Client certificate template, you must now test the CA by manually requesting a certificate. In this exercise, you use the Certificates snap-in on Computer*yy* to request and retrieve a Master Client certificate from the CA running on Computer*xx*.

1. On Computer*yy*, log on to the domain*xxyy* domain as Administrator, using the password **P@ssw0rd**.
2. Open a blank MMC window and add the Certificates snap-in.

   As the console adds the snap-in, a Certificates Snap-in dialog box appears.
3. Leave the default My User Account option selected, and click Finish.
4. In the console tree, expand the Certificates–Current User node and select Personal.

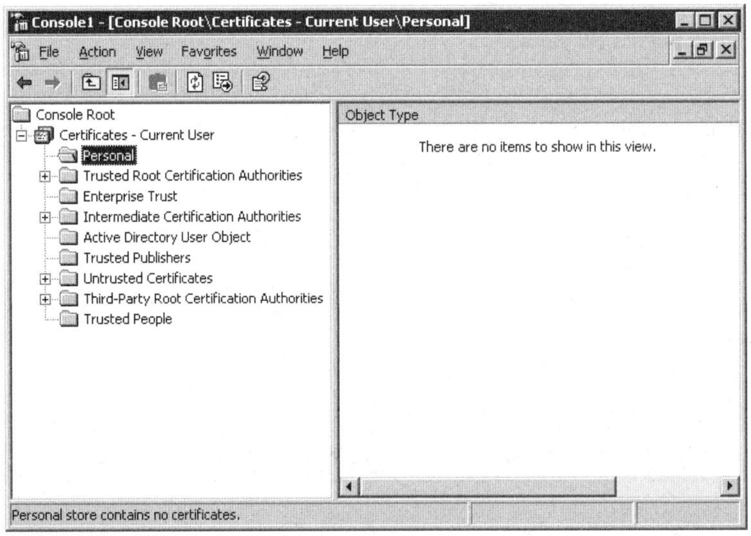

5. On the Action menu, point to All Tasks and click Request New Certificate.

QUESTION What happens?

6. Click OK.
7. On Computer*xx*, click Start, point to Administrative Tools, and select Certification Authority.

   The Certification Authority console appears.

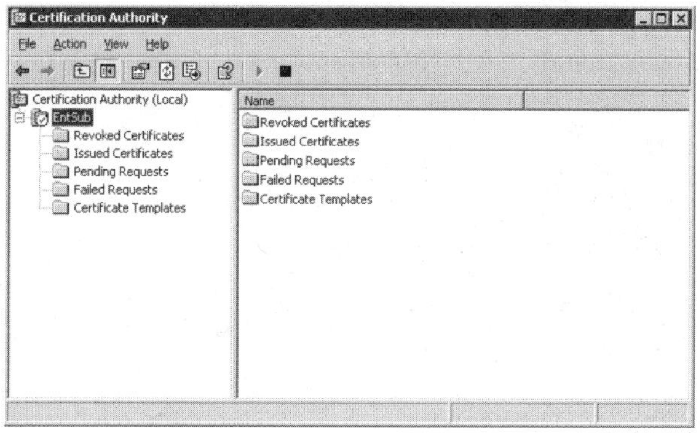

8. Expand the EntSub node and select the Certificate Templates folder.

   QUESTION *How many certificate templates are available for issue by the CA?*

9. On the Action menu, point to New and select Certificate Template To Issue.

   The Enable Certificate Templates dialog box appears.

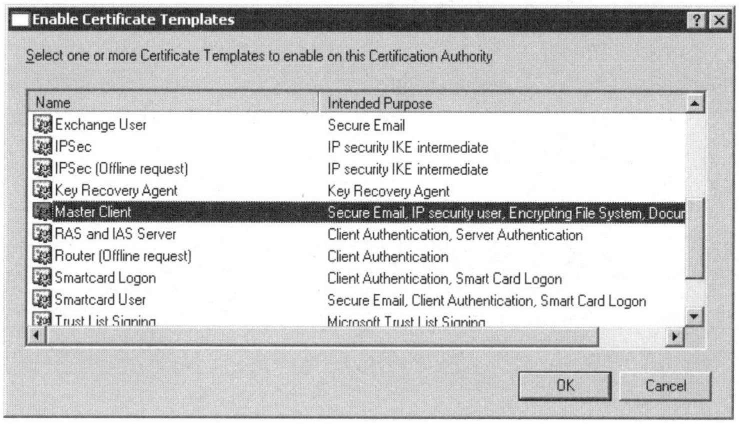

10. Scroll down and select the Master Client template you created, then click OK.

    The Master Client template is added to the list in the Certification Authority console.

11. Close the Certification Authority console.

12. Back on Computeryy, repeat step 5 to request a new certificate.

QUESTION *What happens this time?*

13. Click Next to bypass the Welcome page.

    The Certificate Types page appears, with Master Client selected in the Certificate Types box.

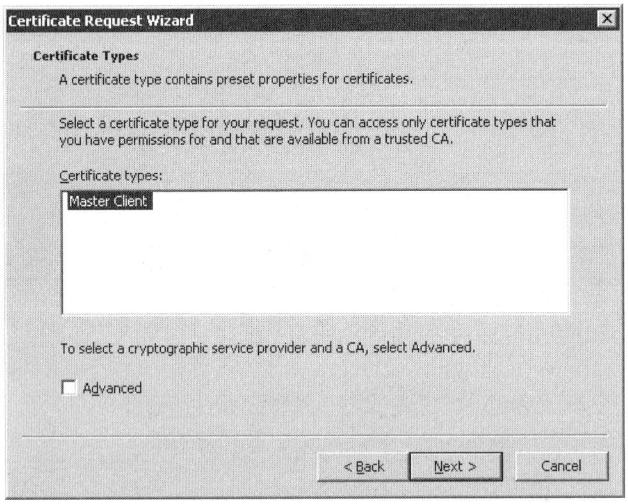

14. Select the Advanced check box and click Next.

    The Cryptographic Service Provider page appears.

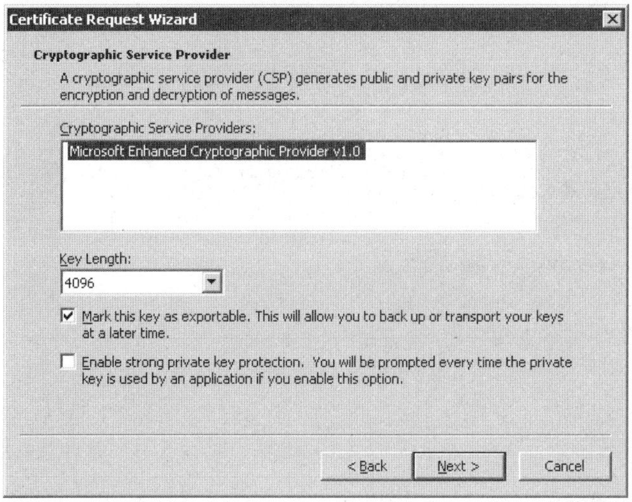

15. Select the Enable Strong Private Key Protection check box and click Next.

    The Certification Authority page appears.

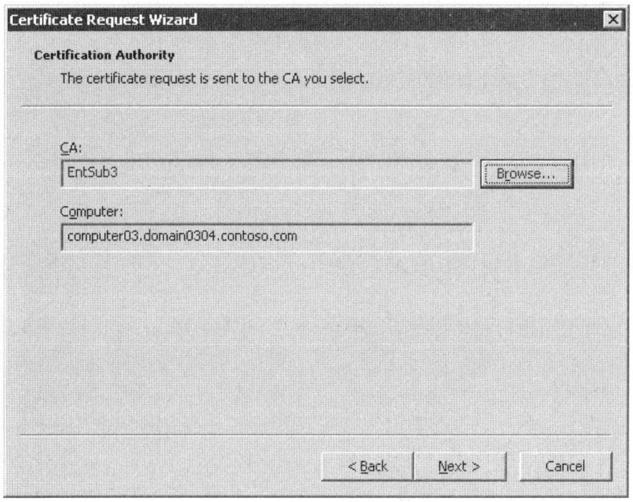

16. Click Next to accept the default settings.

    The Certificate Friendly Name And Description page appears.

17. Leave the text boxes blank and click Next.

    The Completing The Certificate Request Wizard page appears.

18. Click Finish.

    A Creating A New RSA Exchange Key dialog box appears.

19. Click OK.

    A Certificate Request Wizard appears, stating that the certificate request was successful.

20. Click OK.

21. In the Certificates console, under Personal, select the Certificates folder.

22. Double-click the certificate that appears in the folder.

    A Certificate dialog box appears, displaying the contents of the newly issued certificate.

23. Take a screen shot (press ALT+PRINT SCREEN) of the Certificate dialog box, and paste it into a WordPad document named Domain*xxyy*Lab07-2.rtf (where *xx* and *yy* are the numbers assigned to the computers in your student domain), which you will turn in at the end of the lab.

QUESTION *What CA is ultimately responsible for certifying the client? How can you tell?*

24. Close the Certificates console without saving it and leave the computers logged on for later exercises.

EXERCISE 7-5: INSTALLING A STAND-ALONE CA

Estimated completion time: 20 minutes

Contoso's extranet clients do not have credentials in the company's Active Directory directory service, so the CA they will use will be a stand-alone, not an enterprise, CA. In this exercise, you install a stand-alone root CA on Computer*yy* for the extranet clients.

> **NOTE** ***Before You Begin*** *To complete this exercise, you must have IIS installed on Computeryy, as described in Lab 6, "Deploying SUS." If you have not already completed Lab 6, be sure to install IIS on Computeryy before you begin this exercise.*

1. On Computer*yy*, open the Add Or Remove Programs dialog box and launch the Windows Components Wizard.
2. Select Application Server and then click Details.

   The Application Server dialog box appears.
3. Select the Internet Information Services (IIS) check box and then click Details.

   The Internet Information Services (IIS) dialog box appears.
4. Select World Wide Web Service and click Details.

   The World Wide Web Service dialog box appears.
5. Select the Active Server Pages check box and click OK.

6. Click OK to close the Internet Information Services (IIS) dialog box.
7. Click OK to close the Application Server dialog box.
8. In the Windows Components wizard, select Certificate Services and then click Details.

   The Certificate Services dialog box appears.

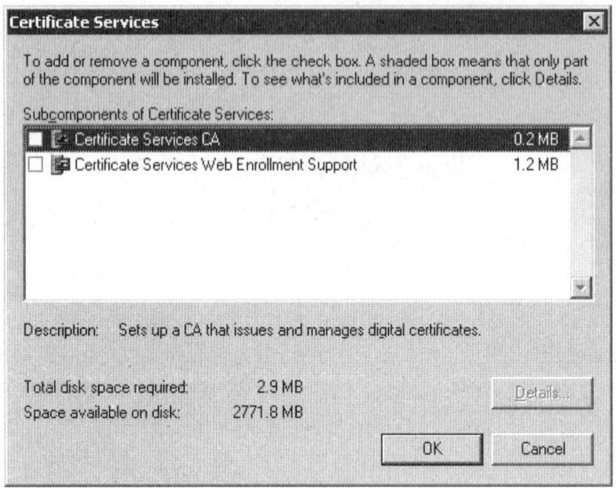

9. Select the Certificate Services CA and Certificate Services Web Enrollment Support check boxes, and then click OK.

   A Microsoft Certificate Services message box appears, warning you that, once you install Certificate Services, you cannot change the computer's machine name or domain membership without affecting the function of the CA.
10. Click Yes to continue.
11. In the Windows Components Wizard, click Next.

    The CA Type page appears.
12. Select the Stand-Alone Root CA option and click Next.

    The CA Identifying Information page appears.

13. In the Common Name For This CA text box, type **StandRoot**, and then click Next.

The Certificate Database Settings page appears.

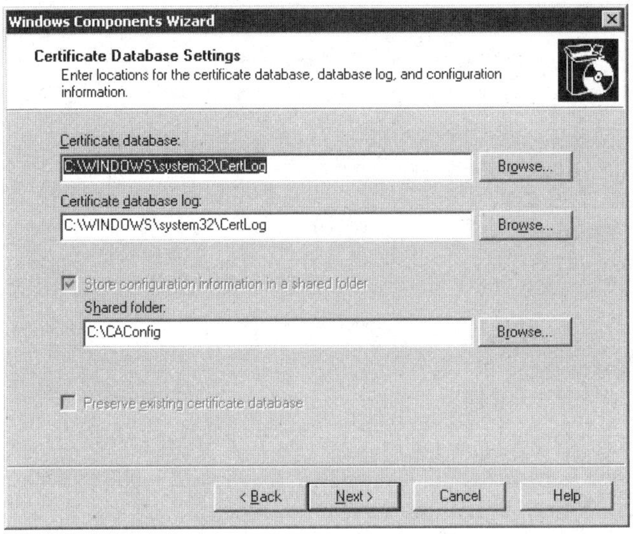

QUESTION *How do the defaults on this Certificate Database Settings page differ from those you accepted in Exercise 7-1?*

14. Click Next to accept the default database settings.

A Microsoft Certificate Services message box appears, stating that the system must temporarily stop the IIS service to complete the installation.

15. Click Yes to proceed.

The Configuring Components page appears, displaying a progress indicator as the wizard installs Certificate Services. Eventually, the Completing The Windows Components Wizard page appears.

16. Click Finish.

17. Close the Add Or Remove Programs dialog box.

18. Click Start, point to Administrative Tools, and click Certification Authority.

    The Certification Authority console appears.

19. Select the StandRoot icon in the console tree and, from the Action menu, select Properties.

    The StandRoot Properties dialog box appears.

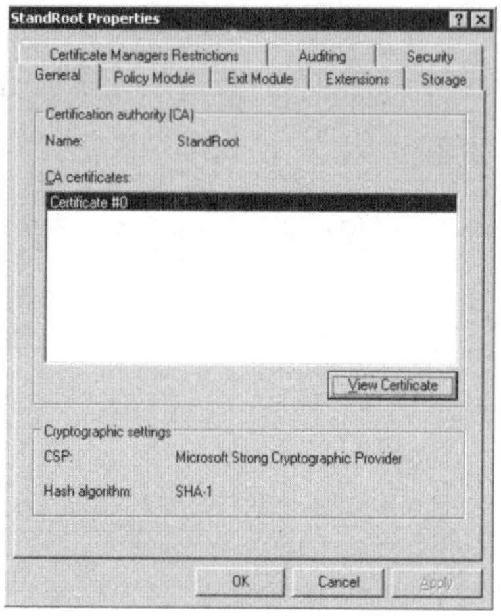

20. Click the View Certificate button and take a screen shot (press ALT+PRINT SCREEN) of the Certificates dialog box. Then, paste it into a WordPad document named Domain*xxyy*Lab07-3.rtf (where *xx* and *yy* are the numbers assigned to the computers in your student domain), which you will turn in at the end of the lab.

21. Leave the Certification Authority console open.

EXERCISE 7-6: USING WEB ENROLLMENT

Estimated completion time: 20 minutes

With the stand-alone CA installed, you must now test it by requesting and issuing a certificate. In this exercise, you use the Web enrollment interface to connect to the stand-alone CA and request a certificate. Then, you manually issue the certificate using the Certification Authority console and return to the Web enrollment interface to retrieve it.

1. On Computer*xx*, open Microsoft Internet Explorer and, in the Address text box, type **http://computer*yy*/certsrv**, where *yy* is the number assigned to the computer, and press ENTER.

   The Microsoft Certificate Services page appears.

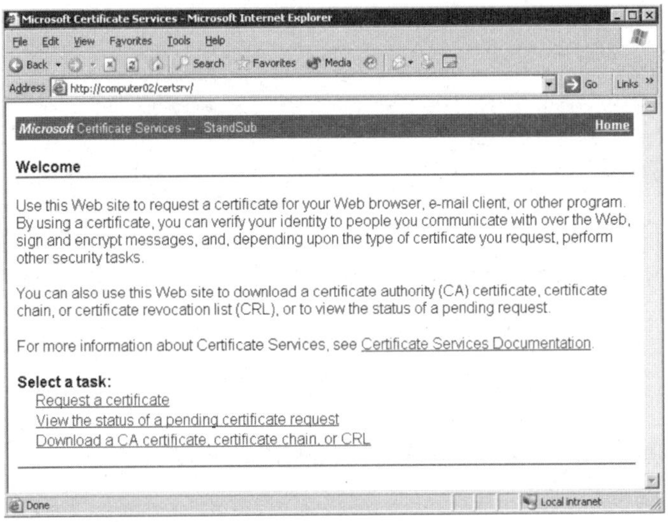

2. Click Request A Certificate.

   The Request A Certificate page appears.

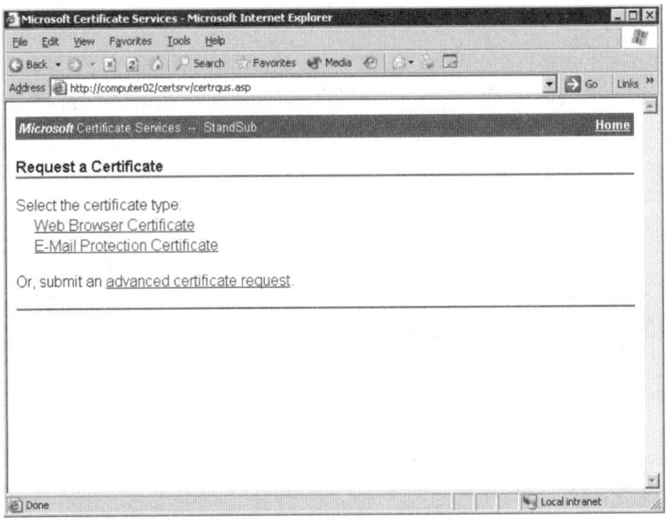

3. Click Advanced Certificate Request.

   The Advanced Certificate Request page appears.

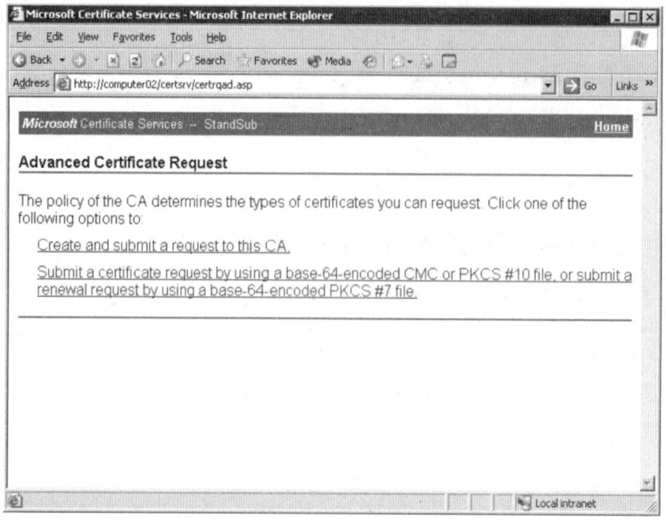

4. Click Create And Submit A Request To This CA.

   The Advanced Certificate Request form appears.

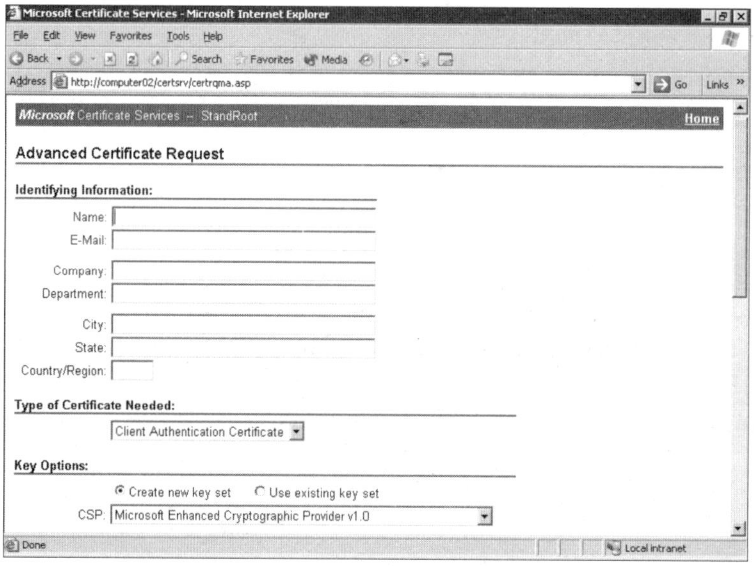

5. In the Name text box, type **Mark Lee**.
6. In the Type Of Certificate Needed drop-down list, leave the default Client Authentication Certificate setting.
7. In the CSP drop-down list, select Microsoft Strong Cryptographic Provider.
8. In the Key Size text box, type **2048**, and then click Submit at the bottom of the form.

   A Potential Scripting Violation message box appears, prompting you to confirm your request.

9. Click Yes.

   The Certificate Pending page appears, informing you that your request has been submitted to the CA and that you must wait for an administrator to issue the certificate.

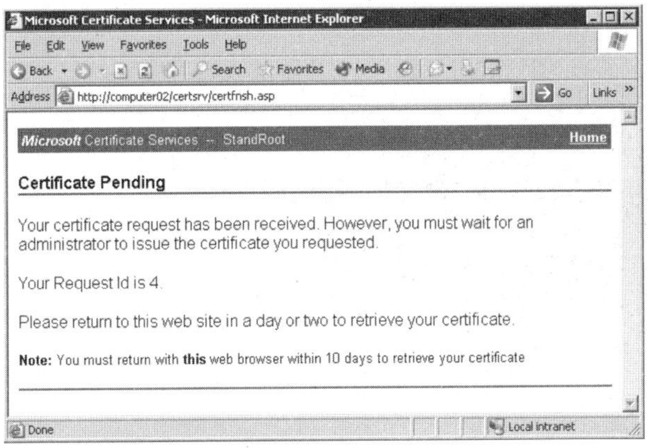

QUESTION *Why was the certificate not issued immediately?*

QUESTION *What is the Request ID assigned to the enrollment request?*

10. On Computeryy, in the Certification Authority console, expand the StandRoot icon in the console tree, and then click the Pending Requests folder.

The request you generated in the first exercise appears in the right pane.

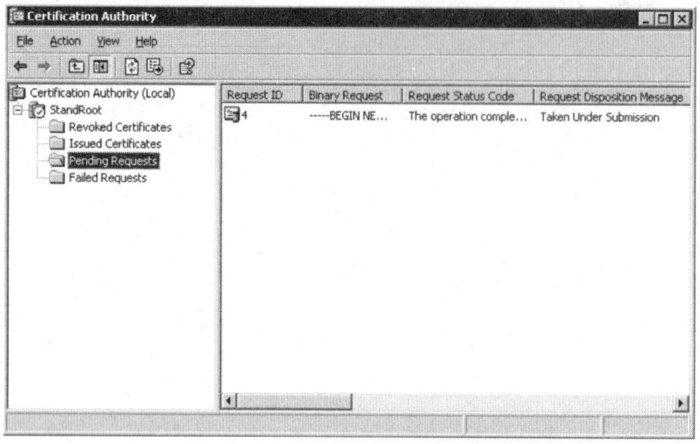

11. Right-click the request, point to All Tasks, and then select Issue.

The request disappears from the folder.

12. Click the Issued Certificates folder.

The request you just approved now appears in the Issued Certificates list.

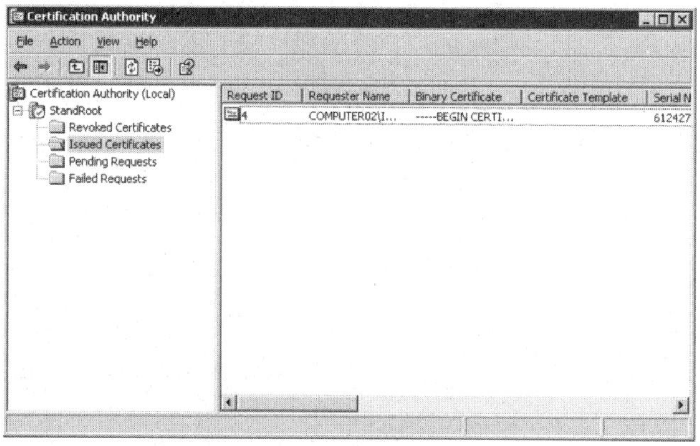

13. Close the Certification Authority console.

14. On Computer*xx*, in the Internet Explorer window, click the Home link.

The Microsoft Certificate Services Web page appears again.

15. Click View The Status Of A Pending Certificate Request.

The View The Status Of A Pending Certificate Request page appears.

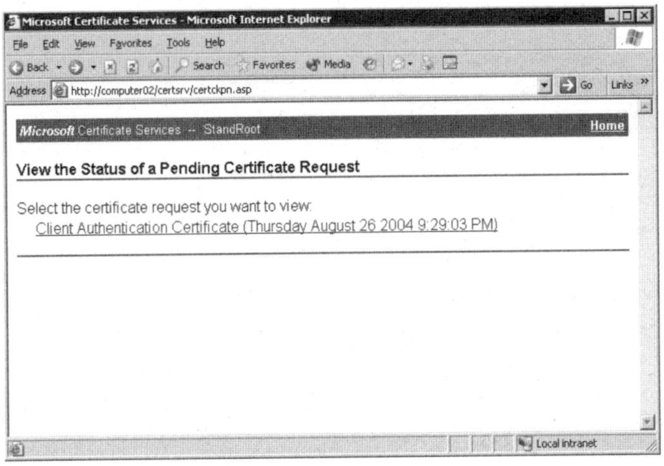

16. Click the Client Authentication Certificate link.

The Certificate Issued page appears, stating that the certificate you requested was issued to you.

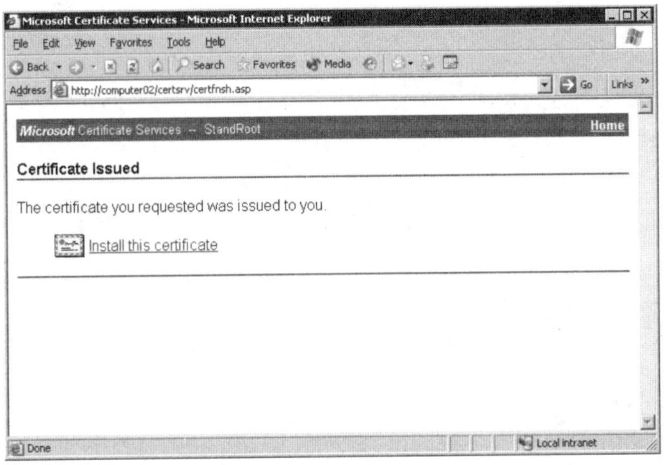

17. Click Install This Certificate.

A Potential Scripting Violation message box appears, prompting you to confirm the installation of the certificate.

18. Click Yes.

A Security Warning page appears, informing you of the potential danger involved in installing the certificate.

19. Click Yes to install the certificate.

    The Certificate Installed page appears.

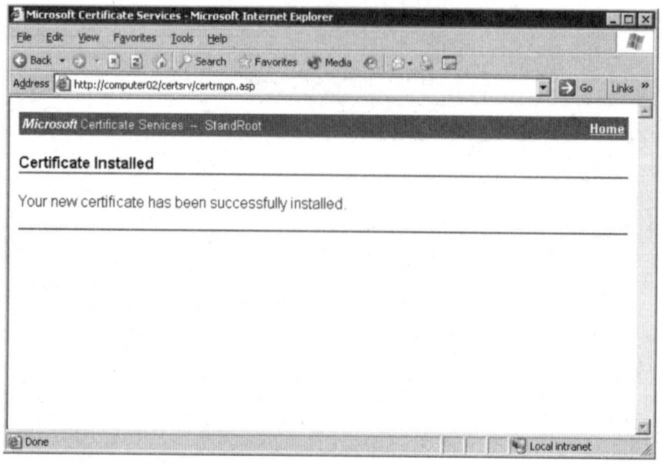

20. Close Internet Explorer.
21. Create an MMC console containing the Certificates snap-in for the current user.
22. Locate the certificate issued to Mark Lee in the \Personal\Certificates folder and open it.
23. Take a screen shot (press ALT+PRINT SCREEN) of the Certificates dialog box, and paste it into a WordPad document named Domain*xxyy*Lab07-4.rtf (where *xx* and *yy* are the numbers assigned to the computers in your student domain), which you will turn in at the end of the lab.

LAB REVIEW QUESTIONS

Estimated completion time: 15 minutes

1. In Exercise 7-2, why was it necessary to log on to the contoso domain instead of the domain*xxyy* domain?
2. In Exercise 7-2, when the CA Certificate Request page appears, what would you have to do next if you selected the Save The Request To A File option instead of Send The Request Directly To A CA Already On The Network?

3. In Exercise 7-4, in the Certificates snap-in, what determines which types of certificates are listed on the Certificate Types page?

4. In Exercise 7-4, what information did the CA use to determine whether or not to issue the requested certificate?

5. If, after installing the enterprise subordinate CA in Exercise 7-2, you were to take Server01's enterprise root CA offline, which of the following statements would be true?

   a. The subordinate CA could no longer issue certificates to clients.

   b. You could not install any more CAs using Server01 as the parent.

   c. All certificates issued by the enterprise root server would be invalidated.

   d. You could not install a subordinate CA using Computer*xx* as its parent.

LAB CHALLENGE 7-1: BACKING UP A CA

Estimated completion time: 30 minutes

On Computer*xx*, using the Certification Authority console, configure the server to audit all CA backup and restore processes. Next, perform a full backup of the CA's private key, CA certificate, certificate database, and certificate database log to a folder named C:\CABackup. Use the password **P@ssw0rd** when you perform the backup. Then, use the Microsoft Windows Server 2003 Backup program to back up the CABackup folder to a single file named C:\CABackup*xxyy*.bkf, where *xx* and *yy* are the numbers assigned to the computers in your student domain. Once the backup is complete, open the Event Viewer console and take a screen shot (press ALT+PRINT SCREEN) of the Event Properties dialog box demonstrating that the CA backup procedure has been successfully completed. Then paste the screen shot into a WordPad document named Domain*xxyy*Lab07-5.rtf (where *xx* and *yy* are the numbers assigned to the computers in your student domain), which you will turn in at the end of the lab along with the C:\CABackup*xxyy*.bkf file.

LAB 8

PLANNING AND CONFIGURING IPSEC

This lab contains the following exercises and activities:

- Lab Exercise 8-1: Preparing the Web Server
- Lab Exercise 8-2: Creating an IP Filter List
- Lab Exercise 8-3: Creating an IP Filter Action
- Lab Exercise 8-4: Creating an IP Security Policy
- Lab Review Questions
- Lab Challenge 8-1: Creating Complex Filter Actions

SCENARIO

The IT director of Contoso, Ltd., wants to install a secure intranet Web server that will enable selected users to access confidential documents without the danger of those documents being intercepted by someone illicitly capturing network traffic. The director has assigned you the task of deploying the Web server and demonstrating to him that it is safe to use the server to transmit sensitive data. In this lab, you will prepare the Web server and configure the Internet Protocol Security (IPSec) policy needed to protect the Web traffic. In Lab 9, "Deploying and Troubleshooting IPSec," you will deploy the IPSec policy on your student domain, test it, and monitor the IPSec traffic.

After completing this lab, you will be able to:

- Create an IP filter list
- Create an IP filter action
- Create an IPSec policy

Estimated lesson time: 75 minutes

BEFORE YOU BEGIN

To complete this lab, you will need the following information:

- The names of the computers in your student domain (Computer*xx* and Computer*yy*)
- The IP addresses of the computers in your student domain. (Run **ipconfig /all** from a command prompt to display this information.)
- The name of your student domain (domain*xxyy*.contoso.com)

EXERCISE 8-1: PREPARING THE WEB SERVER

Estimated completion time: 15 minutes

Before you set about creating a secured intranet server, you must have data to protect, so you create a sample home page on your Web server that will represent the content you want to protect from unauthorized access.

1. On Computer*yy*, log on to domain*xxyy* (where *xx* and *yy* are the numbers assigned to the computers in your lab group by your instructor) as Administrator, using the password **P@ssw0rd**.
2. Click Start, point to All Programs, point to Accessories, and click Notepad.

   The Notepad window appears.

3. In the Notepad window, type the following:

```
<HTML>
<TITLE>W A R N I N G !</TITLE>
<BODY BGCOLOR="FF0000">
<H1>WARNING!</H1>
<H2>You have accessed a secured page on a server belonging to
domainxxyy. Terminate this connection immediately or be prepared to face
departmental sanctions including loss of pay and termination of employ-
ment.</H2>
</BODY>
</HTML>
```

4. Replace the *xxyy* in the fourth line of the code listing with the numbers your administrator assigned to your lab group computers.
5. From the File menu, select Save As and save the file, giving it the name **Default.htm**, in the C:\Inetpub\Wwwroot folder on Computer*yy*.
6. Close Notepad.
7. Click Start, point to Programs, and click Internet Explorer.

   The Internet Explorer window appears.
8. In the Address text box, type **localhost** and press ENTER.

   QUESTION What is the result?

9. Leave the computer logged on for later exercises.

EXERCISE 8-2: CREATING AN IP FILTER LIST

Estimated completion time: 15 minutes

You have decided to use IPSec to secure the intranet Web server that you have been instructed to deploy. As the first step of the process, you must create an IP filter list that causes the computers on the network to encrypt Web traffic only. In this exercise, you will create an IP Security Policy Management console and use it to create a new IP filter list.

1. On Computer*xx*, open a blank Microsoft Management Console (MMC) window and create a custom console containing the IP Security Policy Management snap-in.

2. When the Select Computer Or Domain page appears, choose The Active Directory Domain Of Which This Computer Is A Member.

> **NOTE** ***Creating an MMC Console*** *To review the process of creating a custom MMC console, refer to Exercise 3-1, "Creating a Security Templates Console," in Lab 3.*

3. Save the console using the name **IP Security Policies.msc**.

4. In the console tree, select IP Security Policies On Active Directory. Then, from the Action menu, click Manage IP Filter Lists And Filter Actions.

   The Manage IP Filter Lists And Filter Actions dialog box appears.

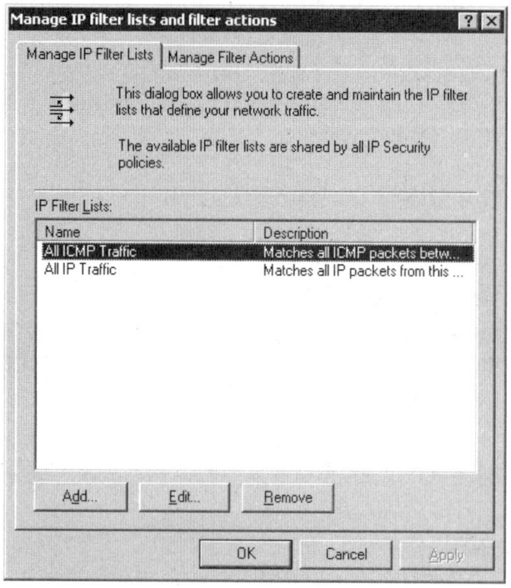

5. In the Manage IP Filter Lists Tab, click Add.

   The IP Filter List dialog box appears.

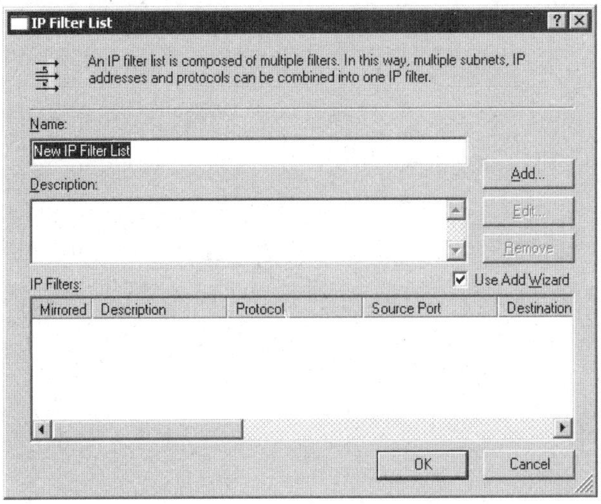

QUESTION *Why is it desirable to create IP filter lists and filter actions in Active Directory before you create local IP security policies or rules?*

6. In the Name text box, type **Intranet Web Traffic**. Then, clear the Use Add Wizard check box and click Add.

   The IP Filter Properties dialog box appears.

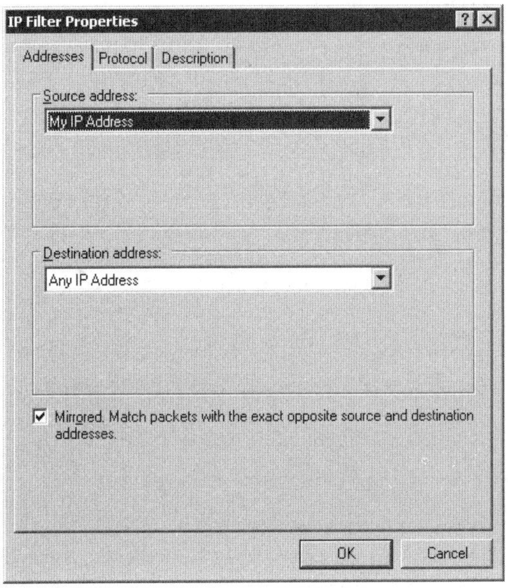

7. In the Source Address drop-down list, select A Specific IP Address.
8. In the IP Address text box that appears, enter the IP address for Computer*yy*.
9. In the Destination Address drop-down list, select A Specific IP Subnet Address.
10. In the IP Address text box that appears, type **10.1.0.0**. In the Subnet Mask text box, type **255.255.0.0**.
11. Leave the Mirrored check box selected, and click the Protocol tab.

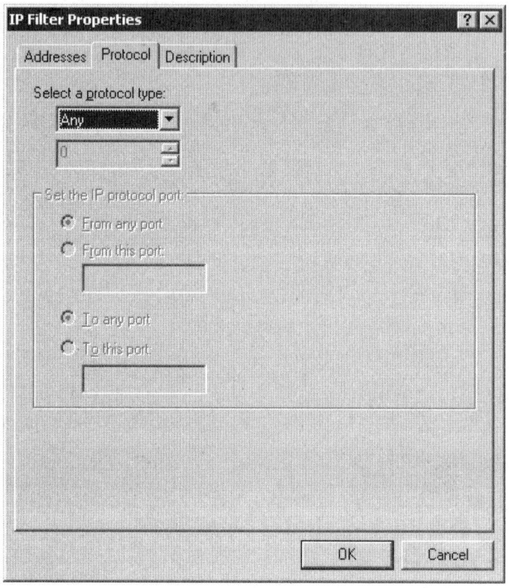

12. In the Select A Protocol Type drop-down list, select TCP.
13. Select From This Port option, and type **80** in the text box provided. Then click OK.

    The new IP filter appears in the IP Filter List dialog box.

14. Take a screen shot (press ALT+PRINT SCREEN) of the IP Filter List dialog box, showing the IP filter you created, and paste it into a WordPad document named Domain*xxyy*Lab08-1.rtf (where *xx* and *yy* are the numbers assigned to the computers in your student domain), which you will turn in at the end of the lab.

15. Click OK to close the IP Filter List dialog box.

    The Intranet Web Traffic filter list appears in the Manage IP Filter Lists And Filter Actions dialog box.

16. Click Close to close the Manage IP Filter Lists And Filter Actions dialog box.

17. Leave the IP Security Policies console open for the next exercise.

EXERCISE 8-3: CREATING AN IP FILTER ACTION

Estimated completion time: 15 minutes

After creating an IP filter list that specifies what traffic IPSec should protect, the next step in your deployment is to create a filter action that specifies how IPSec should protect the selected data. In this exercise, you will use the IP Security Policy Management console to create a filter action with higher security than the Microsoft Windows Server 2003 IPSec defaults.

1. On Computer*xx*, in the IP Security Policies console, open the Manage IP Filter Lists And Filter Actions dialog box. Click the Manage Filter Actions tab.

2. Click Add.

   The IP Security Filter Action Wizard appears.

3. Click Next to bypass the Welcome page.

   The Filter Action Name page appears.

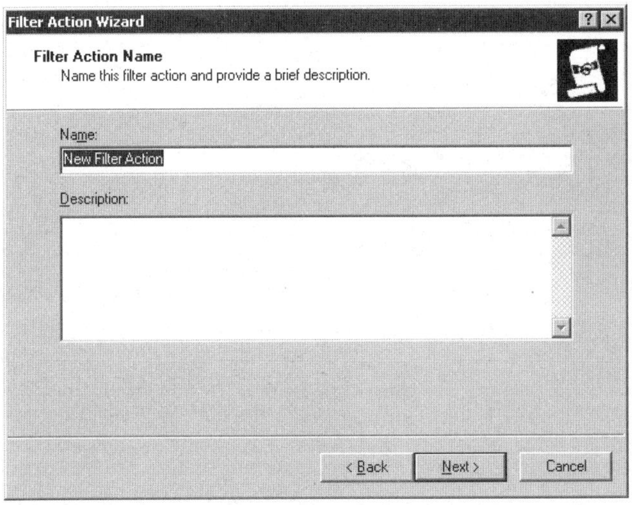

4. In the Name text box, type **High Security** and click Next.

   The Filter Action General Options dialog box appears.

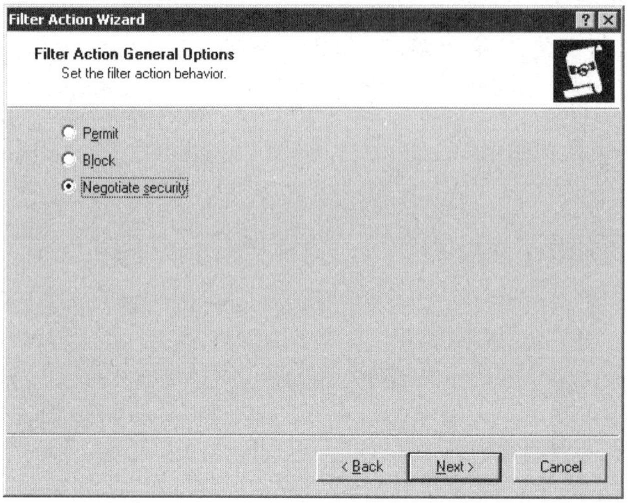

5. Click Next to accept the default Negotiate Security option.

   The Communicating With Computers That Do Not Support IPSec page appears.

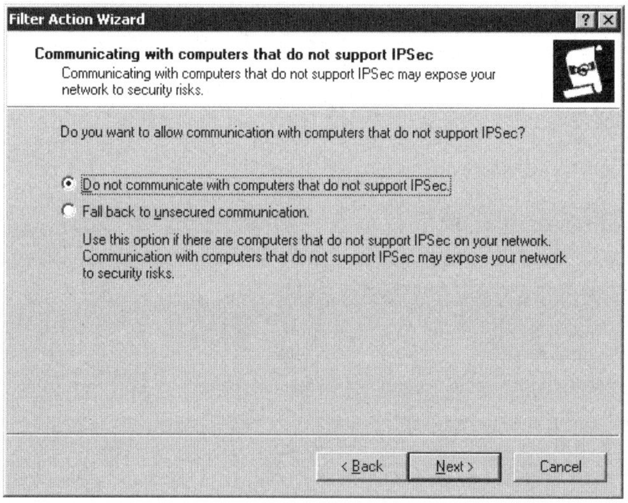

6. Click Next to accept the default Do Not Communicate With Computers That Do Not Support IPSec option.

   The IP Traffic Security page appears.

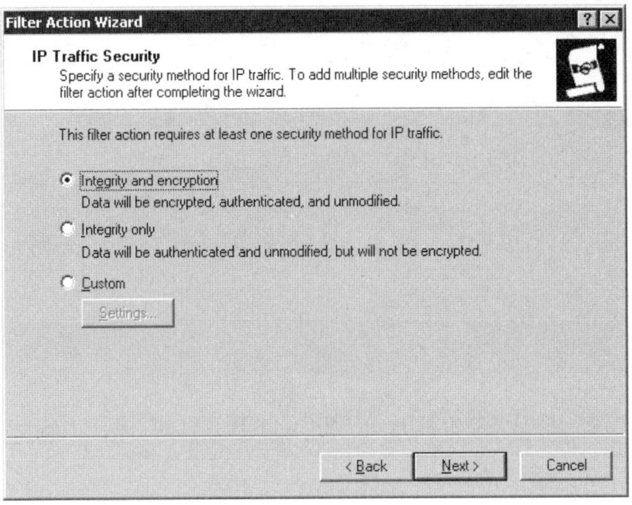

7. Select Custom option, and click Settings.

   The Custom Security Method Settings dialog box appears.

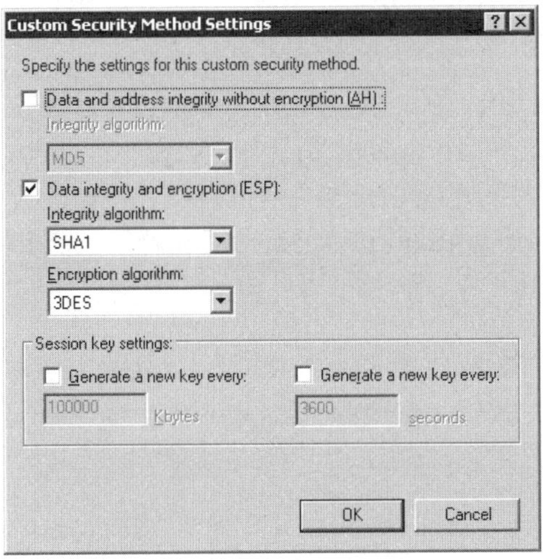

8. Select the Data And Address Integrity Without Encryption (AH) option.

9. In the Integrity Algorithm drop-down list, select SHA1.

QUESTION *Why is the SHA1 algorithm preferable to MD5?*

10. Leave the Data Integrity And Encryption (ESP) check box selected, but change its Integrity Algorithm value to None.

QUESTION *Why do you not need an integrity algorithm for ESP?*

11. In the Session Key Settings box, select the rightmost Generate A New Key Every check box and specify a value of **300** seconds.

12. Click OK to close the Custom Security Method Settings dialog box, and then click Next.

    The Completing The IP Security Filter Action Wizard page appears.

13. Click Finish.

    The new High Security filter action appears in the Manage IP Filter Lists And Filter Actions dialog box.

14. Take a screen shot (press ALT+PRINT SCREEN) of the Manage IP Filter Lists And Filter Actions dialog box, and paste it into a WordPad document named Domain*xxyy*Lab08-2.rtf (where *xx* and *yy* are the numbers assigned to the computers in your student domain), which you will turn in at the end of the lab.

15. Click Close to close the dialog box.

16. Leave the IP Security Policies console open for the next exercise.

EXERCISE 8-4: CREATING AN IP SECURITY POLICY

Estimated completion time: 15 minutes

To deploy the IP filter list and filter action you created in the previous exercises, you must create a new IPSec policy. In this exercise, you will create a new policy using the IP Security Policy Management console and configure it to use the existing IP filter list and filter action.

In this exercise, you create an IP security policy, using the filter list and filter action you created in Exercises 8-2 and 8-3.

1. On Computer*xx*, in the IP Security Policies console, select IP Security Policies On Active Directory and, from the Action menu, select Create IP Security Policy.

   The IP Security Policy Wizard appears.

2. Click Next to bypass the Welcome page.

   The IP Security Policy Name page appears.

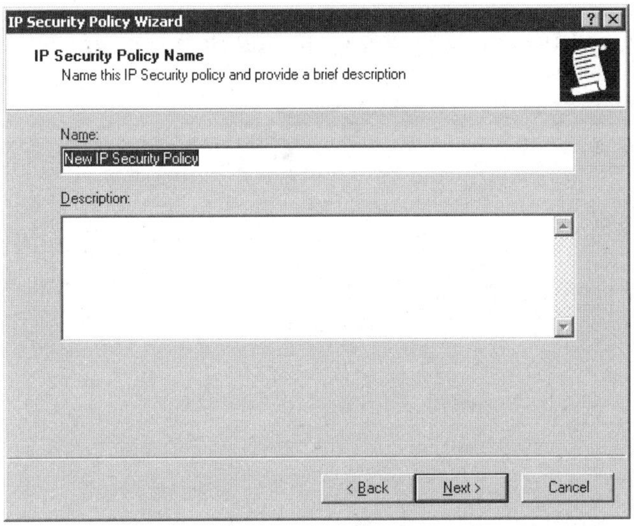

3. In the Name text box, type **Intranet Web Security** and click Next.

   The Requests For Secure Communication page appears.

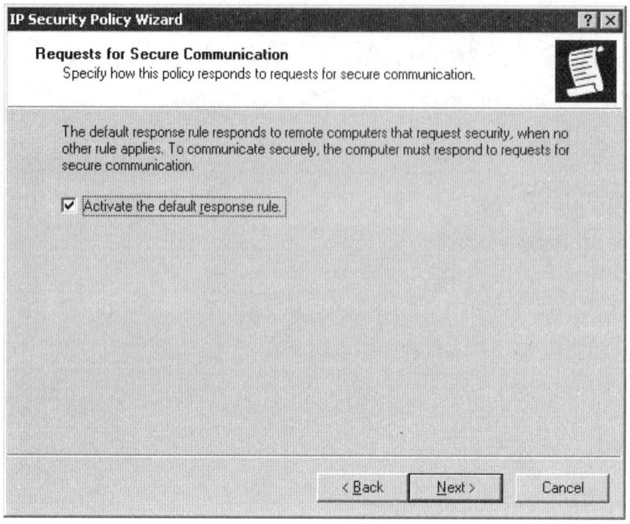

4. Click Next to accept the default Activate The Default Response Rule setting.

   The Default Response Rule Authentication Method page appears.

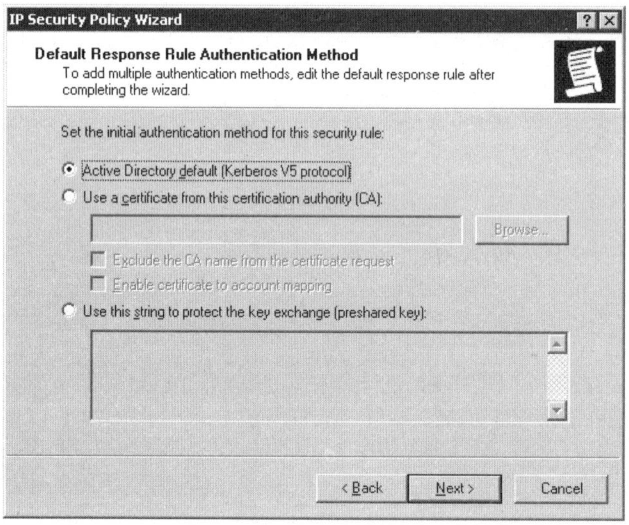

QUESTION What is the function of the default response rule?

5. Click Next to accept the default Kerberos authentication method for the default response rule.

   The Completing The IP Security Policy Wizard page appears.

6. With the Edit Properties check box selected, click Finish.

   The Intranet Web Security Properties dialog box appears.

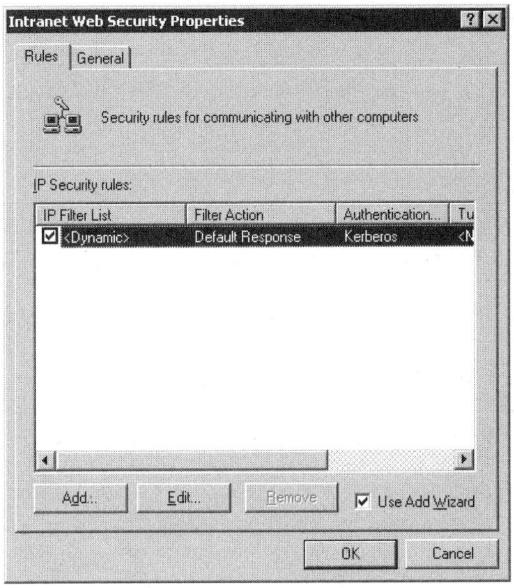

7. Clear the Use Add Wizard check box, and click Add to create a new rule.

   The New Rule Properties dialog box appears.

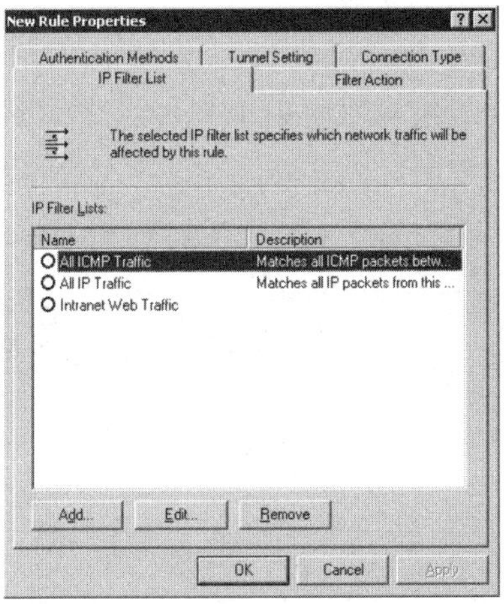

8. In the IP Filter List tab, select the Intranet Web Traffic filter list you created in Exercise 8-2.

9. Click the Filter Action tab.

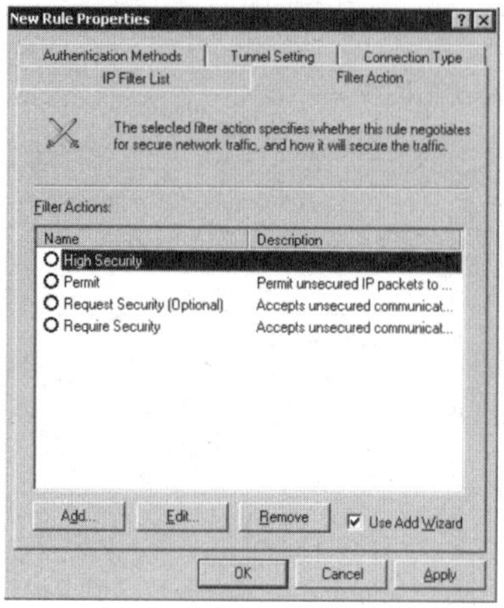

10. Select the High Security filter action you created in Exercise 8-3.

11. Click the Authentication Methods tab.

QUESTION *What is the default authentication method?*

12. Click the Tunnel Setting tab. Leave the This Rule Does Not Specify An IPSec Tunnel option selected.

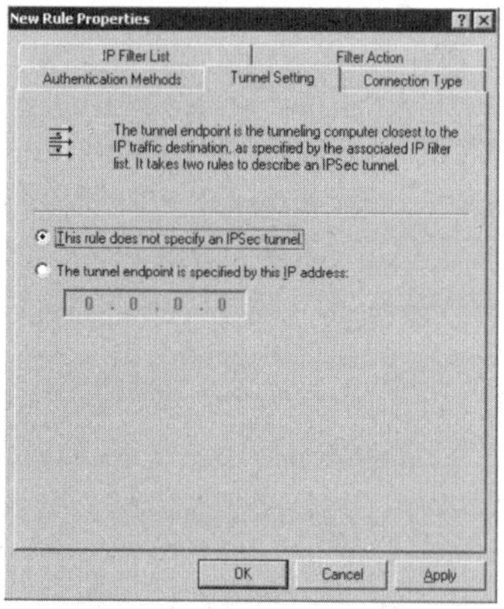

13. Click the Connection Type tab.

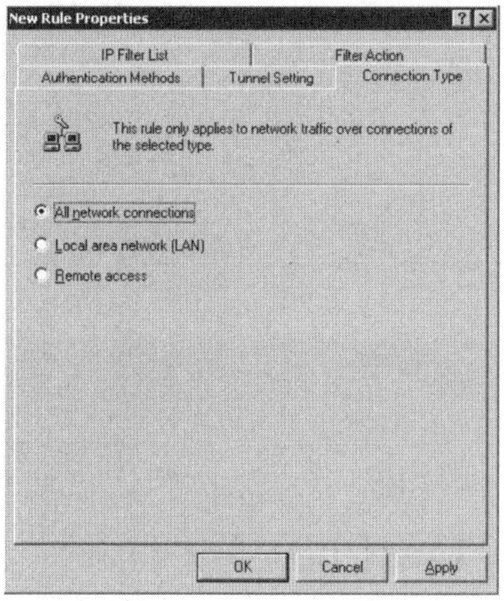

14. Select the Local Area Network (LAN) option and click OK.

    The Intranet Web Traffic rule you created appears in the Intranet Web Security Properties dialog box.

15. Click OK to close the Intranet Web Security Properties dialog box.

    The Intranet Web Security policy is added to the IP Security Policies list.

16. Take a screen shot (press ALT+PRINT SCREEN) of the console showing the IP Security Policies list, and paste it into a WordPad document named Domain*xxyy*Lab08-3.rtf (where *xx* and *yy* are the numbers assigned to the computers in your student domain), which you will turn in at the end of the lab.

17. Close the IP Security Policies console.

LAB REVIEW QUESTIONS

Estimated completion time: 15 minutes

1. When creating the IP filter list in Exercise 8-2, what would be the result if, for the Source Address, you selected A Specific IP Subnet and specified the network address of your student domain, and, for the Destination Address, you specified Computer*yy*'s IP Address? Explain your answer.

2. Assume that you are going to assign the Intranet Web Security policy to the domain*xxyy* domain. If so, why would clearing the Mirrored check box while creating the IP filter list in Exercise 8-2 have no apparent effect on the communications between Computer*xx* and Computer*yy*?

3. Throughout this lab, you have configured IPSec to use the default authentication method, which is the Kerberos authentication protocol. It is also possible to use preshared keys for authentication. Give two reasons why Microsoft recommends against using preshared keys.
4. In Exercise 8-4, for what type of system would you specify a tunnel endpoint while creating a rule?
5. What kind of network traffic is the IP filter list you created in Exercise 8-2 designed to isolate? Explain how you can tell.

LAB CHALLENGE 8-1: CREATING COMPLEX FILTER ACTIONS

Estimated completion time: 30 minutes

In Exercise 8-3, you created a relatively simple filter action using the IP Security Filter Action Wizard. In this challenge, you will create a more complex filter action without using the wizard. The primary limitation of the wizard is that you can specify only one custom security method. To support a fleet of clients with varying capabilities, it can be beneficial to create a filter action with multiple security methods. To complete this challenge, create a filter action called **Compatible Security** that includes eight custom security methods, as shown in the following table:

Security Method Order	AH Integrity Algorithm	ESP Integrity Algorithm	ESP Encryption Algorithm	Session Key Settings (Kbytes)	Session Key Settings (Seconds)
1	SHA1	None	3DES	Default	Default
2	SHA1	None	DES	Default	500
3	MD5	None	3DES	Default	2000
4	MD5	None	DES	Default	500
5	None	SHA1	3DES	Default	1000
6	None	SHA1	DES	Default	500
7	None	MD5	3DES	Default	1000
8	None	MD5	DES	Default	500

Be sure to create the security methods in the order specified in the table. When you are finished, take a screen shot (press ALT+PRINT SCREEN) of the Security Methods tab in the filter action's Properties dialog box, and paste it into a WordPad document named Domain*xxyy*Lab08-4.rtf (where *xx* and *yy* are the numbers assigned to the computers in your student domain), which you will turn in at the end of the lab.

LAB 9
DEPLOYING AND TROUBLESHOOTING IPSEC

This lab contains the following exercises and activities:

- Lab Exercise 9-1: Capturing Unencrypted Web Traffic
- Lab Exercise 9-2: Assigning an IP Security Policy
- Lab Exercise 9-3: Testing IPSec Connectivity
- Lab Exercise 9-4: Capturing IPSec Traffic
- Lab Review Questions
- Lab Challenge 9-1: Creating an IPSec Policy Using Netsh.exe

SCENARIO

The IT director of Contoso, Ltd., wants to install a secure intranet Web server that will enable selected users to access confidential documents without the danger of those documents being intercepted by someone illicitly capturing network traffic. The director has assigned you the task of deploying the Web server and demonstrating to him that it is safe to transmit sensitive data over the network. In this lab, you will deploy the IPSec policy on your student domain, test it, and monitor the IPSec traffic.

After completing this lab, you will be able to:

- Assign an IPSec policy to a Microsoft Active Directory object
- Capture and analyze IPSec traffic

Estimated lesson time: 75 minutes

BEFORE YOU BEGIN

To complete this lab, you will need the following information:

- The names of the computers in your student domain (Computer*xx* and Computer*yy*)
- The name of your student domain (domain*xxyy*.contoso.com)

EXERCISE 9-1: CAPTURING UNENCRYPTED WEB TRAFFIC

Estimated completion time: 15 minutes
For the purposes of demonstrating the security of the new intranet server, you will capture a sample of the Web server's traffic in its unprotected state, which you can later compare with a sample taken while the IPSec security measures are in place. In this exercise, you use Network Monitor to capture the traffic running to and from the Web server and examine the contents of the data packets.

1. On Computer*xx*, log on to domain*xxyy* as Administrator, using the password **P@ssw0rd**.
2. Open Network Monitor and configure the program to capture traffic from the Local Network Connection interface.

> **NOTE Using Network Monitor** To review the process of capturing data with Network Monitor, see Lab 1, "Planning an Authentication Strategy."

3. Start capturing data from the network.

> **NOTE Clearing the Browser Cache** If you are working at the same computer you used to test the Web server connection in the previous exercises, be sure to clear the browser cache before you perform step 4 by selecting Internet Options from the Tools menu, clicking the Delete Files button, and then clicking OK in the Delete Files dialog box.

4. Open Microsoft Internet Explorer and, in the Address box, type **http://computer*yy*** (where *yy* is the number assigned to the computer). Press ENTER.

   QUESTION What is the result?

5. In Network Monitor, select Stop And View from the Capture menu.

   A Capture Summary window appears, containing a list of the packets captured from the network.

6. Create a display filter isolating only the packets containing the Hypertext Transfer Protocol (HTTP).

   MORE INFO ***Creating a Display Filter*** See Exercise 1-3, "Capturing Kerberos Traffic," to review the process of creating a display filter in Network Monitor.

7. Double-click the first packet in the capture summary list.

   The window splits into Summary, Detail, and Hex panes.

8. Examine the HTTP packets in the captured sample and locate the one containing the home page you created in Exercise 8-1.

   The packet you are seeking should display the warning message you typed earlier in the Hex pane, in clear text.

9. Take a screen shot (press ALT+PRINT SCREEN) of the Network Monitor display showing the data in the Hex pane, and paste it into a WordPad document named Domain*xxyy*Lab09-1.rtf (where *xx* and *yy* are the numbers assigned to the computers in your student domain), which you will turn in at the end of the lab.

10. Close the Capture Summary window without saving it to a file.

11. Leave the computer logged on for the next exercise.

EXERCISE 9-2: ASSIGNING AN IP SECURITY POLICY

Estimated completion time: 15 minutes

In Lab 8, "Planning and Configuring IPSec," you created an IPSec policy called Intranet Web Security, but the policy can have no effect until you assign it to a computer or an Active Directory object. In this exercise, you create a new organizational unit (OU) in your Active Directory domain and deploy your new IPSec policy to that OU.

1. On Computer*xx*, click Start, point to Administrative Tools, and select Active Directory Users And Computers.

   The Active Directory Users And Computers console appears.

2. In the console tree, select the domain*xxyy*.contoso.com domain object and, on the Action menu, point to New and select Organizational Unit.

   The New Object–Organizational Unit dialog box appears.

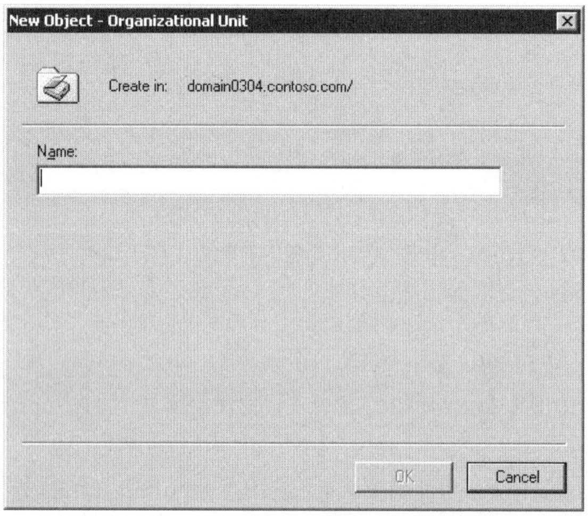

3. In the Name text box, type **Intranet** and click OK.

   The new Intranet OU appears in the domain tree.

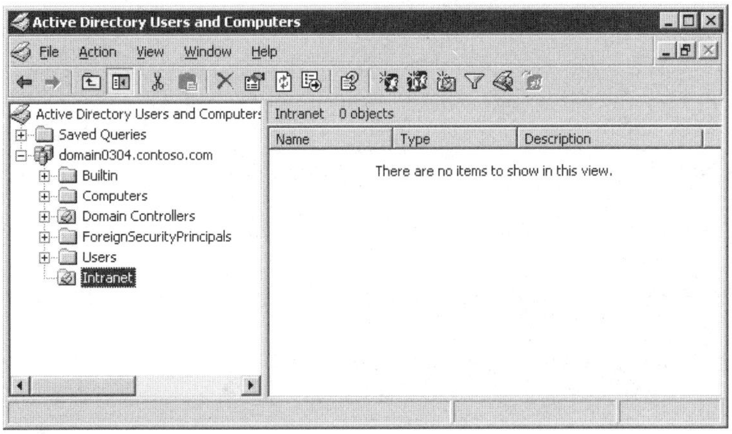

4. In the console tree, click the Computers container.
5. Drag the Computeryy computer object from the Computers container to the Intranet OU you just created.

QUESTION *Why is it necessary to create a new OU object for Computeryy?*

6. Select the Intranet OU and, from the Action menu, choose Properties.

   The Intranet Properties dialog box appears.
7. Click the Group Policy tab.

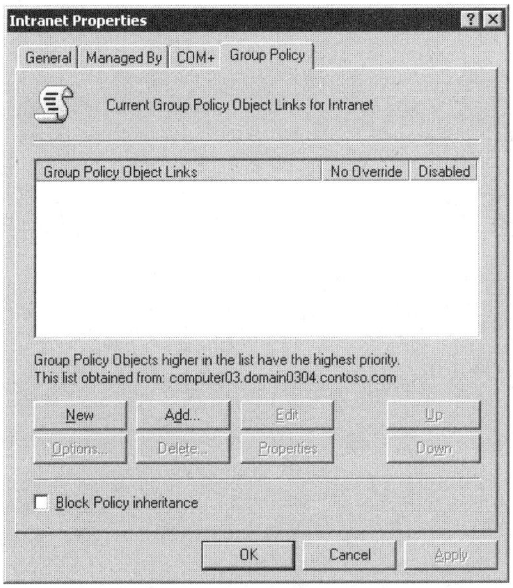

8. Click New.

   A new Group Policy Object (GPO) appears in the Group Policy Object Links list.

9. Give the new GPO the name **Intranet Policies**. Then click Edit.

   The Group Policy Object Editor console appears.

10. Under Computer Configuration, expand the Windows Settings and Security Settings nodes. Select the IP Security Policies On Active Directory (domain*xxyy*.contoso.com) node.

   A list of IP security policies appears in the right pane.

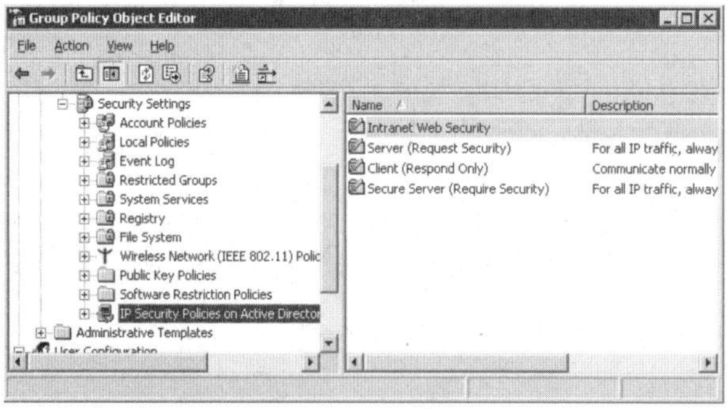

11. In the right pane, select the Intranet Web Security policy you created in Lab 8 and, from the Action menu, choose Assign.

   The value in the Policy Assigned column for the Intranet Web Security policy changes to Yes.

12. Close the Group Policy Object Editor console.
13. Click Close to close the Intranet Properties dialog box.
14. Leave the Active Directory Users And Computers console open for the next exercise.

EXERCISE 9-3: TESTING IPSEC CONNECTIVITY

Estimated completion time: 20 minutes

The next step in your IPSec deployment is to test whether the computers in your lab domain can communicate using IPSec. In this exercise, you use the IP Security Monitor snap-in to gather information about the IPSec activities on your computers.

1. On Computer*yy*, log on to the domain*xxyy* domain as Administrator, using the password **P@ssw0rd**.
2. Open a Command Prompt window and, at the prompt, type **gpupdate /force**. Press ENTER.

   After a few moments, messages appear stating that user and computer policies have been refreshed.

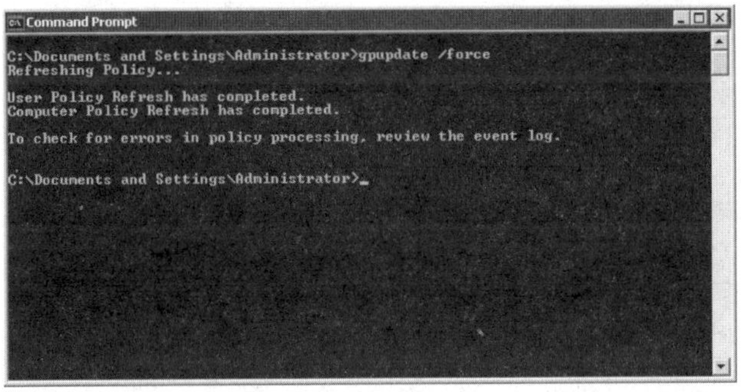

3. Open a blank Microsoft Management Console (MMC) window and add the IP Security Monitor snap-in. Then save the console as **IPSec Monitor.msc**.
4. In the console tree, expand the IP Security Monitor and Computer*yy* nodes and click Active Policy.

QUESTION Based on the information shown in the IP Security Monitor snap-in, what IPSec policy is currently operative on Computer*yy*? How was it assigned to the computer?

5. Take a screen shot (press ALT+PRINT SCREEN) of the IP Security Monitor console, showing the Active Policy display, and paste it into a WordPad document named Domain*xxyy*Lab09-2.rtf (where *xx* and *yy* are the numbers assigned to the computers in your student domain), which you will turn in at the end of the lab.

6. On Computer*xx*, launch Internet Explorer and, in the Address text box, type **http://computeryy** (where *yy* is the number assigned to the Web server computer). Press ENTER.

QUESTION What happens?

7. Create an IP Security Monitor console on Computer*xx*, just as you did on Computer*yy*, and display the Active Policy node.

QUESTION What IPSec policy is currently active on Computer*xx*? Why?

8. On Computer*xx*, click Start, point to Administrative Tools, and select Domain Security Policy.

   The Default Domain Security Settings console appears.

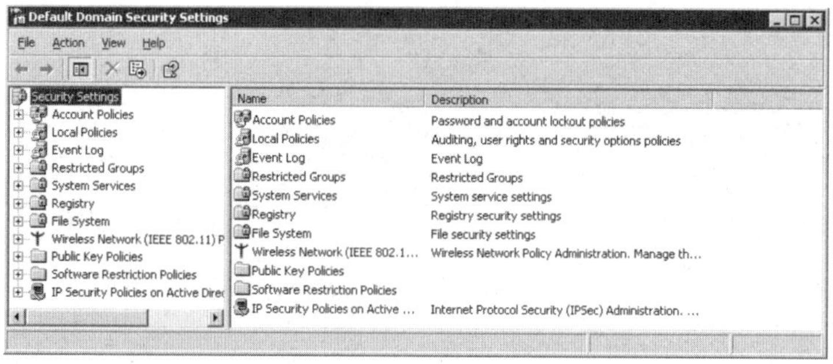

9. In the console tree, select the IP Security Policies On Active Directory (domain*xxyy*.contoso.com) node.

10. In the right pane, click the Server (Request Security) policy and, from the Action menu, select Assign.

    The value in the Policy Assigned column changes to Yes.

11. Open a Command Prompt window and run the **gpupdate /force** command.

12. After the gpupdate command completes, return to the IP Security Monitor console you created, right-click the Active Policy node, and select Refresh from the context menu.

    QUESTION What happens?

13. Take a screen shot (press ALT+PRINT SCREEN) of the IP Security Monitor console, showing the Active Policy display, and paste it into a WordPad document named Domain*xxyy*Lab09-3.rtf (where *xx* and *yy* are the numbers assigned to the computers in your student domain), which you will turn in at the end of the lab.

14. In Internet Explorer, click the Refresh button.

    QUESTION What happens? Why?

EXERCISE 9-4: CAPTURING IPSEC TRAFFIC

Estimated completion time: 10 minutes

To verify that the network traffic exchanged by the computers in your IPSec deployment is truly protected, you must actually look at the contents of a packet using a protocol analyzer. In this exercise, you use Network Monitor to capture an IPSec traffic sample and compare it to the traffic you captured in Exercise 9-1.

1. On Computer*xx*, run Network Monitor and start capturing traffic from the Local Area Network Connection interface.

2. Switch to Internet Explorer and clear the browser cache by opening the Internet Options dialog box and clicking Delete Files.

   The Delete Files dialog box appears.

3. Click OK to close the Delete Files dialog box.
4. Click OK to close the Internet Options dialog box.
5. Click the Refresh button.
6. In Network Monitor, from the Capture menu, select Stop And View.

   A Capture Summary window appears.

> **QUESTION** How is the data you captured this time different from that which you captured in Exercise 9-1?

7. Locate one of the Encapsulating Security Payload (ESP) packets sent from Computer*yy* to Computer*xx* (using the Src Other Addr and Dst Other Addr values) and examine its data in the Hex pane, as you did in Exercise 9-1.

> **QUESTION** How is the Hex data display different from that of the HTTP packet you examined earlier?

8. Take a screen shot (press ALT+PRINT SCREEN) of the Network Monitor display showing the contents of the ESP packet, and paste it into a WordPad document named Domain*xxyy*Lab09-4.rtf (where *xx* and *yy* are the numbers assigned to the computers in your student domain), which you will turn in at the end of the lab.

LAB REVIEW QUESTIONS

Estimated completion time: 15 minutes

1. In Exercise 9-3, you used the IP Security Monitor snap-in to find out which IPSec policies are operating on your computers. List two other methods for determining which policy is active on a Microsoft Windows Server 2003 computer.
2. In Exercise 9-3, why is the Intranet Web Security policy not assigned to Computer*xx*?
3. In Exercise 9-3, when you assign the Server (Request Security) policy to the domain*xxyy* domain, why does Computer*yy* continue to use the Intranet Web Security policy?

4. In Exercise 9-1, you created a display filter that isolated the HTTP packets in your captured traffic sample. What would be the result if you applied the same display filter to the traffic sample you captured in Exercise 9-4? Why?

LAB CHALLENGE 9-1: CREATING AN IPSEC POLICY USING NETSH.EXE

Estimated completion time: 45 minutes

In Lab 8, you created an IPSec policy using the graphical interface supplied by the IP Security Policy Management snap-in. In this challenge, you must create another IPSec policy, but this time using only Netsh.exe from the Windows Server 2003 command prompt. For the purposes of this challenge, assume that Computer*yy* in your lab domain is configured to function as a File Transfer Protocol (FTP) server as well as a Web server. The IPSec policy you create must be designed to protect all of the FTP traffic running to and from Computer*yy*, and only that traffic.

To complete the challenge, you must write a script with Netsh commands that creates all of the components for a new IPSec policy, including the policy itself, an IP filter list with appropriate filters, a filter action, and a rule. Use the online help for the Netsh.exe program if you need help with the program's command syntax. The policy must protect all TCP traffic using ports 20 and 21 originating from or destined to Computer*yy*, using ESP with its default settings and the Kerberos authentication. Do not activate the default response rule, and use the following names for your components:

- Policy: FTPpolicy
- Filter list: FTP
- Filter action: secureFTP
- Rule: FTPrule

When you have completed your script, execute each of the commands on Computer*yy* to verify that there are no syntax errors. Then run the following command:

```
netsh ipsec static show policy name=FTPpolicy level=verbose > domainxxyyLab09-5.txt
```

This command will generate a detailed summary of the policy you have created. Save it as a file called Domain*xxyy*Lab09-5.txt, which you can submit at the end of the lab.

LAB 10

PLANNING AND IMPLEMENTING SECURITY FOR WIRELESS NETWORKS

This lab contains the following exercises and activities:

- Lab Exercise 10-1: Configuring an Active Directory Infrastructure for Wireless Access
- Lab Exercise 10-2: Installing IAS
- Lab Exercise 10-3: Configuring IAS
- Lab Exercise 10-4: Configuring Wireless Networking Clients Using Group Policy
- Lab Review Questions
- Lab Challenge 10-1: Configuring a WAP

SCENARIO

You have been assigned the task of deploying a wireless networking solution for your company, Contoso, Ltd. For the initial deployment, the company has purchased a single wireless access point (WAP), but others are expected to be added later. The clients are laptop computers running Microsoft Windows XP Professional, all of which are members of the domain*xxyy*.contoso.com domain. The primary concerns of company management when they approved the project were that all traffic on the wireless network be secured by encryption and that access to the wireless network be limited to a specific group of users. It is your job to see to it that all of the components are configured properly.

After completing this lab, you will be able to:

- Create a Microsoft Active Directory hierarchy for the wireless network infrastructure
- Install and configure Internet Authentication Services (IAS)
- Configure a WAP
- Configure wireless networking client settings using Group Policy

Estimated lesson time: 85 minutes

BEFORE YOU BEGIN

To complete this lab, you will need the following information:

- The names of the computers in your student domain (Computer*xx* and Computer*yy*)
- The name of your student domain (domain*xxyy*.contoso.com)
- A copy of the Wireless Access Point Configuration handout, provided by your instructor

EXERCISE 10-1: CONFIGURING AN ACTIVE DIRECTORY INFRASTRUCTURE FOR WIRELESS ACCESS

Estimated completion time: 20 minutes

Your wireless network deployment project will rely on Active Directory for authentication and access control, so you must first create the appropriate group objects for these purposes. You are also going to create new user and computer objects for testing purposes, make them members of the appropriate groups, and configure them to provide access to the wireless network.

1. On Computer*xx*, log on to the domain*xxyy* domain as Administrator by typing the password **P@ssw0rd**.
2. Open the Active Directory Users And Computers console.

3. In the console tree, expand the domain*xxyy*.contoso.com domain object.

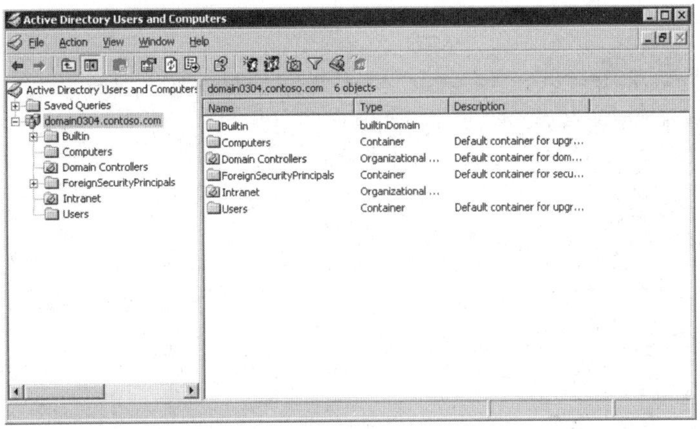

4. Select the Users container and, on the Action menu, point to New and select Group.

   The New Object–Group dialog box appears.

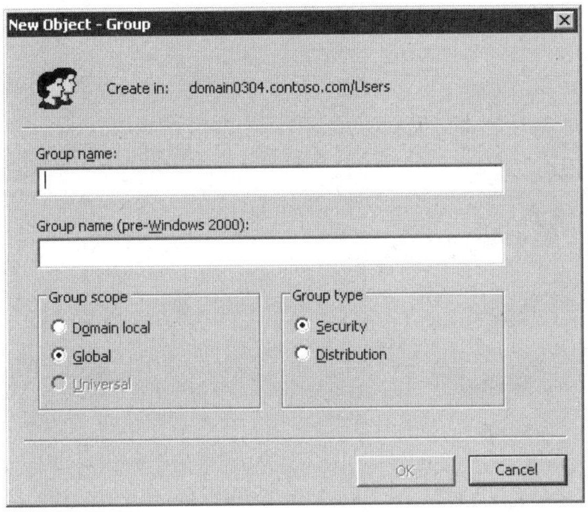

5. In the Group Name text box, type **WirelessComputers**.

6. Make sure that the Global scope and the Security type are selected and click OK.

   The WirelessComputers group appears in the Users container.

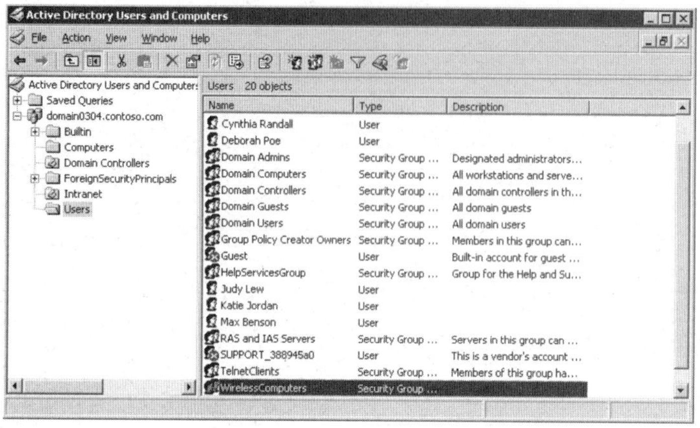

7. Create another global security group in the Users container and give it the name **WirelessUsers**.
8. In the console tree, select the Computers container and, on the Action menu, point to New and select Computer.

   The New Object–Computer wizard appears.

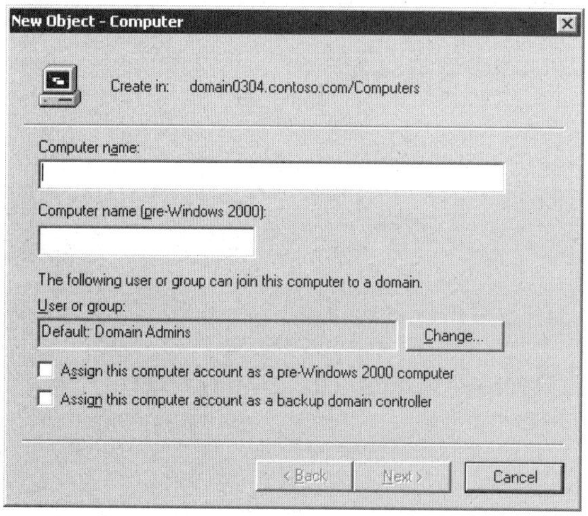

9. In the Computer Name text box, type **WirelessClient**. Then click Next.
10. Click Next to bypass the Managed page.
11. Click Finish to create the new computer object.
12. Locate the WirelessClient object you created in the Computers container, select it and, from the Action menu, select Properties.

    The WirelessClient Properties dialog box appears.

13. Click the Dial-In tab.

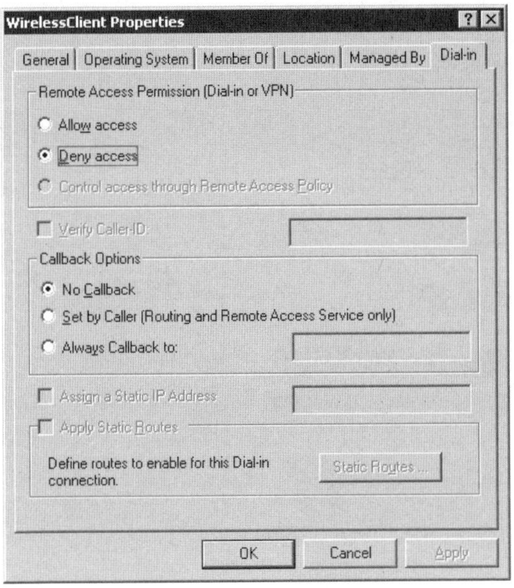

14. Select the Allow Access option.

> **NOTE** **Setting Dial-In Properties** Even though the computer is not actually dialing in to the network, this setting is required for wireless access.

15. Click the Member Of tab.

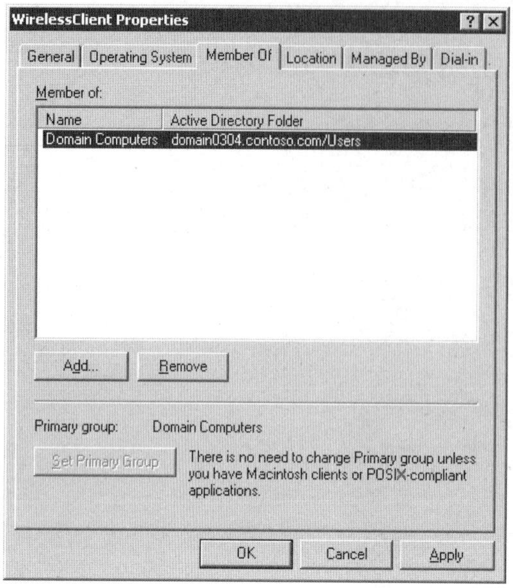

16. Click Add.

The Select Groups dialog box appears.

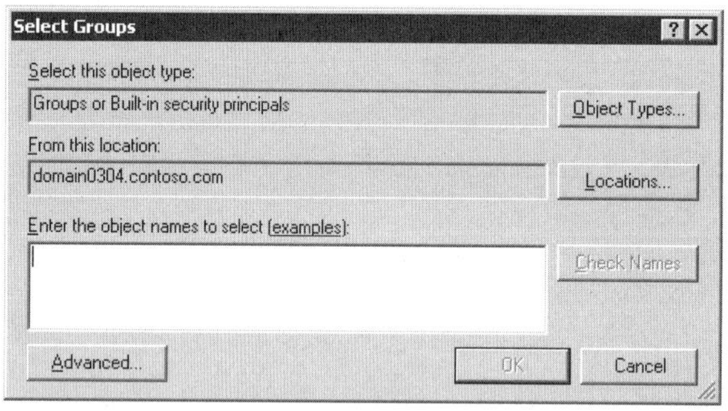

17. In the Enter The Object Names To Select box, type **WirelessComputers** and click OK.

The WirelessComputers group is added to the Member Of list.

18. Click OK to close the WirelessClient Properties dialog box.

19. In the console tree, select the Users container and, on the Action menu, point to New and select User.

The New Object–User dialog box appears.

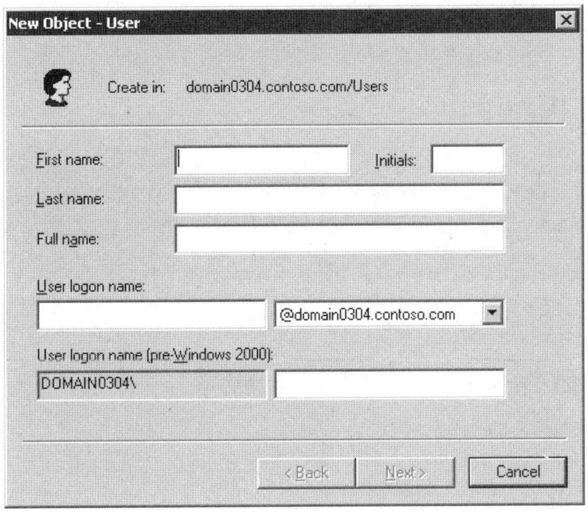

20. Type **WirelessUser** in the First Name text box and then type **WirelessUser** in the User Logon Name text box. Click Next.

21. In the Password and Confirm Password text boxes, type **P@ssw0rd**. Clear the User Must Change Password At Next Logon check box.

22. Click Next, and then click Finish.

    The WirelessUser account is added to the Users container.

23. Select the WirelessUser object and, from the Action menu, select Properties.

    The WirelessUser Properties dialog box appears.

24. Click the Dial-In tab.

25. Select the Allow Access option.

26. Click the Member Of tab, and then click Add.

    The Select Groups dialog box appears.

27. In the Enter The Object Names To Select text box, type **WirelessUsers**, and then click OK.

    The WirelessUsers group appears in the Member Of list.

28. Click OK to close the WirelessUser Properties dialog box.

29. Close the Active Directory Users And Computers console.

EXERCISE 10-2: INSTALLING IAS

Estimated completion time: 10 minutes

The security infrastructure for the wireless network calls for the use of Wired Equivalent Privacy (WEP) for encryption, with IEEE 802.1X, which will provide secure authentication and regular changes of the shared secret key used by WEP to encrypt the network data. To implement 802.1X, you must install the IAS on one of the company's Windows Server 2003 computers.

1. On Computer*xx*, open Add Or Remove Programs in Control Panel and click Add/Remove Windows Components.

   The Windows Components Wizard appears.

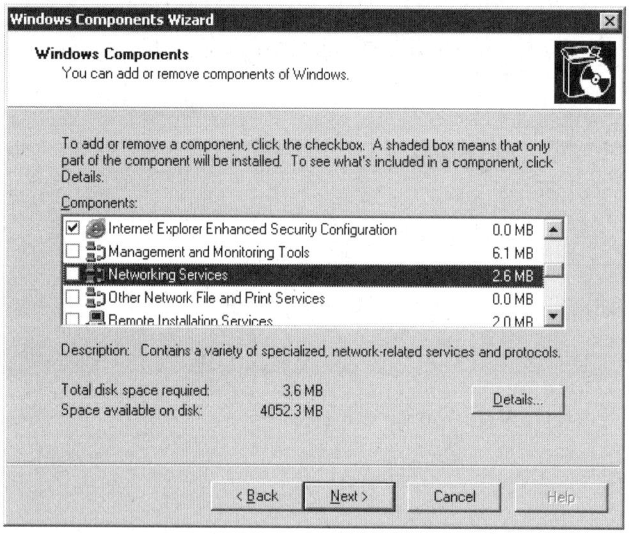

2. Scroll down in the Components list, click Networking Services, and then click Details.

   The Networking Services dialog box appears.

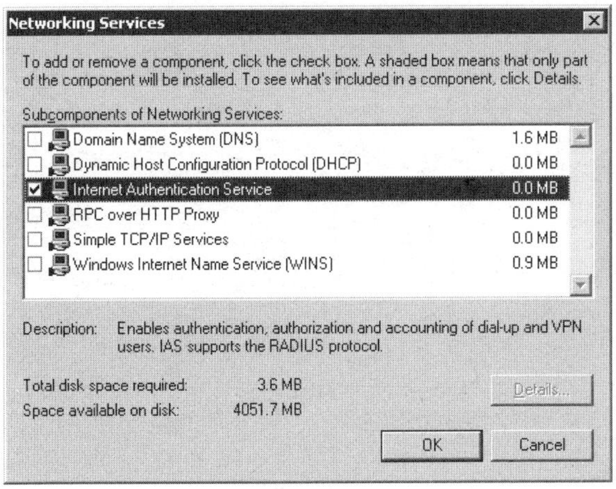

3. Select the Internet Authentication Service check box and click OK.
4. In the Windows Components Wizard, click Next.

   The Configuring Components page appears as the wizard installs IAS.

5. If the wizard prompts you to insert the Windows Server 2003 installation CD, browse to the C:\Win2k3 folder instead.

   The Completing the Windows Components Wizard page appears.

6. Click Finish.
7. Close Add Or Remove Programs.

EXERCISE 10-3: CONFIGURING IAS

Estimated completion time: 20 minutes

After installing IAS, your next task is to configure the service with a RADIUS client and create a remote access policy that will limit wireless network access to members of the WirelessUsers and WirelessComputers groups.

1. Click Start, point to Administrative Tools, and select Internet Authentication Service.

   The Internet Authentication Service console appears.

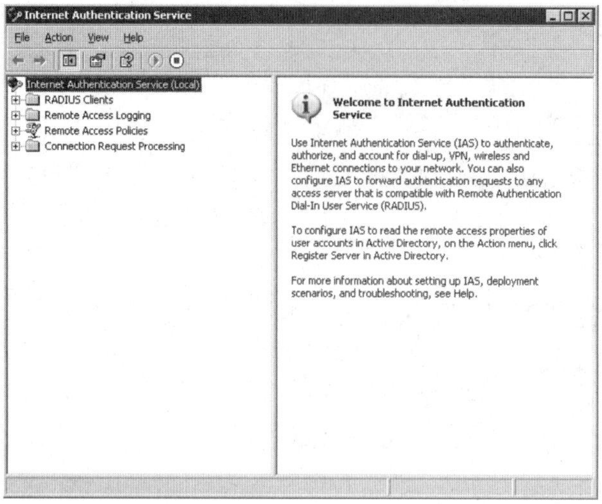

2. In the console tree, select the Internet Authentication Service (Local) node and, from the Action menu, select Register Server In Active Directory.

   A Register Internet Authentication Server In Active Directory message box appears, informing you that IAS must be authorized to access users' dial-in properties in the domain to authenticate them against the Active Directory directory service.

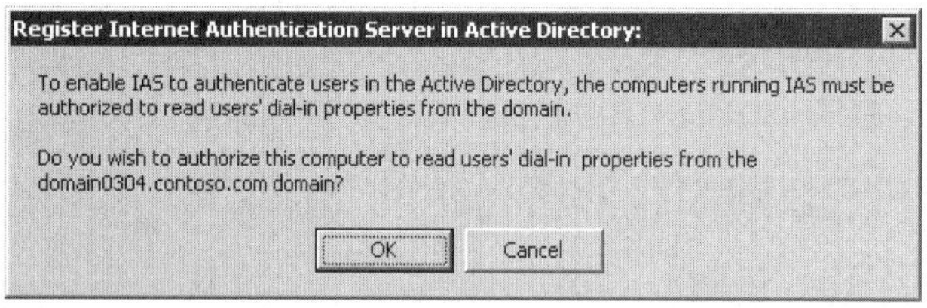

3. Click OK.

   A Server Registered message box appears, informing you that IAS is now authorized to read users' dial-in properties from the domain*xxyy* domain.

4. Click OK.

5. In the console tree, select the RADIUS Clients node and, from the Action menu, select New RADIUS Client.

   The New RADIUS Client Wizard appears, showing the Name And Address page.

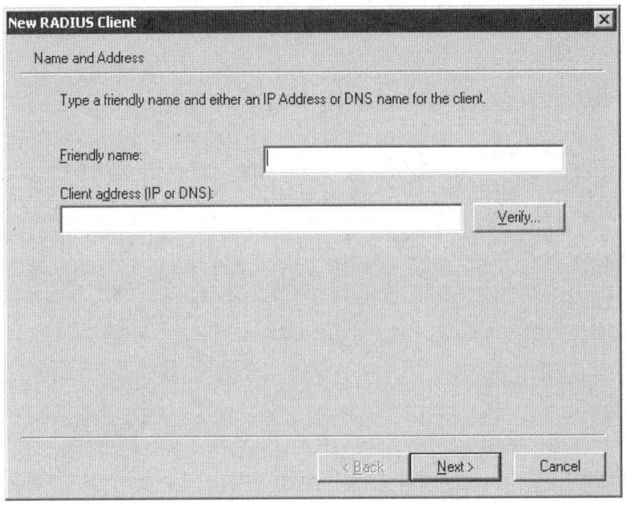

6. In the Friendly Name text box, type **ContosoWAP1**. In the Client Address text box, type **10.1.1.222**, and then click Next.

> **NOTE Naming a WAP** Because there is no actual wireless access point in the lab, the name ContosoWAP1 and the address 10.1.1.222 are fictional identifiers. In an actual deployment, you would assign a name to the WAP and specify its actual IP address, as configured on the device itself.

The Additional Information page appears.

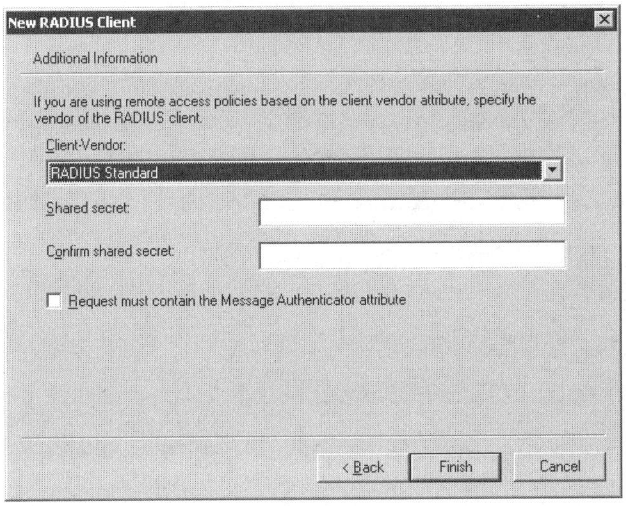

7. Type **C0nt0$0W@p1** in the Shared Secret and Confirm Shared Secret boxes. Then, click Finish.

   The new RADIUS client appears in the right pane of the console.

8. Take a screen shot (press ALT+PRINT SCREEN) of the Internet Authentication Service console showing the RADIUS client you created and paste it into a WordPad document named Domain*xxyy*Lab010-1.rtf (where *xx* and *yy* are the numbers assigned to the computers in your student domain), to turn in at the end of the lab.

9. Select the Remote Access Policies node.

   QUESTION *What remote access policies appear on the server by default?*

10. From the Action menu, select New Remote Access Policy.

    The New Remote Access Policy Wizard appears.

11. Click Next to bypass the Welcome page.

    The Policy Configuration Method page appears.

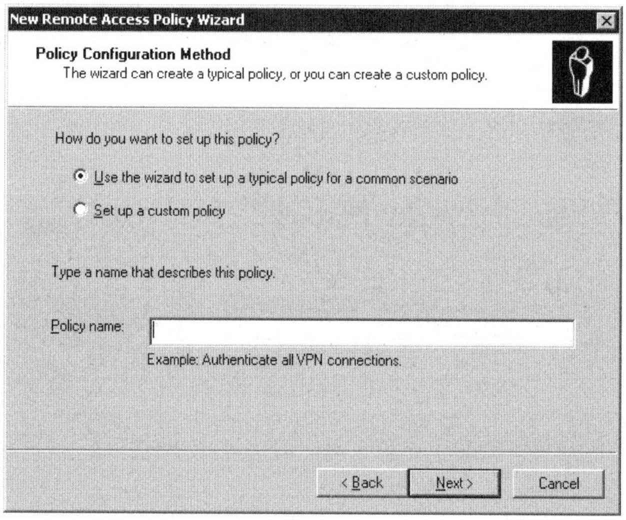

12. In the Policy Name text box, type **Wireless Network Access**, and then click Next.

    The Access Method page appears.

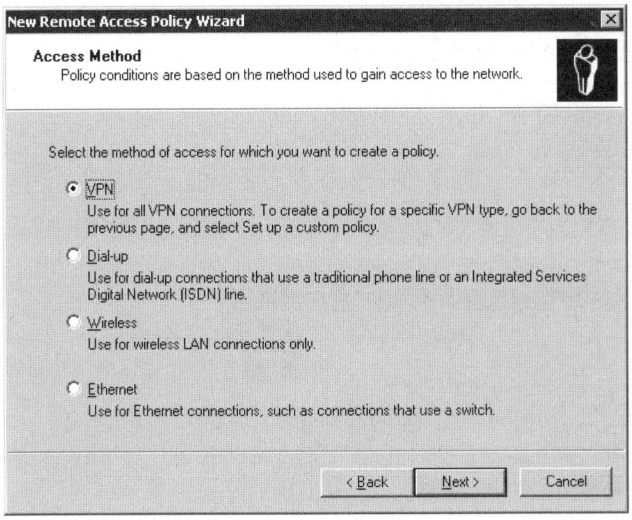

13. Select the Wireless option and then click Next.

    The User Or Group Access page appears.

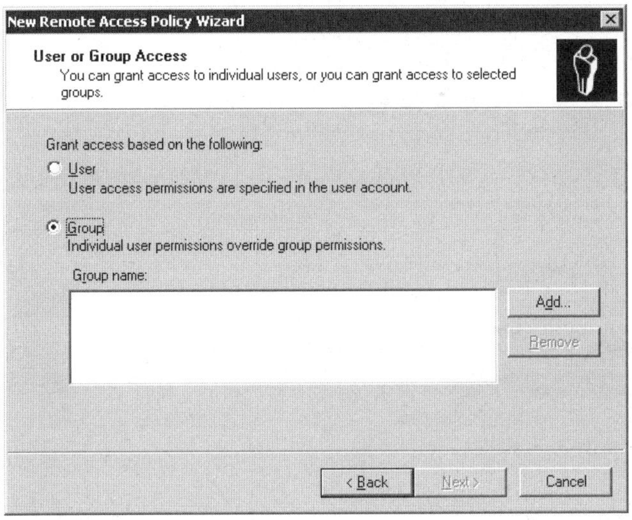

14. Select the Group option, and then click Add.

    The Select Groups dialog box appears.

15. Click the Locations button.

16. Expand the contoso.com domain and select your domain*xxyy*.contoso.com domain. Then, click OK.

17. In the Enter The Object Names To Select text box, type **Wireless-Computers; WirelessUsers** and click OK.

    The two groups are added to the Group Name list.

18. Click Next.

    The Authentication Methods page appears.

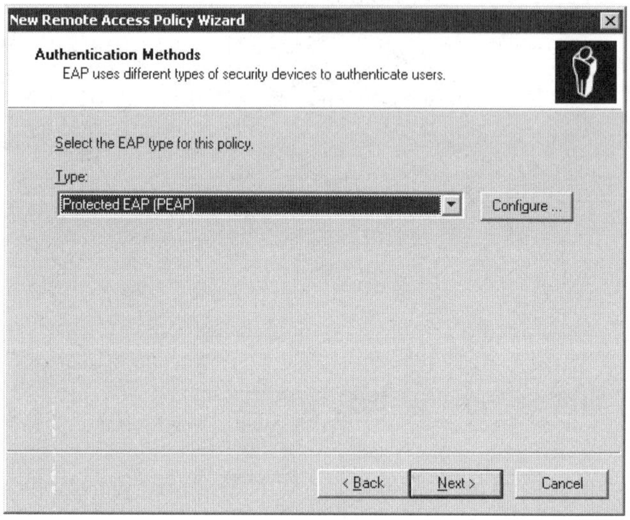

19. With the default Protected EAP type selected in the drop-down list, click Configure.

    The Protected EAP Properties dialog box appears.

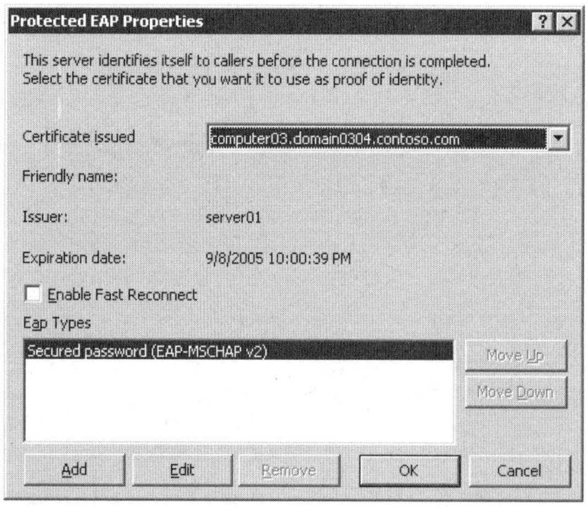

20. Select the Enable Fast Reconnect check box and click OK.

21. Click Next.

    The Completing The New Remote Access Policy Wizard page appears.

22. Check the conditions generated by the wizard, which should read as follows:

```
Conditions: NAS-Port-Type matches "Wireless - Other OR Wireless -
 IEEE 802.11"
AND Windows-Groups matches "DOMAINxxyy\WirelessComputers;DOMAINxxyy
\WirelessUsers"

Authentication: EAP(Protected EAP (PEAP))

Encryption: Basic, Strong, Strongest, No encryption
```

23. Take a screen shot (press ALT+PRINT SCREEN) of the Completing the New Remote Access Policy Wizard page showing the conditions of the policy you created and paste it into a WordPad document named Domain*xxyy*Lab010-2.rtf (where *xx* and *yy* are the numbers assigned to the computers in your student domain), to turn in at the end of the lab.

24. Click Finish.

25. The Wireless Network Access policy you just created appears in the right pane of the console.

26. Close the Internet Authentication Service console.

EXERCISE 10-4: CONFIGURING WIRELESS NETWORKING CLIENTS USING GROUP POLICY

Estimated completion time: 20 minutes

Although it is possible to configure each wireless client computer individually, Contoso, Ltd., deliberately formulated its wireless security plan so that it would be possible to configure all of the clients at once using Group Policy. In this exercise, you create a new organizational unit for the wireless clients and apply a Group Policy object to it that contains a wireless networking policy with the client configuration.

1. On Computer*xx*, open the Active Directory Users and Computers console.

2. In the console tree, select the domain*xxyy*.contoso.com node and, on the Action menu, point to New and select Organizational Unit.

3. Create a new organizational unit with the name **Wireless**.
4. Select the Wireless organizational unit and, from the Action menu, select Properties.

   The Wireless Properties dialog box appears.
5. Click the Group Policy tab and then click New.
6. Name the new Group Policy object by typing **Wireless Networking**, and then click Edit.

   The Group Policy Object Editor console appears.
7. In the console tree, expand the Computer Configuration, Windows Settings, and Security Settings nodes, and then select Wireless Network (IEEE 802.11) Policies.

   QUESTION *What wireless networking policies appear in the Group Policy object by default?*

8. From the Action menu, select Create Wireless Network Policy.

   The Wireless Network Policy Wizard appears.
9. Click Next to bypass the Welcome page.

   The Wireless Network Policy Name page appears.

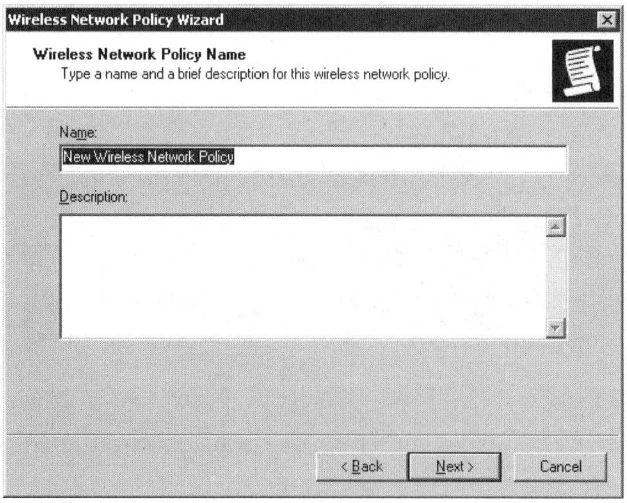

10. In the Name text box, type **Default Wireless Access** and click Next.

    The Completing the Wireless Network Policy Wizard page appears.

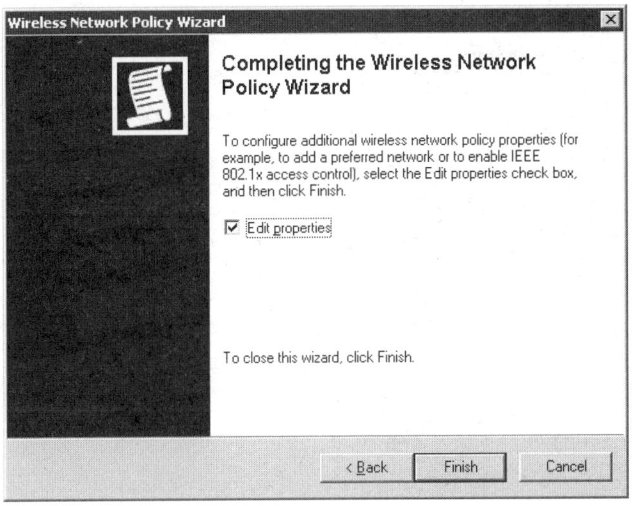

11. Leave the Edit Properties check box selected and click Finish.

    The Default Wireless Access Properties dialog box appears.

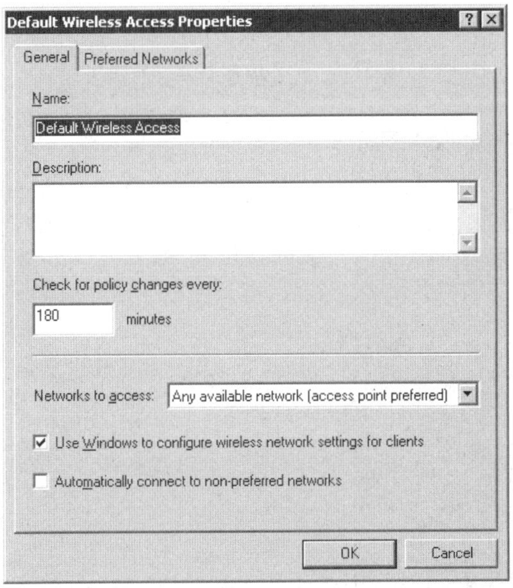

12. On the General tab, in the Networks To Access drop-down list, select Access Point (Infrastructure) Networks Only.

13. Make sure the Automatically Connect to Non-Preferred Networks check box is cleared.

14. Click the Preferred Networks tab.

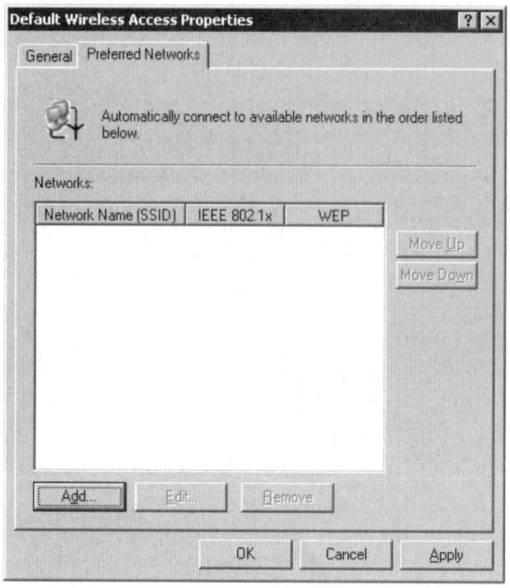

15. Click Add.

The New Preferred Setting Properties dialog box appears.

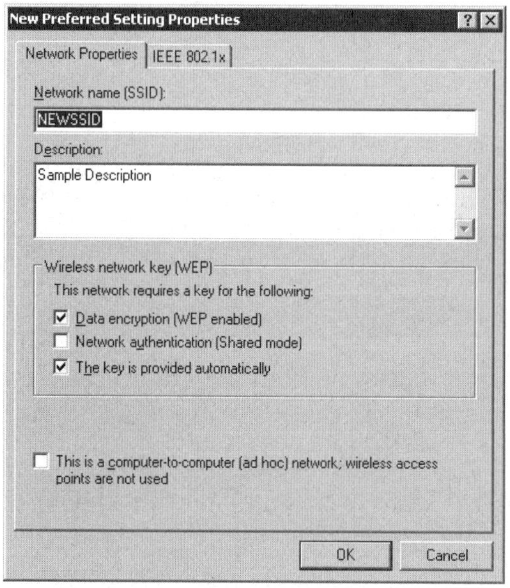

16. In the Network Name (SSID) text box, type **ContosoWAP1**.

17. In the Description text box, type **Authorized Contoso, Ltd. Users Only**.

18. In the Wireless Network Key (WEP) box, make sure that the Data Encryption (WEP Enabled) and The Key Is Provided Automatically check boxes are selected and that the Network Authentication (Shared Mode) check box is cleared.

19. Click the IEEE 802.1x tab.

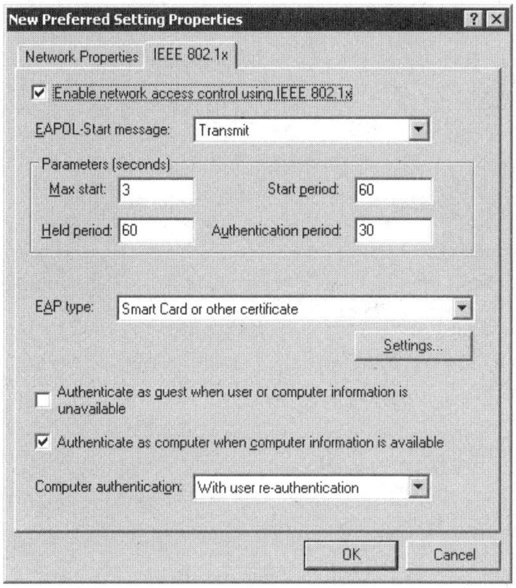

20. Verify that the Enable Network Access Control Using IEEE 802.1x check box is selected.

21. In the EAP Type drop-down list, select Protected EAP (PEAP) and then click Settings.

The Protected EAP Properties dialog box appears.

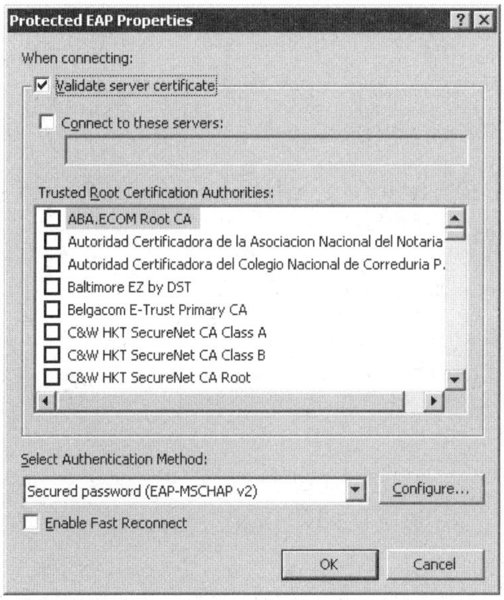

22. In the Select Authentication Method drop-down list, make sure that Secured Password (EAP-MSCHAP v2) is selected.
23. Select the Enable Fast Reconnect check box and click OK to close the Protected EAP Properties dialog box.
24. Click OK to close the New Preferred Setting Properties dialog box.

    The ContosoWAP1 network appears in the Networks list.
25. Take a screen shot (press ALT+PRINT SCREEN) of the Preferred Networks tab showing the ContosoWAP1 network you just added and paste it into a WordPad document named Domain*xxyy*Lab010-3.rtf (where *xx* and *yy* are the numbers assigned to the computers in your student domain), to turn in at the end of the lab.
26. Click OK to close the Default Wireless Access Properties dialog box.

    The Default Wireless Access policy appears in the right pane of the console.
27. Close the Group Policy Object Editor console.
28. Click Close to close the Wireless Properties dialog box.
29. Locate the WirelessComputer object in the Computers container and drag it to the Wireless organizational unit you created.
30. Close the Active Directory Users and Computers console.
31. Log off the computer.

LAB REVIEW QUESTIONS

Estimated completion time: 15 minutes

1. In Exercise 10-4, why is it preferable to clear the Network Authentication (Shared Mode) check box?
2. In Exercises 10-3 and 10-4, what capability does the Enable Fast Reconnect check box provide to wireless network users?
3. In Exercise 10-3, you selected Protected EAP as the authentication method for the wireless network. What would you need before you could use a different authentication method?

4. In Exercise 10-4, how does selecting Access Point (Infrastructure) Networks Only in the Networks To Access drop-down list enhance the security of the network?

5. In Exercise 10-4, how does clearing the Automatically Connect to Non-Preferred Networks check box enhance the security of the network?

LAB CHALLENGE 10-1: CONFIGURING A WAP

Estimated completion time: 30 minutes

After setting up the WAP and connecting it to the company's wired Ethernet network, you are able to open Internet Explorer on a networked computer and access the configuration home page hosted by the WAP, as shown in the following figure:

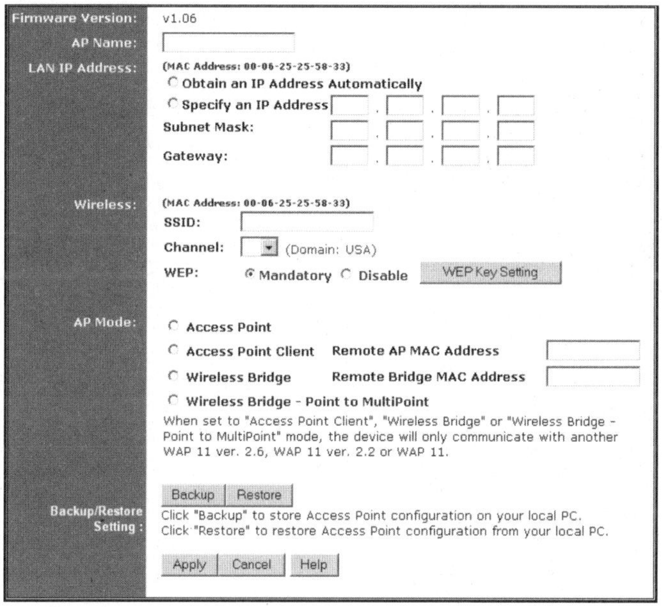

NOTE ***Performing a Virtual Configuration*** Because your lab does not have a WAP, your instructor will provide you with a handout containing a facsimile of a WAP configuration interface. Complete the handout and submit it to your instructor at the end of the lab.

Fill in the appropriate text boxes and option buttons, using the information you have already supplied in this lab's previous exercises. Be sure to configure the WAP to function as an access point only, and to require all WEP encryption for all traffic.

QUESTION Based on your study of wireless networks and your experiences in this lab, it appears as though this WAP might require a firmware upgrade before it can be fully functional on your network. What setting(s) are missing from the interface you configured?

LAB 11
DEPLOYING, CONFIGURING, AND MANAGING SSL CERTIFICATES

This lab contains the following exercises and activities:

- Lab Exercise 11-1: Testing Internal Network Connectivity
- Lab Exercise 11-2: Generating an IIS Server Certificate Request
- Lab Exercise 11-3: Requesting an IIS Server Certificate
- Lab Exercise 11-4: Issuing a Certificate
- Lab Exercise 11-5: Installing a Certificate
- Lab Exercise 11-6: Testing SSL Connectivity
- Lab Exercise 11-7: Configuring SSL Requirements
- Lab Exercise 11-8: Obtaining a Client Certificate
- Lab Review Questions
- Lab Challenge 11-1: Encrypting Active Directory Traffic

SCENARIO

You have been assigned the task of securing your company's Web servers using Secure Sockets Layer (SSL). To develop an SSL deployment strategy, you have constructed a lab network containing Windows Server 2003 computers running Internet Information Services (IIS) and Certificate Services. You intend to experiment on this lab network with the various SSL capabilities available to you and determine what type of deployment is most suitable for your company.

After completing this lab, you will be able to:

- Request and install an SSL server certificate.
- Connect to a Web server using SSL security.
- Configure SSL parameters on a Web server.
- Obtain and install SSL client certificates.

Estimated lesson time: 95 minutes

BEFORE YOU BEGIN

To complete this lab, you will need the following information:

- The names of the computers in your student domain (Computer*xx* and Computer*yy*)
- The name of your student domain (domain*xxyy*.contoso.com)

EXERCISE 11-1: TESTING INTERNAL NETWORK CONNECTIVITY

Estimated completion time: 5 minutes

In this exercise, you prepare your lab network for the subsequent exercises and test its network connectivity.

1. On Computer*xx*, log on to domain*xxyy* as Administrator, using the password **P@ssw0rd**.
2. Open the Active Directory Users And Computers console.
3. Locate the Computer*yy* computer object in the Intranet organizational unit you created in Lab 9 and drag it to the Computers container.
4. Close the Active Directory Users And Computers console.
5. On Computeryy, log on to domain*xxyy* as Administrator, using the password **P@ssw0rd.**
6. Open Internet Explorer.

7. In the Address text box, type **http://computer*xx*.domain*xxyy*.contoso.com**, where *xx* and *yy* are the numbers of the computers in your lab group, and click Go.

   QUESTION What happens?

8. Close Internet Explorer and leave the computer logged on.

EXERCISE 11-2: GENERATING AN IIS SERVER CERTIFICATE REQUEST

Estimated completion time: 15 minutes

As the first step in configuring your lab network servers to use IIS, you must obtain and install a server certificate for the computer running IIS. In order to observe and document each phase of the process, you plan to create a certificate request file and then manually submit it to the certification authority (CA).

1. On Computer*xx*, log on to the domain*xxyy* domain as Administrator, using the password **P@ssw0rd**.

2. Click Start, point to Administrative Tools, and click Internet Information Services (IIS) Manager.

   The Internet Information Services (IIS) Manager console appears.

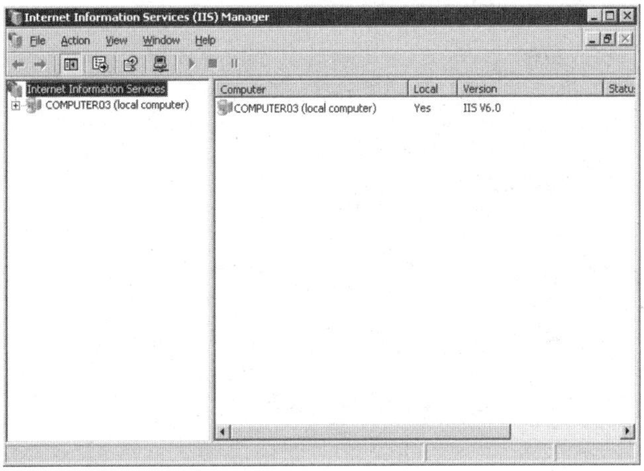

3. In the console tree, expand the Computer*xx* (Local Computer) node and the Web Sites folder.

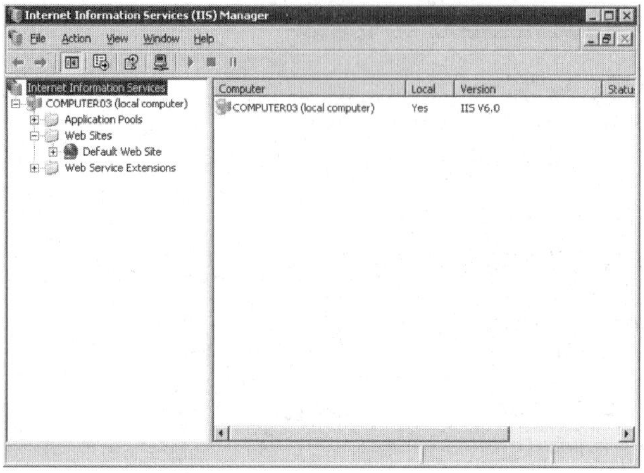

4. Select the Default Web Site and, from the Action menu, select Properties.

   The Default Web Site Properties dialog box appears.

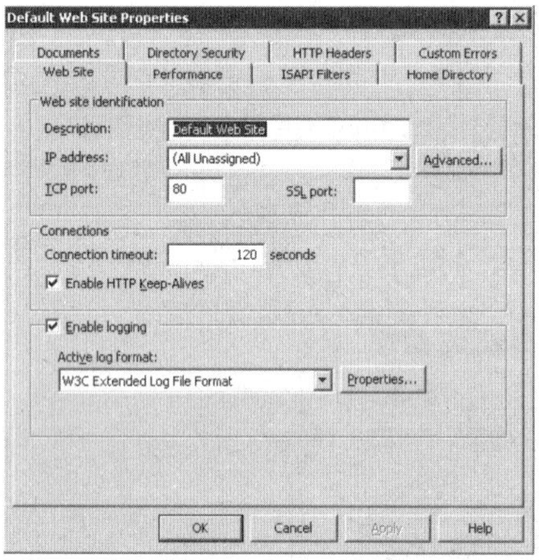

5. Click the Directory Security tab.

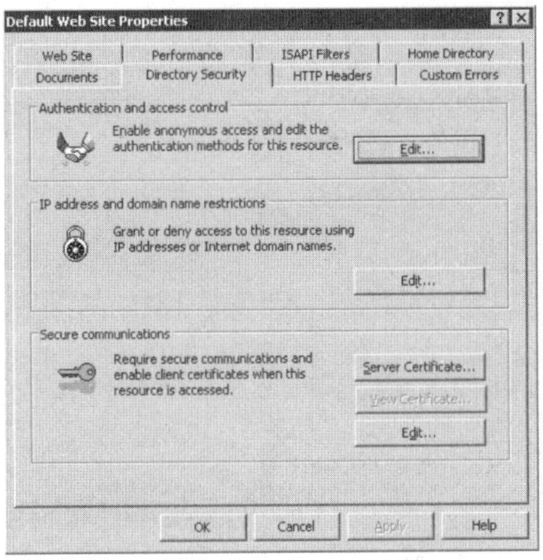

6. In the Secure Communications check box, click Server Certificate.

   The Web Server Certificate Wizard appears.

7. Click Next to bypass the Welcome page.

The Server Certificate page appears.

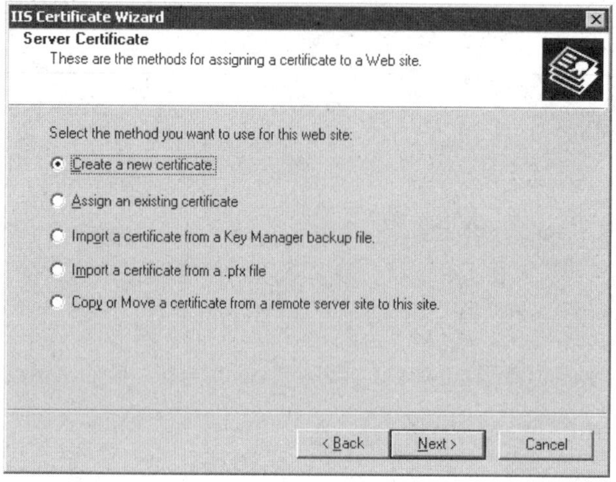

8. With the default Create A New Certificate option selected, click Next.

The Delayed Or Immediate Request page appears.

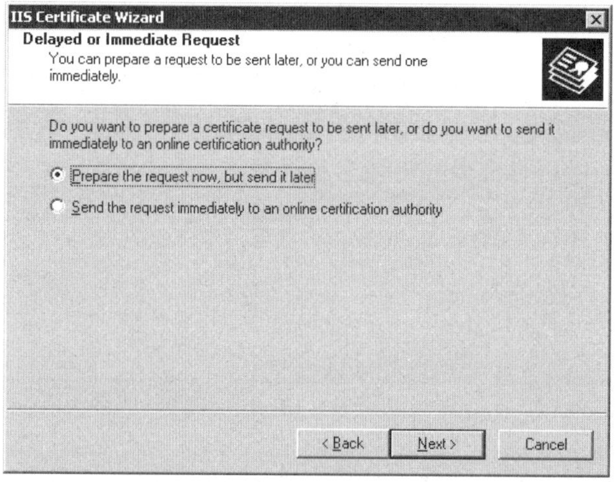

9. With the default Prepare The Request Now, But Send It Later option selected, click Next.

   The Name And Security Settings page appears.

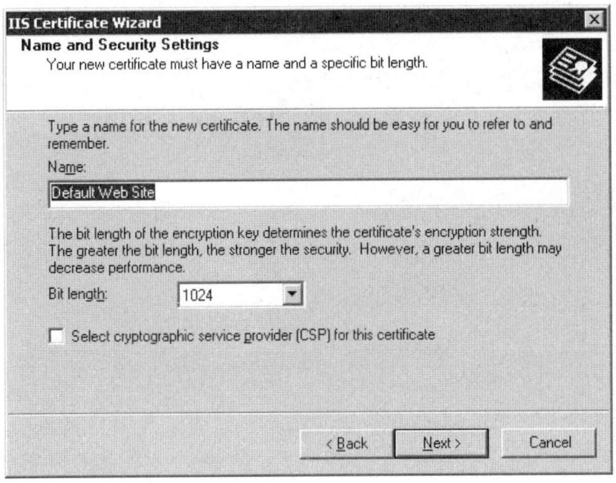

10. In the Name text box, type **Computer*xx* Web Site** and click Next.

   The Organization Information page appears.

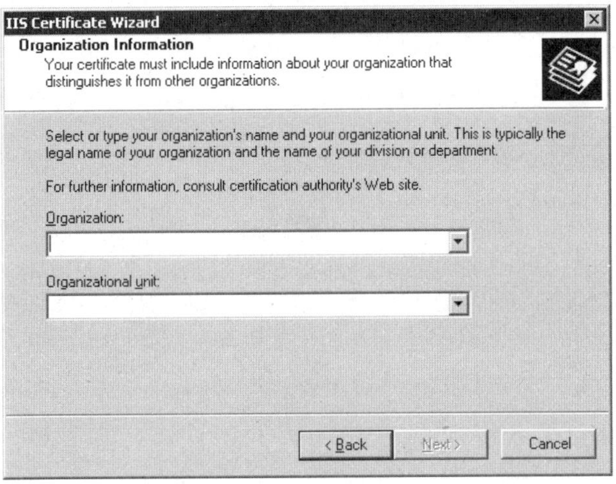

11. In the Organization text box, type **Contoso Ltd**.
12. In the Organizational Unit text box, type **Online Services**. Then click Next.

    The Your Site's Common Name page appears.

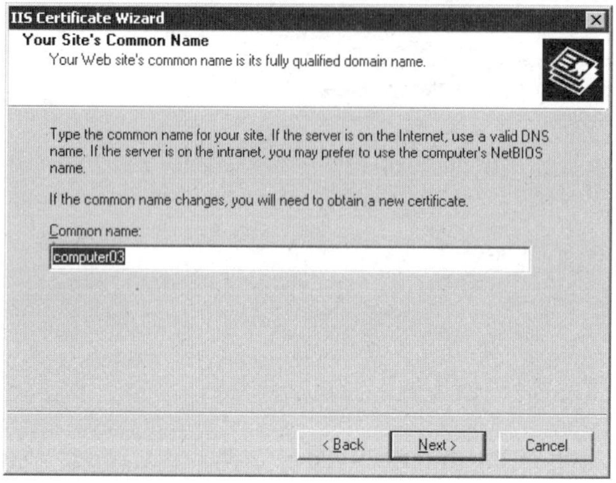

13. In the Common Name text box, type **computer*xx*.domain*xxyy*.contoso.com**, where *xx* and *yy* are the numbers assigned to your lab group computers, and click Next.

    The Geographical Information page appears.

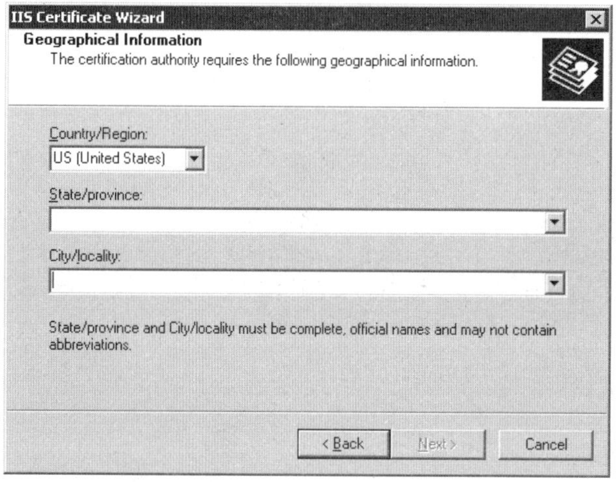

14. In the State/Province text box, type **Washington**.

15. In the City/Locality text box, type **Redmond**. Then click Next.

    The Certificate Request File Name page appears.

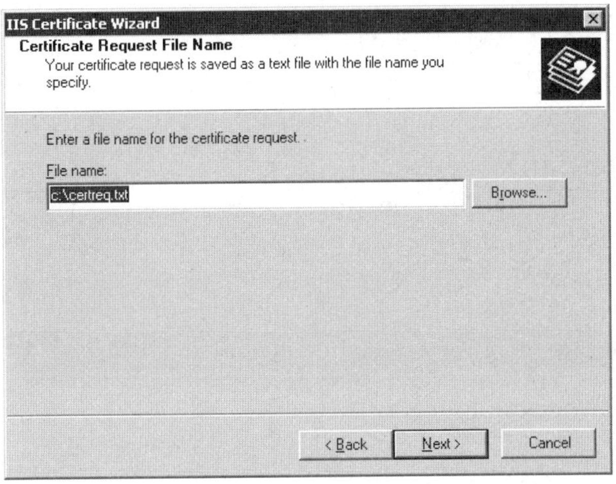

16. In the File Name text box, type **c:\webcertreq.txt** and click Next.

    The Request File Summary page appears.

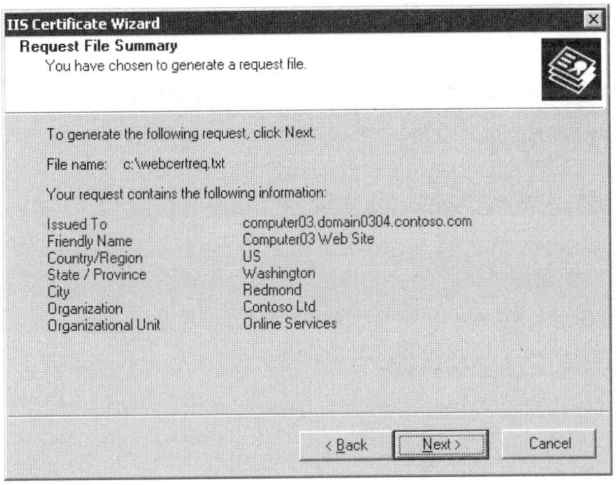

17. Click Next to continue.

    The Completing The Web Server Certificate Wizard page appears.

18. Click Finish to complete the wizard and create the certificate request file.

19. Click OK to close the Default Web Site Properties dialog box.
20. Leave the Internet Information Services (IIS) console open and the computer logged on for the next exercise.

EXERCISE 11-3: REQUESTING AN IIS SERVER CERTIFICATE

Estimated completion time: 10 minutes

To manually submit the certificate request file you created in Exercise 11-2 to the CA, you intend to use the Web enrollment home page supplied with Certificate Services.

1. On Computer*xx*, open Internet Explorer.

   The Internet Explorer window appears.

2. In the Address text box, type **http://computer*yy*/certsrv**, where *yy* is the number assigned to the computer by your instructor, and then click Go.

   The Microsoft Certificate Services page for the CA you installed on Computer*yy* in Lab 7 appears.

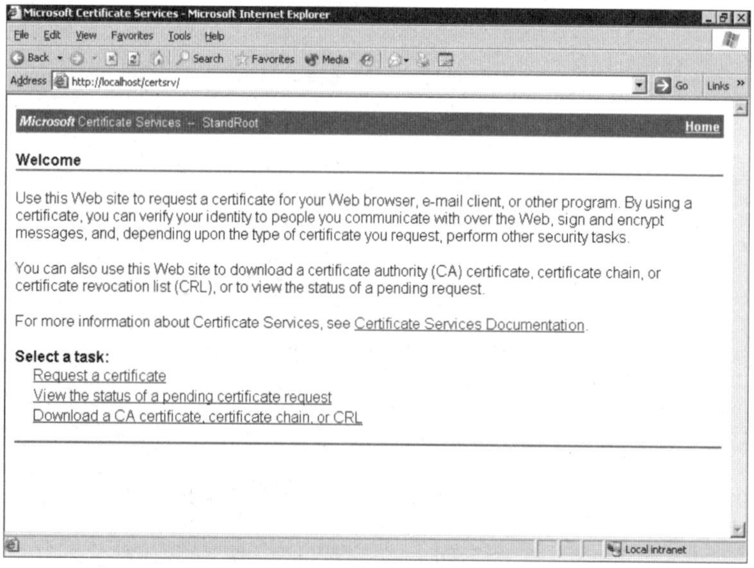

3. Click the Request A Certificate link.

   The Request A Certificate page appears.

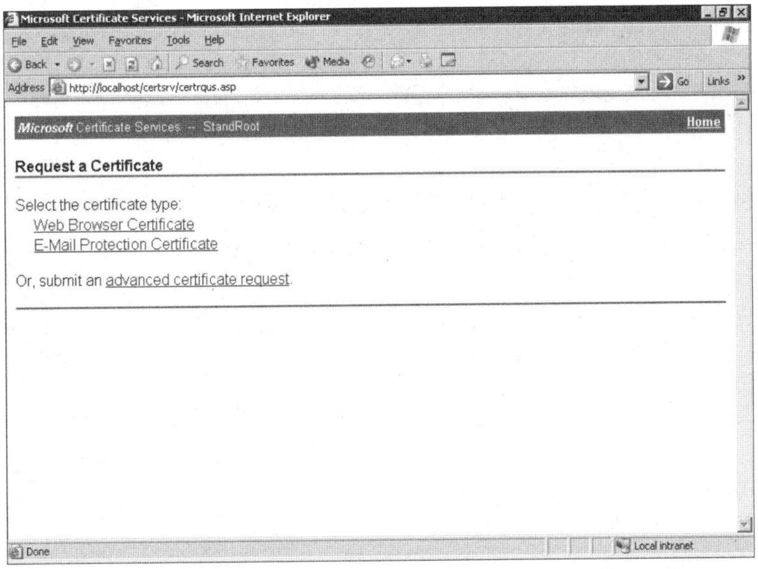

4. Click the Advanced Certificate Request link.

   The Advanced Certificate Request page appears.

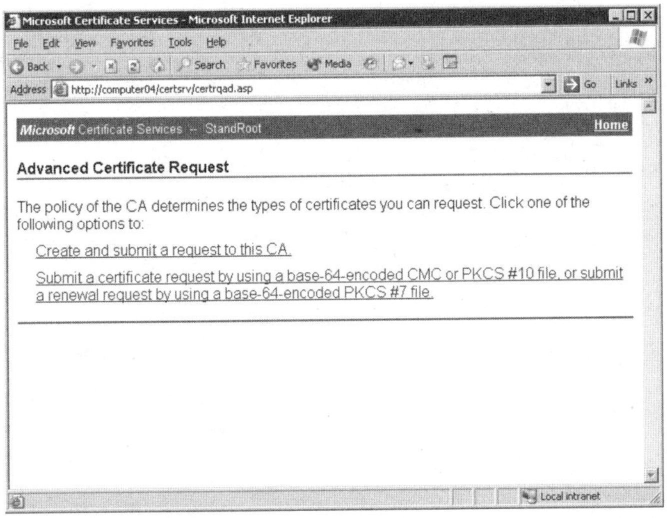

5. Click the Submit A Certificate Request By Using A Base-64-Encoded CMC Or PKCS #10 File, Or Submit A Renewal Request By Using A Base-64-Encoded PKCS #7 File link.

   The Submit a Certificate Request Or Renewal Request page appears.

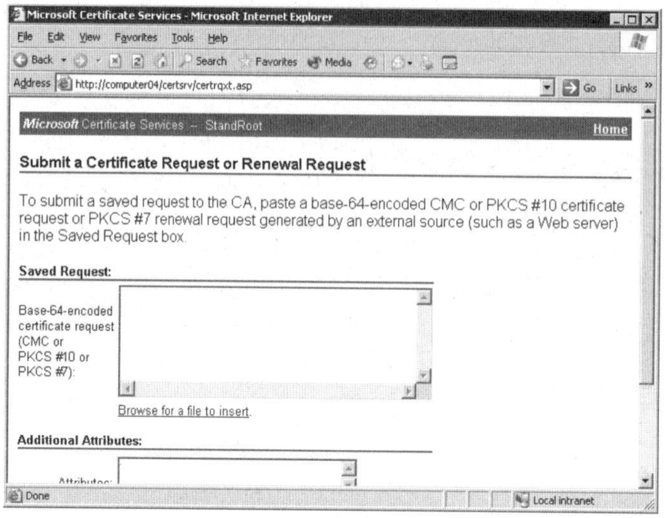

6. Click Start, and then click Run.

   The Run dialog box appears.

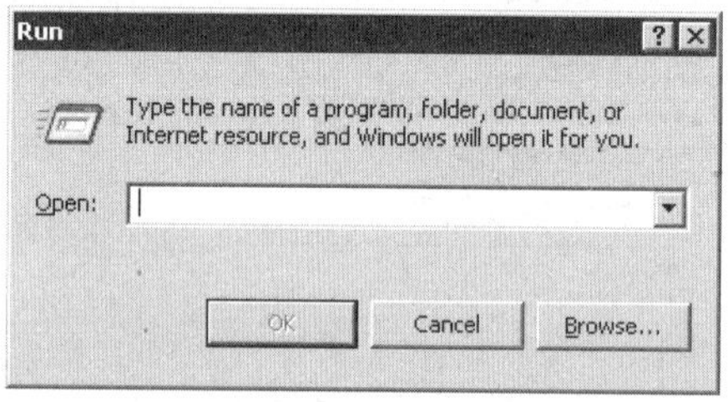

7. In the Open text box, type **c:\webcertreq.txt** and click OK.

   A Notepad window appears, containing the encoded certificate request.

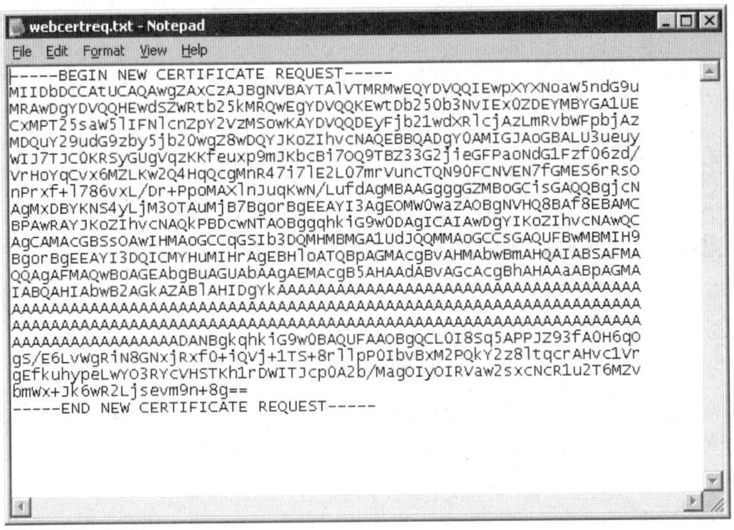

8. From the Edit menu, choose Select All. Then, again from the Edit menu, select Copy.

9. Switch back to Internet Explorer and click your cursor in the Base-64-Encoded Certificate Request (CMC or PKCS #10 or PKCS #7) text box.

10. From the Edit menu, select Paste.

    The encoded certificate request appears in the text box.

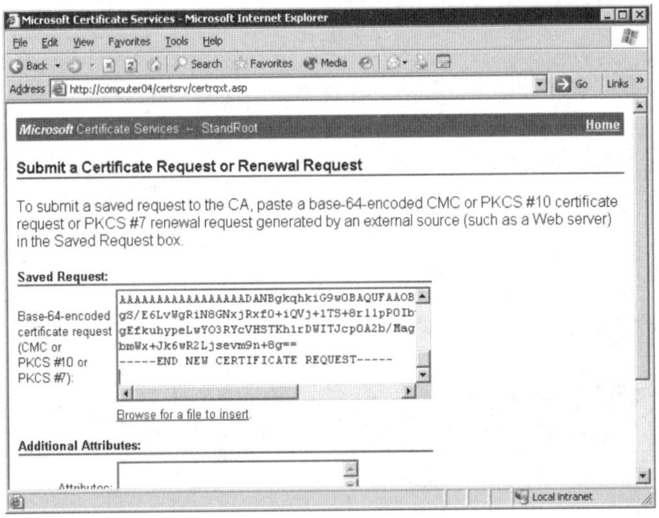

11. Click the Submit button at the bottom of the page.

    The Certificate Pending page appears.

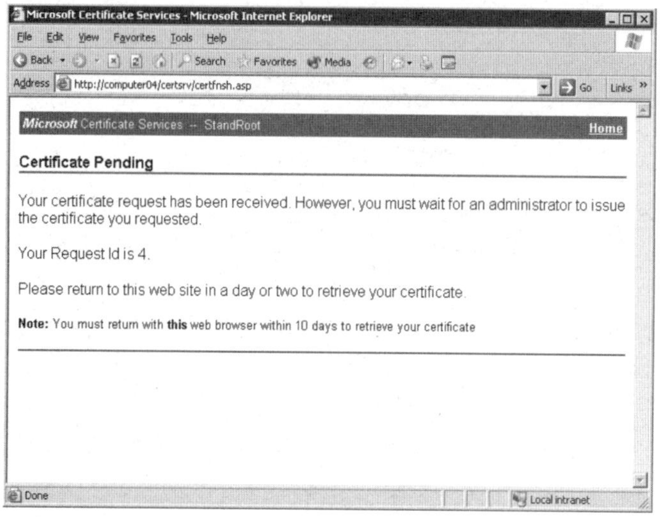

QUESTION *What is the Request ID specified on the page?*

12. Leave Internet Explorer open for later exercises.

EXERCISE 11-4: ISSUING A CERTIFICATE

Estimated completion time: 5 minutes

After submitting the certificate request to the CA, you must manually issue the certificate using the Certification Authority console.

1. On Computeryy, click Start, point to Administrative Tools, and select Certification Authority.

   The Certification Authority console appears.

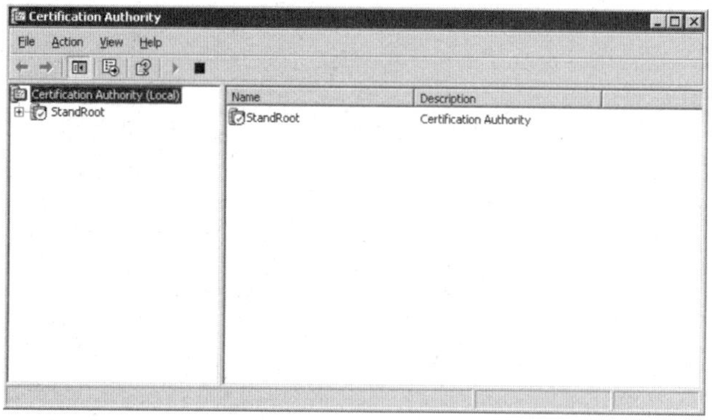

2. In the console tree, expand the StandRoot node and click the Pending Requests folder.

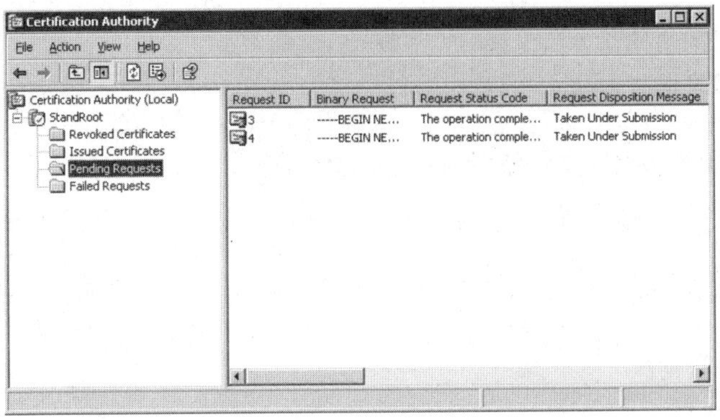

3. In the right pane, locate and select the entry with the Request ID matching the one assigned to you by the Microsoft Certificate Services Web page.
4. On the Action menu, point to All Tasks and click Issue.

QUESTION What happens?

5. Take a screen shot (press ALT+PRINT SCREEN) to turn in at the end of the lab of the Certification Authority console showing the contents of the Issued certificates folder. Paste the screen shot into a WordPad document named Domain*xxyy*Lab11-1.rtf (where *xx* and *yy* are the numbers assigned to the computers in your student domain).

EXERCISE 11-5: INSTALLING A CERTIFICATE

Estimated completion time: 10 minutes

After you have issued the certificate, you must retrieve it from the CA and install it, again using the Web enrollment interface.

1. On Computer*xx*, in Internet Explorer, click the Home link.

   The Microsoft Certificate Services home page appears again.

2. Click the View The Status Of A Pending Certificate Request link.

   The View The Status Of A Pending Certificate Request page appears.

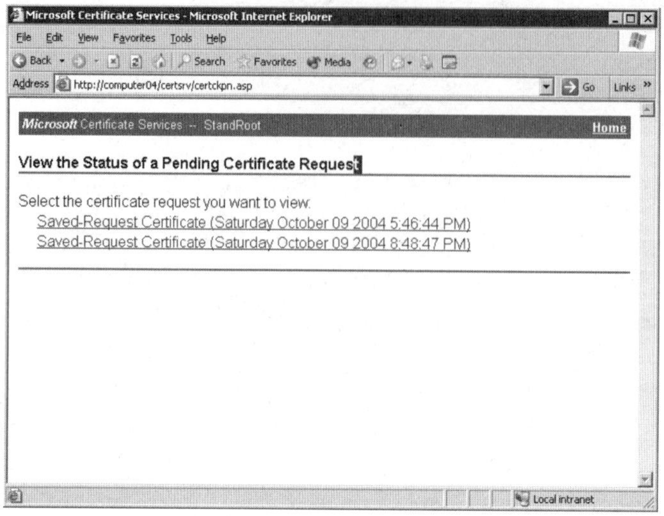

3. Click the link containing the date and time that you submitted your certificate request in Exercise 11-3.

   A Certificate Issued page appears.

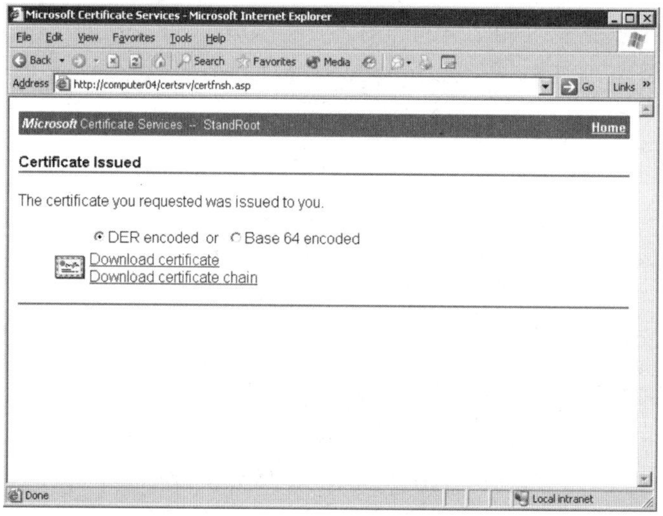

4. With the DER Encoded option selected, click the Download Certificate link.

   A File Download dialog box appears.

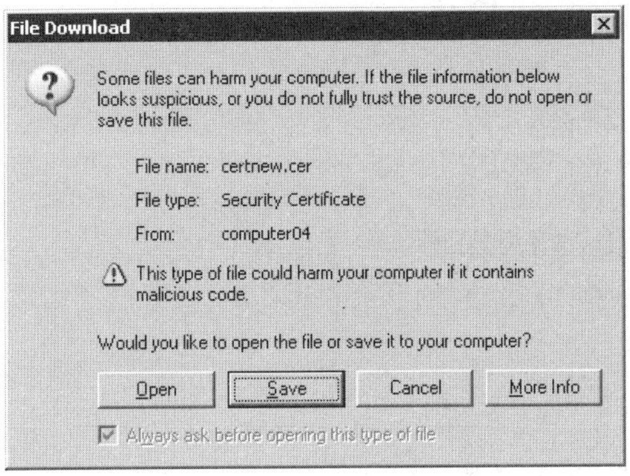

5. Click Save.

   A Save As dialog box appears.

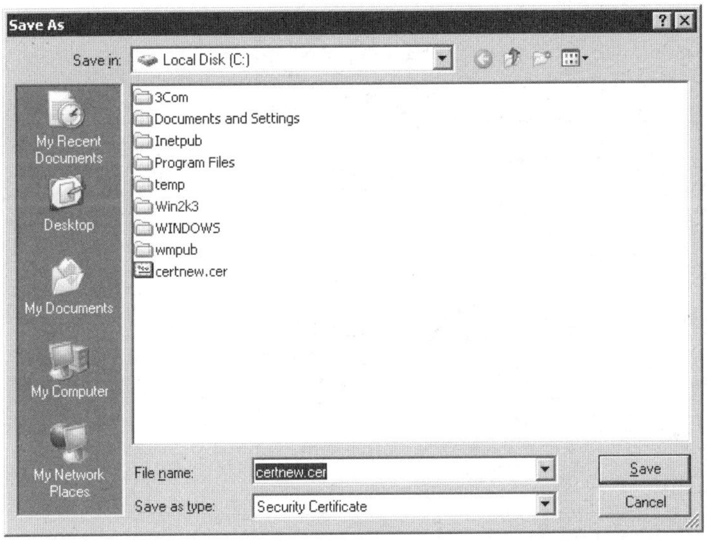

6. In the File Name text box, type **c:\webcertnew.cer** and click Save.

   The certificate is saved to the file.

7. Click Close to close the Download Complete dialog box.

8. Switch back to the Internet Information Services (IIS) Manager console.
9. Open the Default Web Site Properties dialog box, as you did in Exercise 11-2, click the Directory Security tab, and click Server Certificate.

   The Web Server Certificate Wizard appears.
10. Click Next to bypass the Welcome page.

   The Pending Certificate Request page appears.

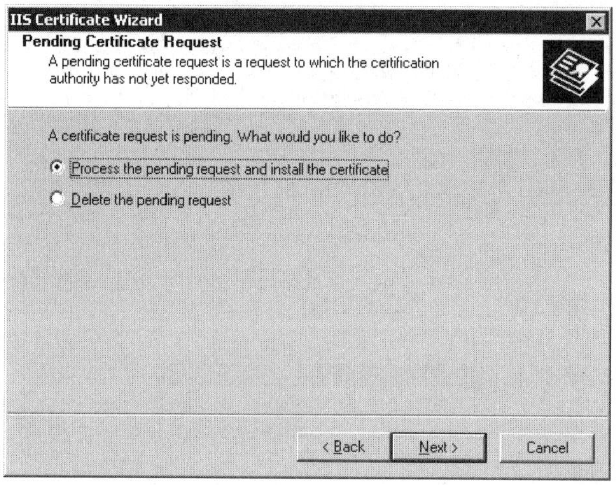

11. With the default Process The Pending Request And Install The Certificate option selected, click Next.

   The Process a Pending Request page appears.

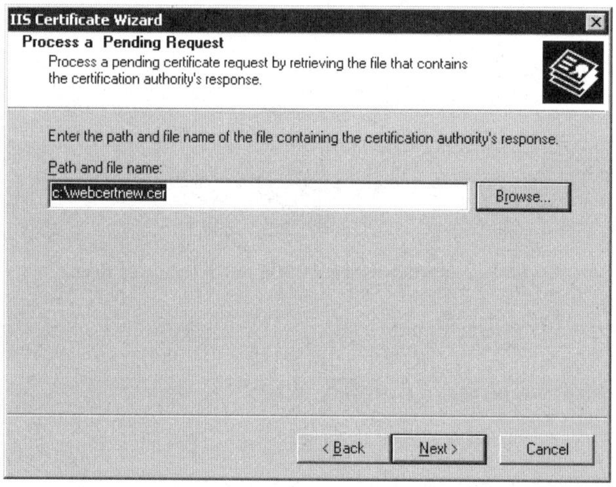

12. In the Path and File Name text box, type **c:\webcertnew.cer** and click Next.

    The SSL Port page appears.

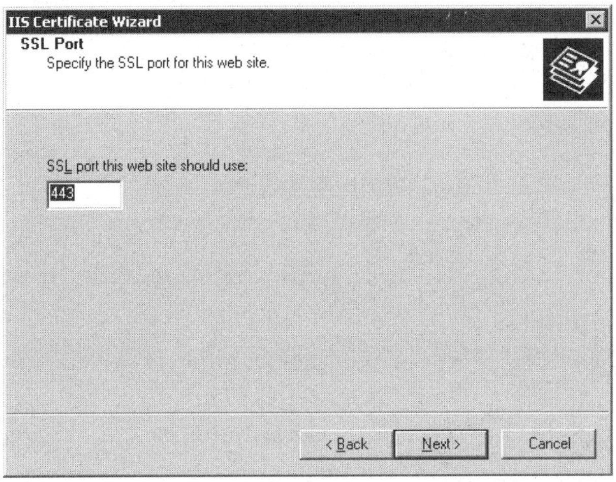

13. Leave the default 443 value in place and click Next.

    The Certificate Summary page appears.

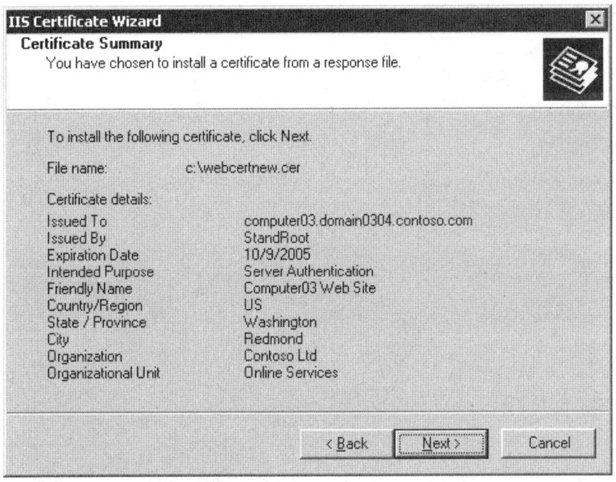

14. Click Next to continue.

    The Completing the Web Server Certificate Wizard page appears.

15. Click Finish to complete the wizard and install the certificate.

16. Click OK to close the Default Web Site Properties dialog box.

EXERCISE 11-6: TESTING SSL CONNECTIVITY

Estimated completion time: 10 minutes

Now that the IIS Web server has the certificate needed to use SSL, you can test the capabilities of the server by connecting to it with a browser, using both the http:// and https:// prefixes.

1. On Computeryy, open Internet Explorer.
2. In the Address text box, type **http://computer*xx*.domain*xxyy*.contoso.com**, where *xx* and *yy* are the numbers of the computers in your lab group, and click Go.

   QUESTION What happens?

3. In the Address box, type **https://computer*xx*.domain*xxyy*.contoso.com** and click Go.

   A Security Alert message box appears, stating that you are about to view pages over a secure connection.

   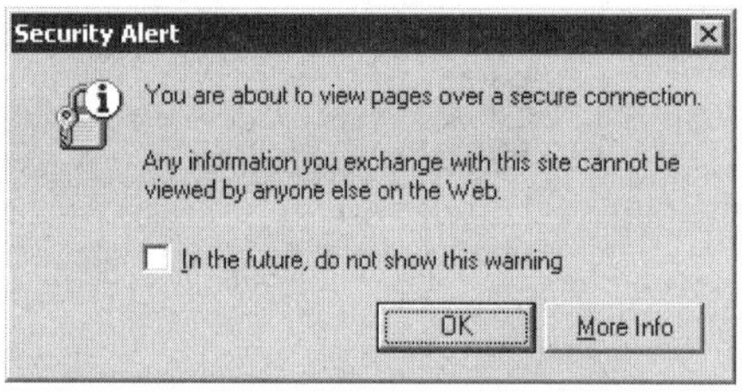

4. Select the In The Future, Do Not Show This Warning check box and click OK.

   QUESTION What happens now?

   QUESTION How can you tell that the browser has established a secure connection to the Web server?

   QUESTION What level of encryption is the browser using for its connection to the server? How can you tell?

5. In the Address box, type **https://computer*xx*** and click Go.

   A Security Alert dialog box appears.

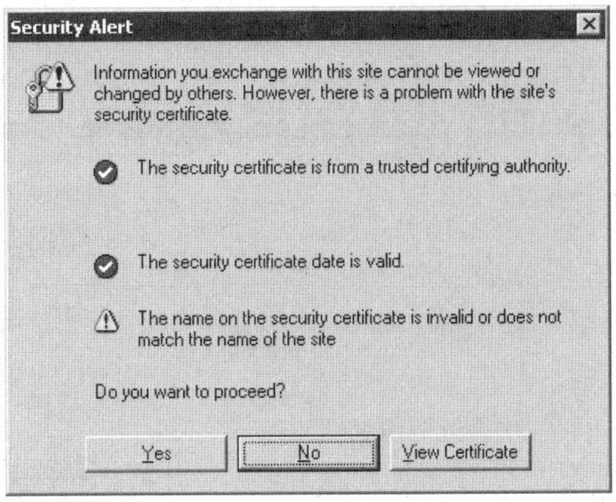

QUESTION What is the problem with the certificate that caused the dialog box to appear?

6. Click the View Certificate button.

   A Certificate dialog box appears.

7. Take a screen shot (press ALT+PRINT SCREEN) of the Certificate dialog box and paste it into a WordPad document named Domain*xxyy*Lab011-2.rtf (where *xx* and *yy* are the numbers assigned to the computers in your student domain), to turn in at the end of the lab.
8. Click OK to close the Certificate dialog box.
9. Click Yes in the Security Alert dialog box.

QUESTION What happens?

10. Leave Internet Explorer open and the computer logged on for later exercises.

EXERCISE 11-7: CONFIGURING SSL REQUIREMENTS

Estimated completion time: 10 minutes

SSL is now functional on your IIS server, and clients are able to connect to the Web site using either a protected or an unprotected connection. The next step in your lab deployment is to determine what SSL requirements you should configure the server to use, if any.

1. On Computer*xx*, in the Internet Information Services (IIS) Manager console, open the Default Web Site Properties dialog box and click the Directory Security tab.
2. In the Secure Communications box, click Edit.

   The Secure Communications dialog box appears.

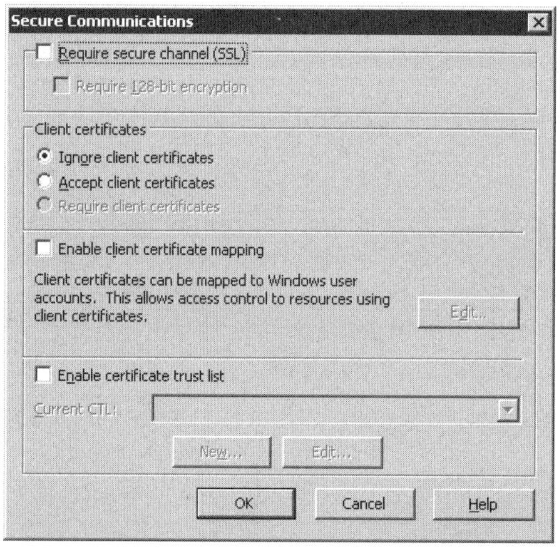

3. Select the Require Secure Channel (SSL) check box and click OK.
4. Click OK to close the Default Web Site Properties dialog box.
5. On Computer*yy*, in Internet Explorer, attempt to connect to the Computer*xx* Web server using the URL **http://computer*xx*.domain*xxyy*.contoso.com**.

6. Click the Refresh button to ensure that the browser is establishing a new connection to the server.

   QUESTION What is the result?

7. Now try to connect using the URL **https://computer*xx*.domain*xxyy*.contoso.com**.

   QUESTION What is the result?

8. On Computer*xx*, in the Internet Information Services (IIS) Manager console, open the Secure Communications dialog box again and select the Require Client Certificates option.
9. Click OK twice to close the dialog boxes.
10. On Computer*yy*, try again to connect to the Computer*xx* Web server using the URL **https://computer*xx*.domain*xxyy*.contoso.com.**
11. Click the Refresh button.

    QUESTION What happens?

12. Click Cancel.
13. Take a screen shot (press ALT+PRINT SCREEN) to turn in at the end of the lab of the Internet Explorer window that shows the error page requiring you to have a client certificate. Paste the screen shot into a WordPad document named Domain*xxyy*Lab11-3.rtf (where *xx* and *yy* are the numbers assigned to the computers in your student domain).
14. Close Internet Explorer and leave the computer logged on for the next exercise.

EXERCISE 11-8: OBTAINING A CLIENT CERTIFICATE

Estimated completion time: 15 minutes

Before clients can connect to your IIS server, they must have client certificates, because the server is now configured to require them. To obtain a client certificate for the computer running the Web browser, you must again request one using the Certificate Services Web enrollment interface.

1. On Computer*yy*, open Internet Explorer and in the Address text box, type **http://localhost/certsrv** and click Go.

   The Microsoft Certificate Services home page appears.

2. Click the Request Certificate link.

   The Request A Certificate page appears.

3. Click the Web Browser Certificate link.

   The Web Browser Certificate – Identifying Information page appears.

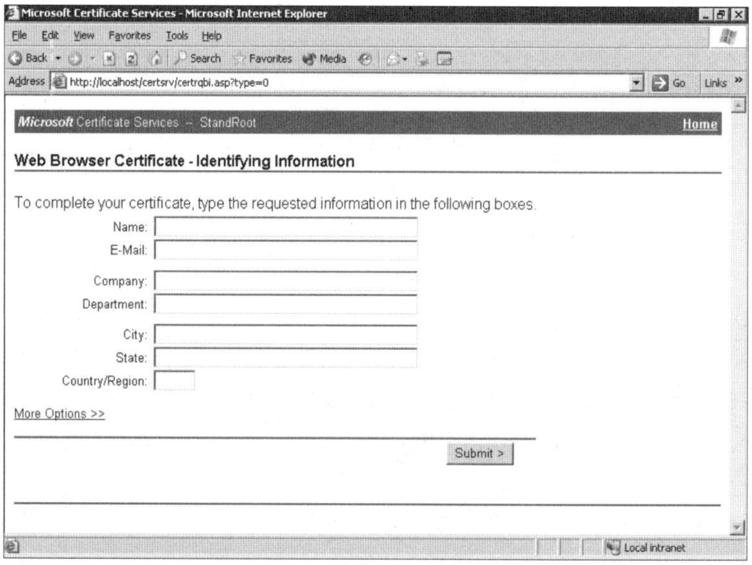

4. Type your name in the Name text box and click Submit.

   A Potential Scripting Violation message box appears.

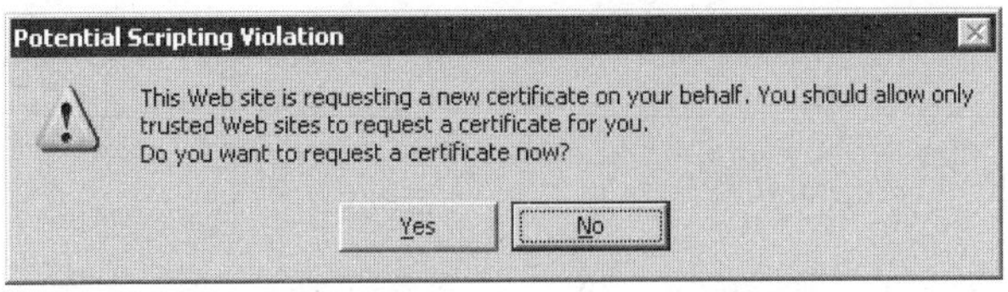

5. Click Yes to continue.

   The Certificate Pending page appears.

QUESTION What is the Request ID for the certificate request?

6. Open the Certification Authority console on Computeryy, locate the certificate request you just created in the Pending Requests folder, and issue the certificate, just as you did in Exercise 11-4.
7. In Internet Explorer, connect to the Web Enrollment server again by clicking the Home link.
8. Click the View The Status Of A Pending Certificate Request link.

   The View The Status Of A Pending Certificate Request page appears.

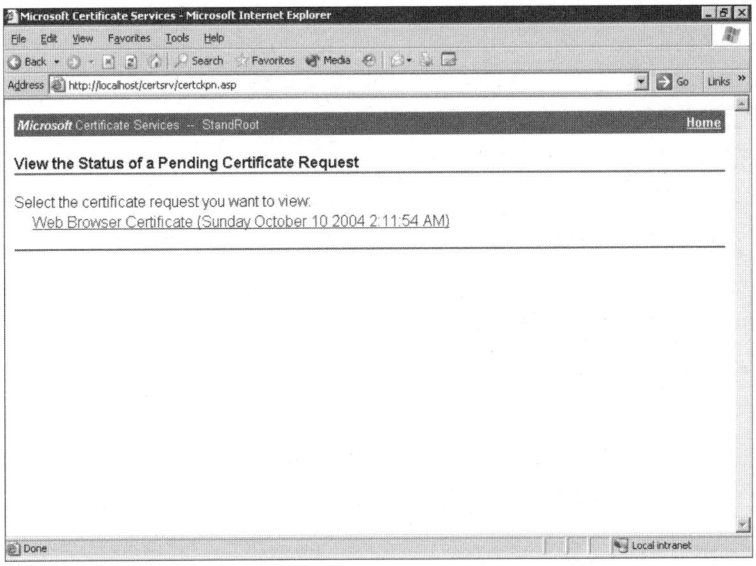

9. Click the Web Browser Certificate link corresponding to the certificate you just issued.

   The Certificate Issued page appears.

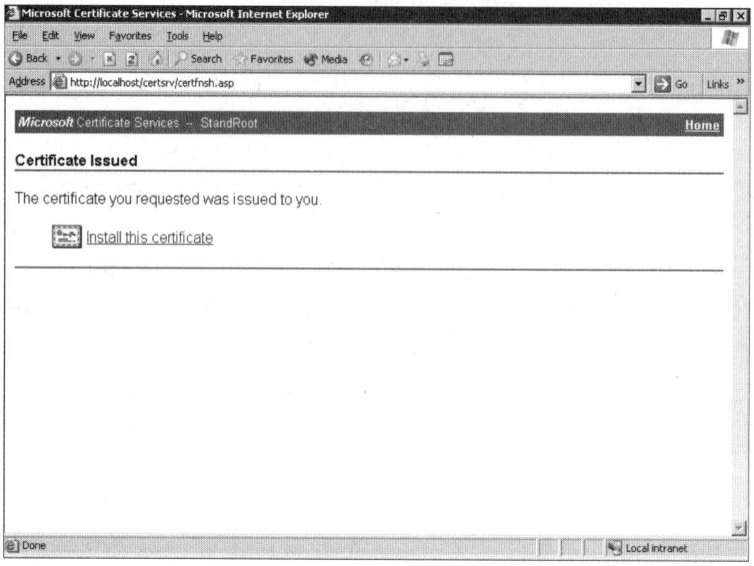

10. Click the Install This Certificate link.

    Another Potential Scripting Violation message box appears.

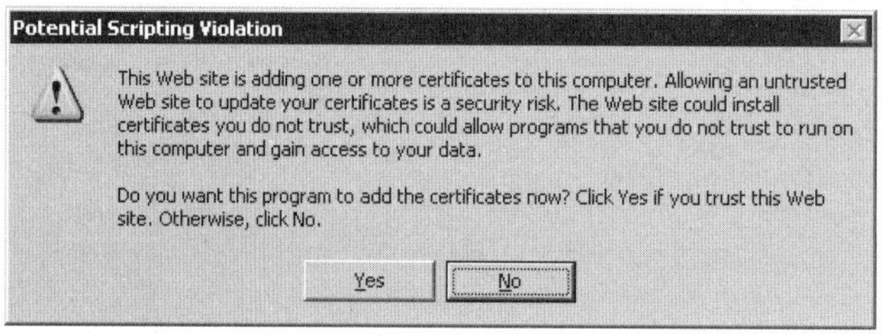

11. Click Yes to continue.

    The Certificate Installed page appears.

12. Close all Internet Explorer windows.

13. Open a new Internet Explorer window and, as you did in Exercise 11-7, try to connect to the Computer*xx* Web server using the URL **https://computer*xx*.domain*xxyy*.contoso.com.**

    The Client Authentication dialog box appears again.

    QUESTION *What has changed in this attempt to connect to the Computerxx Web server?*

14. Take a screen shot (press ALT+PRINT SCREEN of the Client Authentication dialog box and paste it into a WordPad document named Domain*xxyy*Lab11-4.rtf (where *xx* and *yy* are the numbers assigned to the computers in your student domain), to turn in at the end of the lab.
15. Select Users and click OK.

    QUESTION *What happens?*

16. Close Internet Explorer and log off both computers.

LAB REVIEW QUESTIONS

Estimated completion time: 15 minutes

1. In Exercise 11-2, what would be the result if you typed **computer*xx*** in the Common Name text box instead of **computer*xx*.domain*xxyy*.contoso.com?**
2. In Exercise 11-7, when the Client Authentication dialog box appears, why are you unable to connect to the server?
3. In Exercise 11-3 and Exercise 11-4, why is it necessary to submit the request for the server certificate through the Web enrollment home page and manually issue the certificate using the Certification Authority console?
4. How could the process of obtaining a certificate for the Web server be streamlined if the certification authority was an enterprise CA instead of a stand-alone CA?
5. How could you increase the security provided by configuring the IIS server to require client certificates, as you did in Exercise 11-7?

LAB CHALLENGE 11-1: ENCRYPTING ACTIVE DIRECTORY TRAFFIC

Estimated completion time: 30 minutes

The Address Book application included in Windows Server 2003 is a Lightweight Directory Access Protocol (LDAP) client that you can use to send queries for Microsoft Active Directory information to a domain controller. Address Book is also capable of sending these queries in encrypted form using SSL. To complete this challenge, you must accomplish the following tasks:

1. Use Network Monitor on Computer*xx* to capture a sample of standard, unencrypted LDAP traffic generated by the Address Book application running on Computer*yy*.
2. Configure Address Book on Computer*yy* to encrypt its LDAP communications.
3. Use Network Monitor on Computer*xx* to capture a sample of the encrypted LDAP traffic and compare the packets with the unencrypted ones.

Write out the procedure you used to configure Address Book and, for each captured traffic sample, create a display filter in Network Monitor to isolate the packets containing the LDAP queries and replies. Then take a screen shot (press ALT+PRINT SCREEN) of Network Monitor's three-paned display, showing the header information demonstrating that the selected packet contains LDAP traffic. Paste the screen shots into two separate WordPad documents named Domain*xxyy*Lab011-5.rtf and Domain*xxyy*Lab011-6.rtf (where *xx* and *yy* are the numbers assigned to the computers in your student domain), to turn in at the end of the lab.

> **IMPORTANT Hint** To ensure that Address Book sends its queries to the Computerxx server where Network Monitor can capture them, you must configure the Search Base parameter with the name of the domain for your lab group, in LDAP notation. LDAP notation consists of a header and value for each level of the domain hierarchy, separated by commas. For example, the LDAP name for the domainxxyy.contoso.com domain would be DC=domainxxyy,DC=contoso,DC=com.

LAB 12
SECURING REMOTE ACCESS

This lab contains the following exercises and activities:

- Lab Exercise 12-1: Creating a Remote Access User
- Lab Exercise 12-2: Configuring RRAS
- Lab Exercise 12-3: Configuring a VPN Client
- Lab Exercise 12-4: Establishing a VPN Connection
- Lab Exercise 12-5: Creating a Remote Access Policy
- Lab Review Questions
- Lab Challenge 12-1: Capturing Remote Access Traffic

SCENARIO

You are a network administrator at Contoso, Ltd., who has been instructed to configure a Microsoft Windows Server 2003 computer to function as a remote access server for VPN clients. The clients are members of the sales department who will use laptops while traveling so they can connect to the company network and access e-mail and other resources. To test your VPN server configuration, you are using the company's lab network to install a RRAS server and a VPN client.

After completing this lab, you will be able to:

- **Install and configure RRAS to function as a remote access VPN server**
- **Configure a VPN client**
- **Establish a VPN connection**
- **Create a remote access policy**

Estimated lesson time: 85 minutes

BEFORE YOU BEGIN

To complete this lab, you will need the following information:

- The names of the computers in your student domain (Computer*xx* and Computer*yy*)
- The name of your student domain (domain*xxyy*.contoso.com)

> **NOTE** **Raising the Domain Functional Level** To complete Exercise 12-5, you must have raised the domain functional level of your student domain to Windows Server 2003, as specified in Lab Challenge 2-1. If you have not completed that lab challenge, you must raise the domain functional level using the Active Directory Domains and Trusts console before you can complete Exercise 12-5.

EXERCISE 12-1: CREATING A REMOTE ACCESS USER

Estimated completion time: 10 minutes

To connect the VPN client to the RRAS server, you must supply a user name and password. In this exercise, you create a test user account, which you will use later to log on to the RRAS server.

1. On Computer*xx*, log on to the domain*xxyy* domain as Administrator, and type the password **P@ssw0rd**.
2. Open the Active Directory Users and Computers console.
3. In the console tree, select the Users container and, on the Action menu, point to New and select User.

   The New Object–User wizard appears.

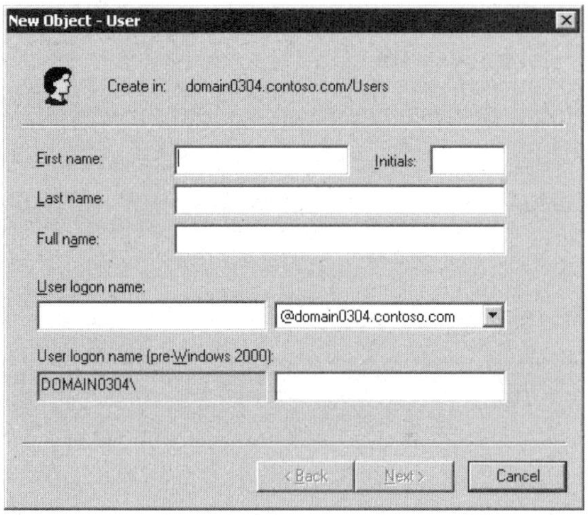

4. In the Full Name text box, type **Tina O'Dell**.
5. In the User Logon Name text box, type **tinao** and click Next.

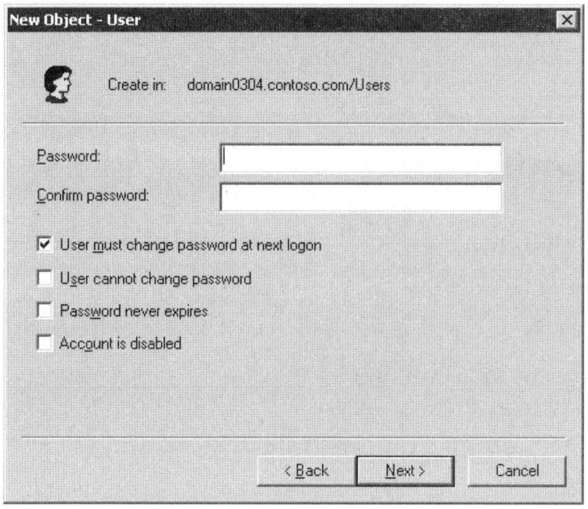

6. In the Password and Confirm Password fields, type **P@ssw0rd**.
7. Clear the User Must Change Password At Next Logon check box, and then click Next.
8. Click Finish to create the new user account.
9. On the Action menu, point to New and select Group.

   The New Object–Group dialog box appears.

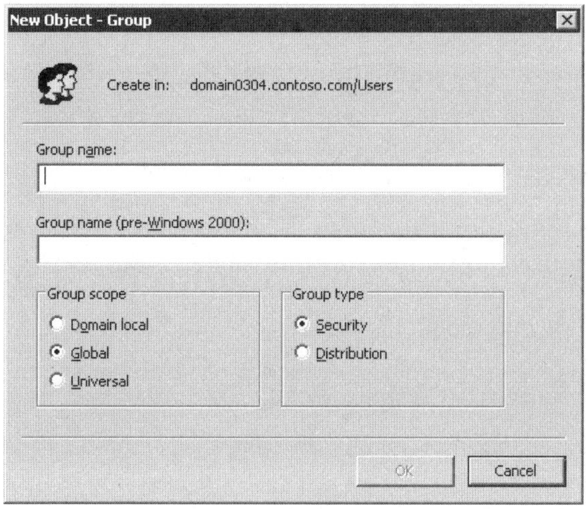

10. In the Group Name text box, type **Remote Users** and click OK to create a new global security group.

    The Remote Users group appears in the Users container.

11. Close the Active Directory Users and Computers console.

EXERCISE 12-2: CONFIGURING RRAS

Estimated completion time: 15 minutes

For Windows Server 2003 to function as a remote access server, you must configure the Routing and Remote Access service. In this exercise, you create a custom RRAS configuration that will enable you to implement a VPN on your lab network.

1. On Computer*xx*, click Start, point to Administrative Tools, and click Routing And Remote Access.

   The Routing and Remote Access console appears.

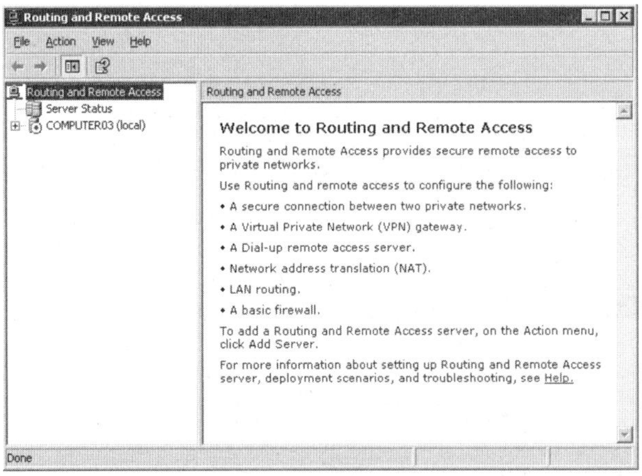

2. In the console tree, select the Computer*xx* (Local) node and, from the Action menu, select Configure and Enable Routing and Remote Access.

   The Routing and Remote Access Server Setup Wizard appears.

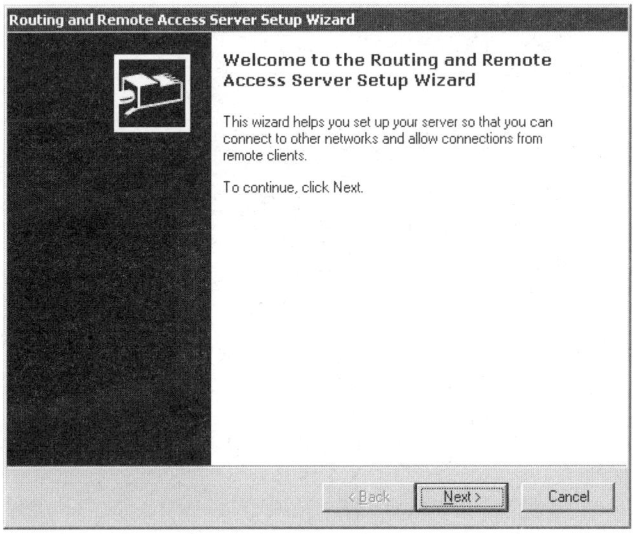

3. Click Next to bypass the Welcome page.

   The Configuration page appears.

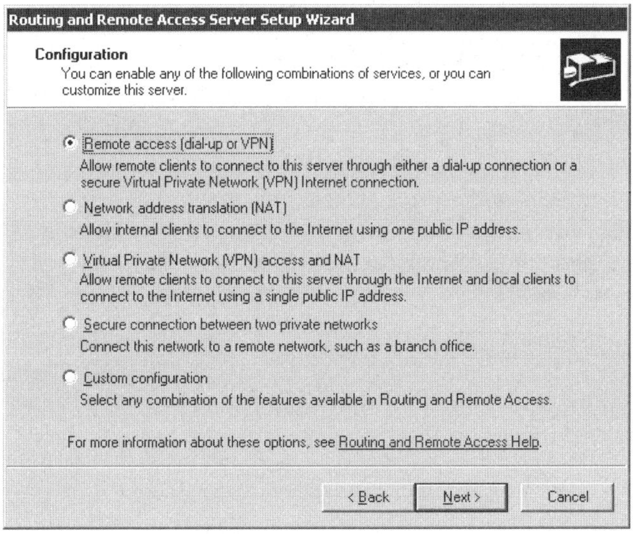

4. Select Custom Configuration and click Next.

   The Custom Configuration page appears.

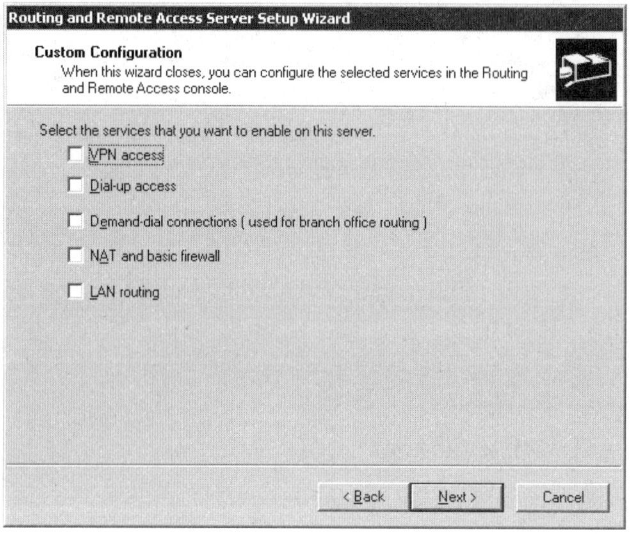

5. Select the VPN Access check box and click Next.

> **NOTE** ***Configuring a Remote Access Server*** To configure RRAS as a VPN server on a production computer, you can usually select the Remote Access (Dial-up or VPN) option on the Configuration page and then choose the VPN option. This option, however, requires the computer to have two network interfaces, one for the internal, private network, and one for the Internet connection. Because your lab server does not have two interfaces and because you will be establishing a VPN connection over the LAN, instead of through the Internet, you must use the Custom Configuration option instead.

   The Completing The Routing And Remote Access Server Setup Wizard page appears.

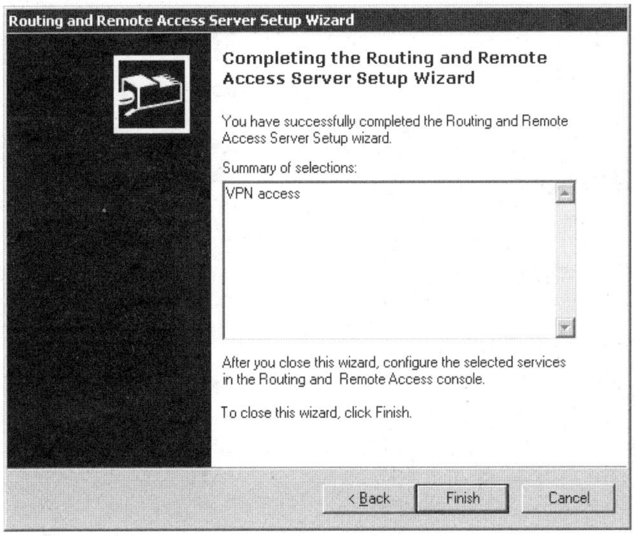

6. Click Finish to complete the wizard.

   A Routing And Remote Access message box appears, asking if you want to start the Routing And Remote Access service.

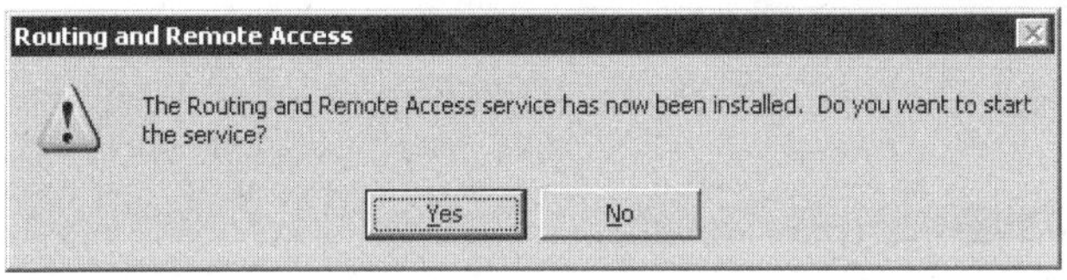

7. Click Yes to start the service.

   The Routing and Remote Access console tree expands to display the server subheadings.

8. Take a screen shot (press ALT+PRINT SCREEN) of the Routing and Remote Access console and paste it into a WordPad document named Domain*xxyy*Lab12-1.rtf (where *xx* and *yy* are the numbers assigned to the computers in your student domain), which you will turn in at the end of the lab.

9. In the console tree, select the Computer*xx* (Local) node and, from the Action Menu, select Properties.

   The Computer*xx* (Local) Properties dialog box appears.

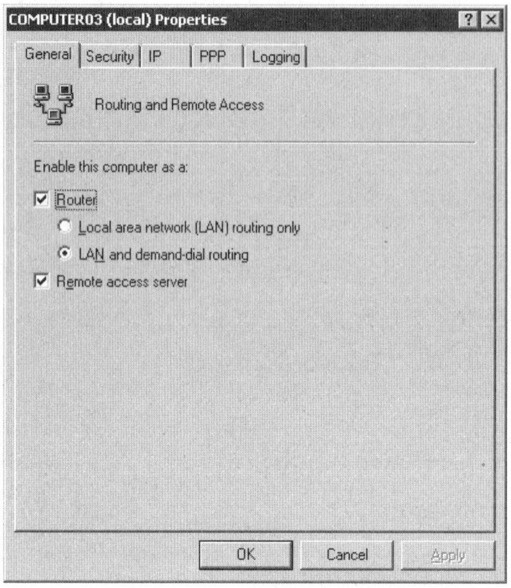

10. Click the Security tab.

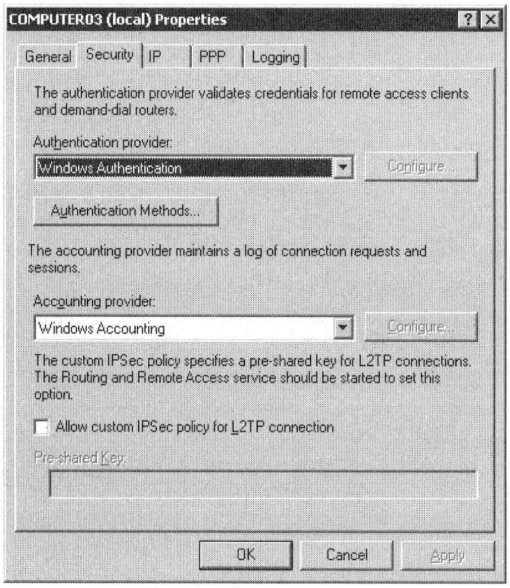

11. Click the Authentication Methods button.

    The Authentication Methods dialog box appears.

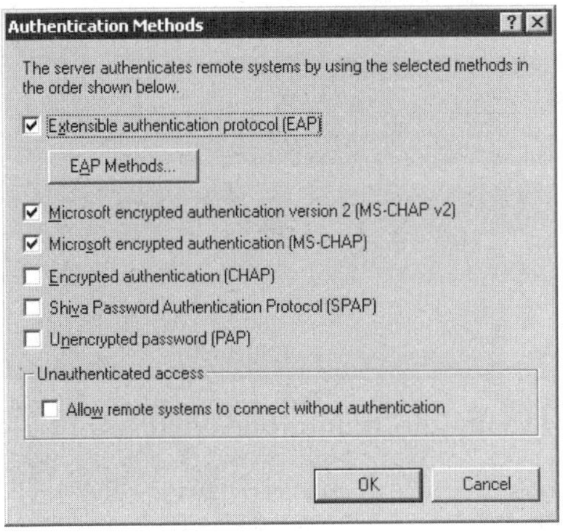

12. Clear the Extensible Authentication Protocol (EAP) check box.
13. Select the Unencrypted Password (PAP) check box and click OK.
14. Click OK to close the Computer*xx* (Local) Properties dialog box.
15. A Routing And Remote Access message box appears, offering to display Help pages about the selected authentication methods.
16. Click No.
17. Leave the Routing and Remote Access console open for later exercises.

EXERCISE 12-3: CONFIGURING A VPN CLIENT

Estimated completion time: 15 minutes

Windows Server 2003 is capable of functioning as a remote access client, using either a dial-up or VPN connection. In this exercise, you configure a computer to connect to the RRAS server by creating a VPN network connection.

1. On Computer*yy*, log on to the domain*xxyy* domain as Administrator by typing the password **P@ssw0rd**.

2. Click Start, point to Control Panel, right-click Network Connections, and select Open from the context menu.

   The Network Connections window appears.

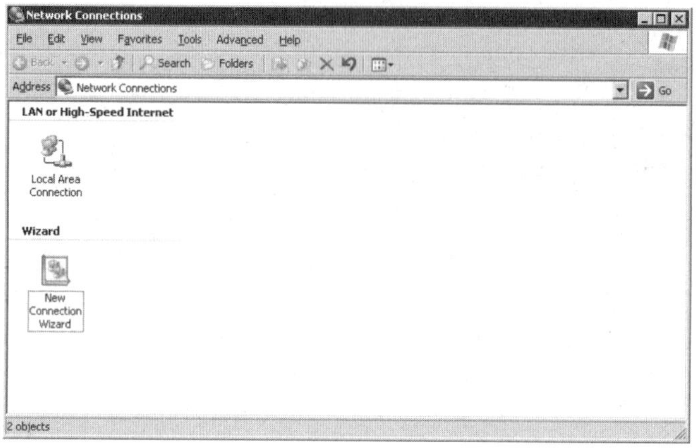

3. Double-click the New Connection Wizard icon.

   The New Connection Wizard appears.

4. Click Next to bypass the Welcome page.

   The Network Connection Type page appears.

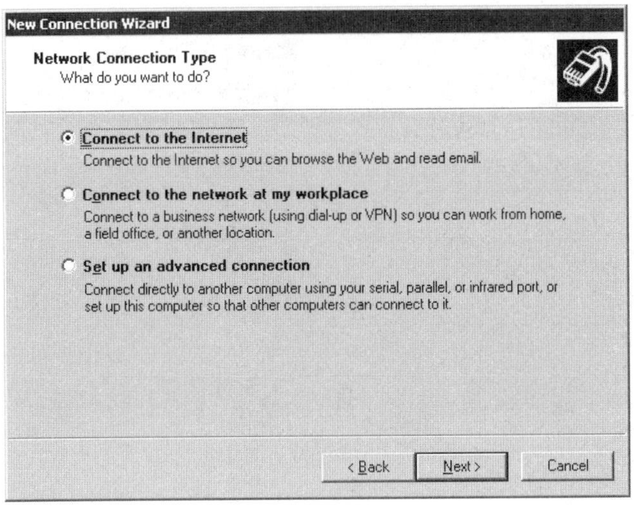

5. Select the Connect To The Network At My Workplace option and click Next.

   The Network Connection page appears.

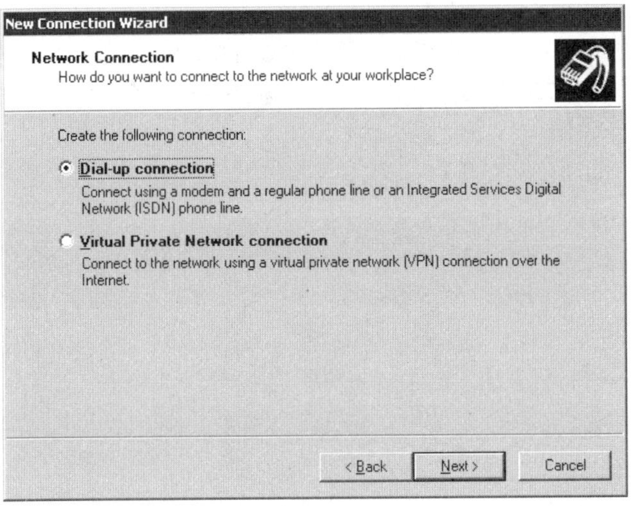

6. Select the Virtual Private Network Connection option and click Next.

   The Connection Name page appears.

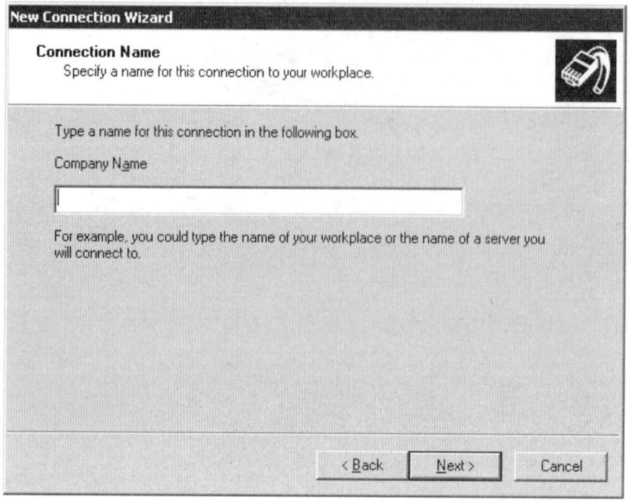

7. In the Company Name text box, type **Computer*xx***, where *xx* is the number assigned to the computer by your instructor. Then click Next.

   The VPN Server Selection page appears.

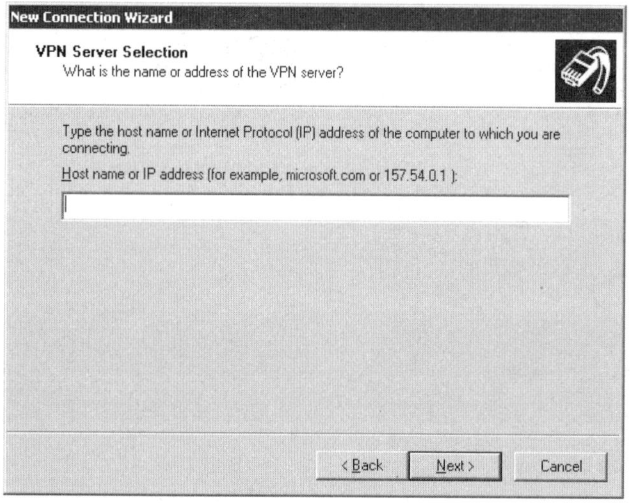

8. In the Host Name Or IP Address text box, type **computerxx** and click Next.

   The Connection Availability page appears.

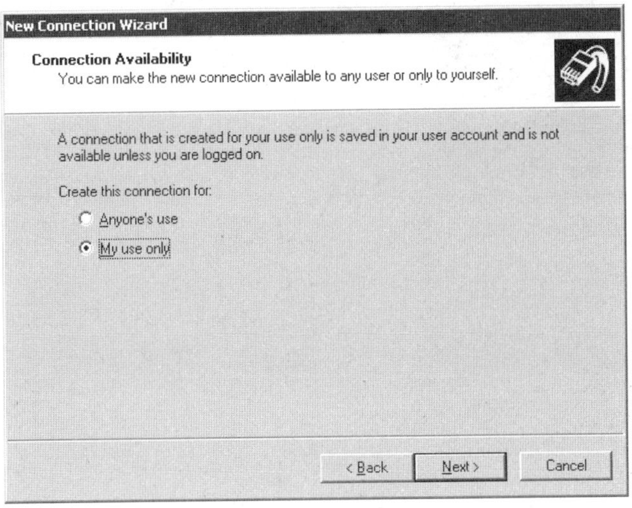

9. Select the Anyone's Use option and click Next.

   The Completing The New Connection Wizard page appears.

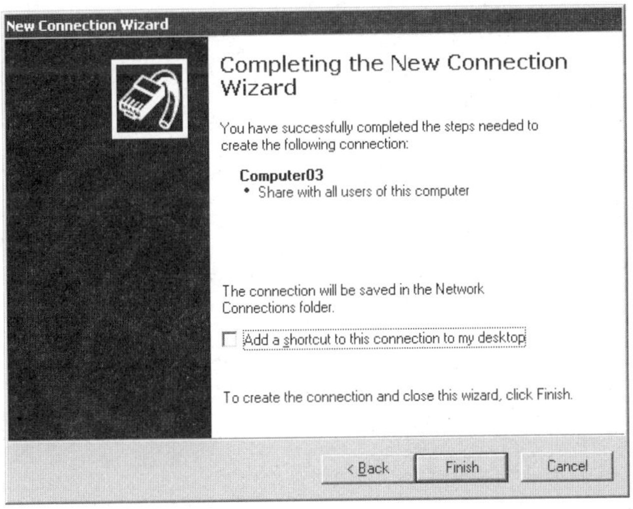

10. Click Finish to complete the wizard and create the connection.

The Connect Computer*xx* dialog box appears.

11. Click Properties.

The Computer*xx* Properties dialog box appears.

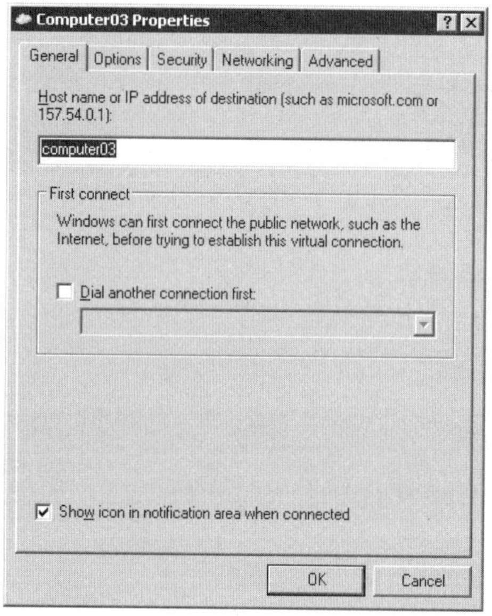

12. Click the Security tab.

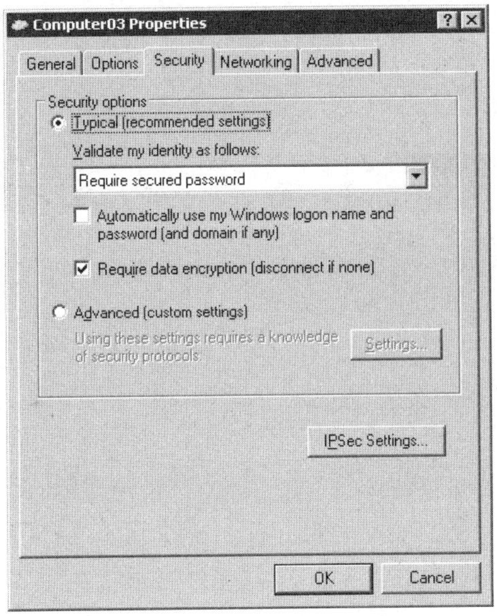

13. Select the Advanced (Custom Settings) option and click Settings.

    The Advanced Security Settings dialog box appears.

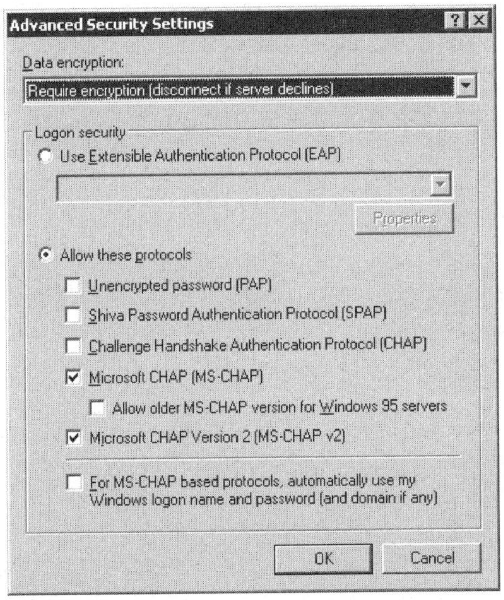

14. In the Data Encryption drop-down list, select Optional Encryption.

15. Under Allow These Protocols, select the Unencrypted Password (PAP) check box and leave the Microsoft CHAP (MS-CHAP) and Microsoft CHAP Version 2 (MS-CHAP v2) check boxes selected. Then click OK.

    A Network Connections message box appears.

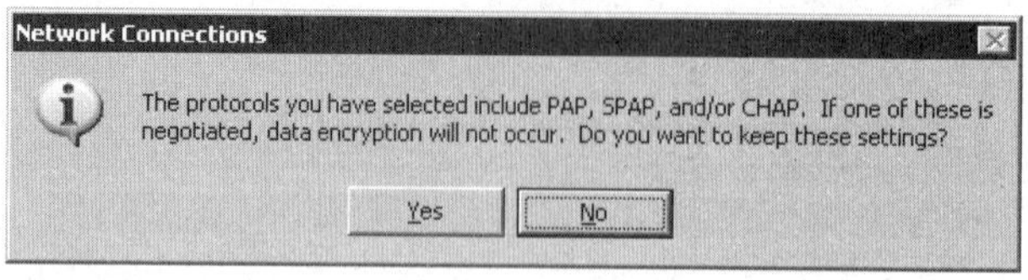

16. Click Yes.
17. Click OK to close the Computer*xx* Properties dialog box.
18. In the Connect Computer*xx* dialog box, click Cancel.
19. Leave the Network Connections window open for the next exercise.

EXERCISE 12-4: ESTABLISHING A VPN CONNECTION

Estimated completion time: 15 minutes

In this exercise, you test the VPN connection on your lab network by using the client computer in your lab to log on to the RRAS computer.

1. On Computer*yy*, in the Network Connections window, double-click the Computer*xx* icon.
2. The Connect Computer*xx* dialog box appears.

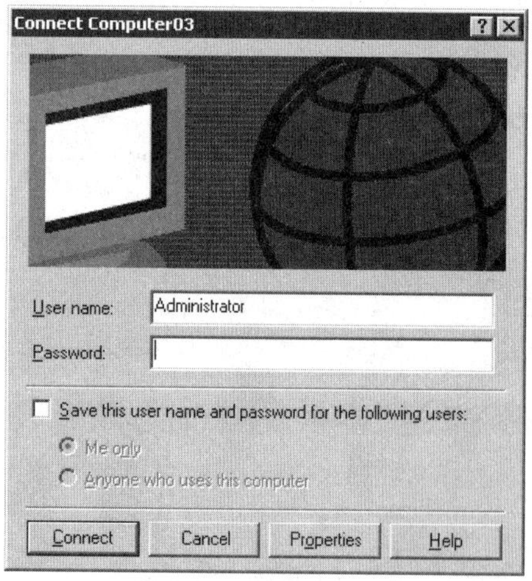

3. In the User Name text box, type **tinao**.
4. In the Password text box, type **P@ssw0rd** and then click Connect.

QUESTION Why is the client unable to connect to the server?

5. Take a screen shot (press ALT+PRINT SCREEN) of the Error Connecting To Computer*xx* dialog box and paste it into a WordPad document named Domain*xxyy*Lab12-2.rtf (where *xx* and *yy* are the numbers assigned to the computers in your student domain), which you will turn in at the end of the lab.
6. Click Close.
7. On Computer*xx*, open the Active Directory Users and Computers console.
8. In the Users container, double-click the Tina O'Dell user object you created in Exercise 12-1.
9. The Tina O'Dell Properties dialog box appears.

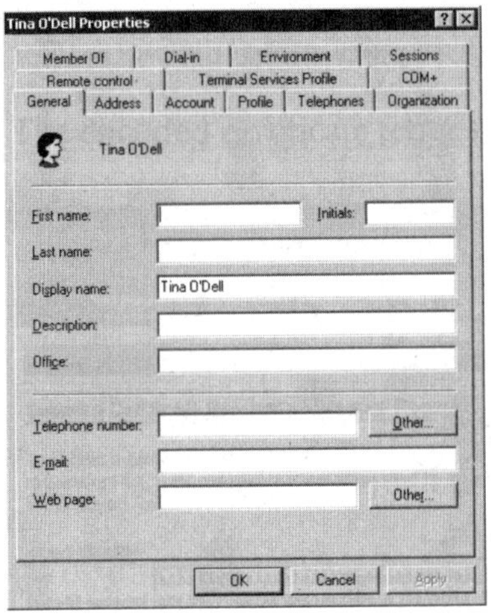

10. Click the Dial-in tab.

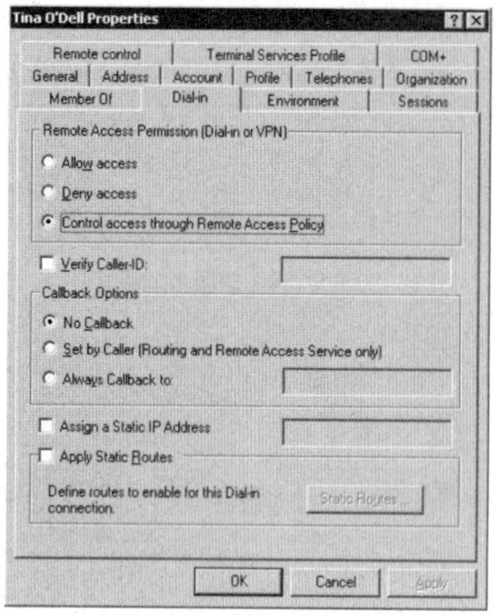

11. In the Remote Access Permission box, select the Allow Access option and click OK.

12. On Computer*yy*, try again to connect to the remote access server.

QUESTION What is the result?

13. On Computer*xx*, in the Routing and Remote Access console, click the Remote Access Clients node in the console tree.

14. In the right pane, double-click the domain*xxyy*\tinao connection.

15. A Status dialog box appears.

16. Take a screen shot (press ALT+PRINT SCREEN) of the Status dialog box and paste it into a WordPad document named Domain*xxyy*Lab12-3.rtf (where *xx* and *yy* are the numbers assigned to the computers in your student domain), which you will turn in at the end of the lab.

17. Click the Disconnect button. Then click Close.

EXERCISE 12-5: CREATING A REMOTE ACCESS POLICY

Estimated completion time: 15 minutes

To provide more granular control over the capabilities of the remote access clients on the Contoso, Ltd., remote access server, you intend to use remote access policies. Now that you have proven that the client can connect to the server, you will create and implement a RAP that controls access to the RRAS server.

1. On Computer*xx*, in the Routing and Remote Access console, click the Remote Access Policies node in the console tree.
2. From the Action menu, select New Remote Access Policy.

   The New Remote Access Policy Wizard appears.

3. Click Next to bypass the Welcome page.

   The Policy Configuration Method page appears.

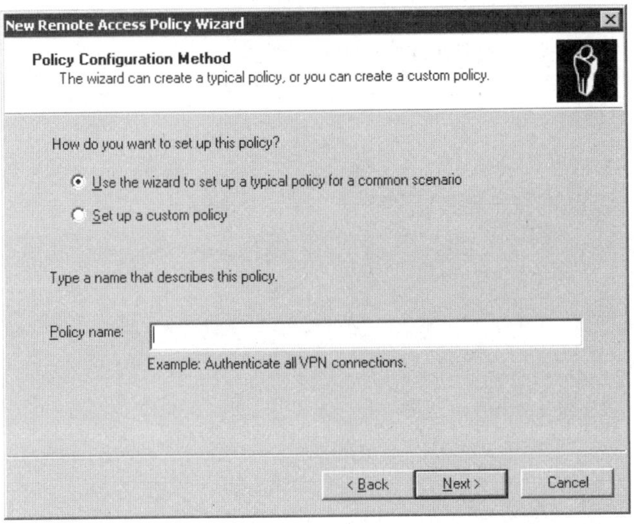

4. In the Policy Name text box, type Remote Users and click Next.

   The Access Method page appears.

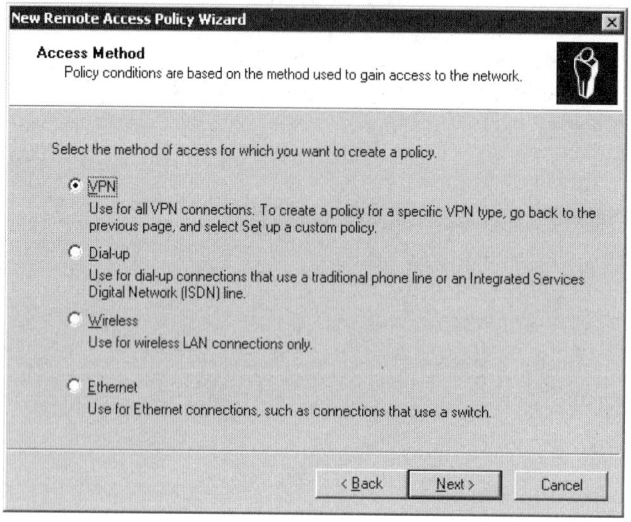

5. Leave the VPN option selected and click Next.

   The User Or Group Access page appears.

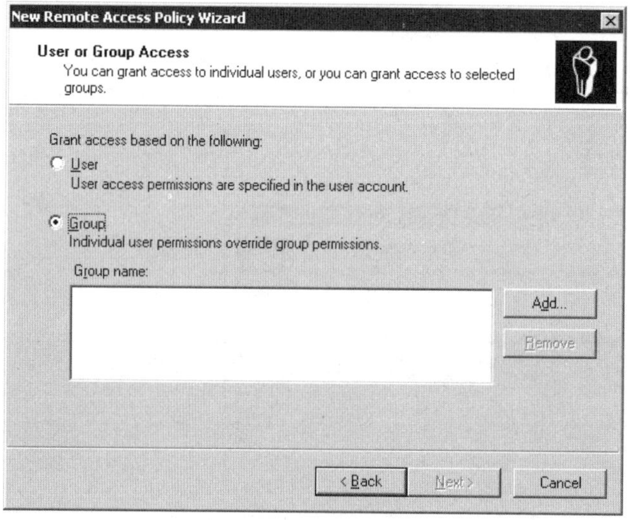

6. With the Group option selected, click Add.

   The Select Groups dialog box appears.

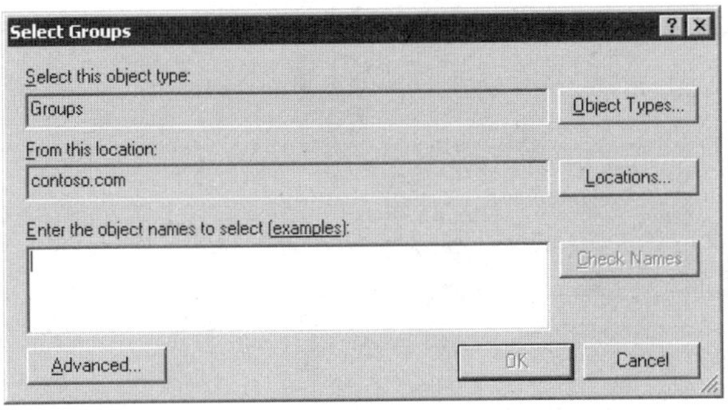

7. In the Enter The Object Names To Select text box, type **Domain*xxyy*\Remote Users** and click OK.
8. The Domain*xxyy*\Remote Users group appears in the Group Name list.

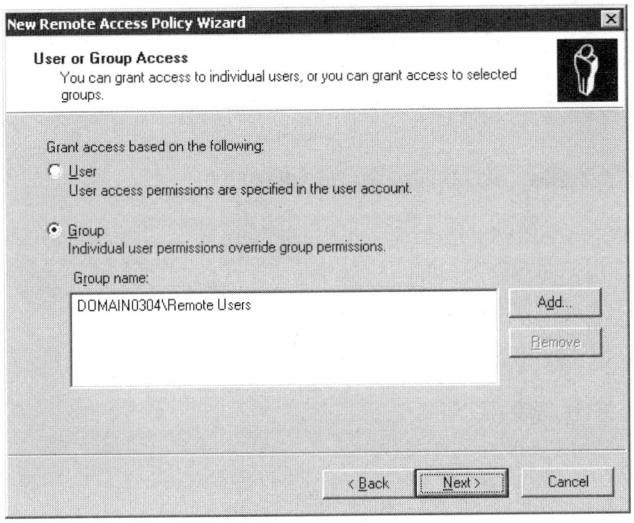

9. Click Next.

   The Authentication Methods page appears.

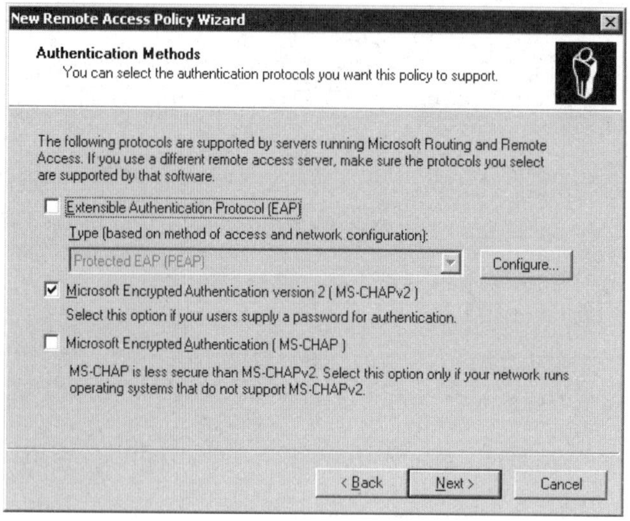

10. Click Next to accept the default settings.

    The Policy Encryption Level page appears.

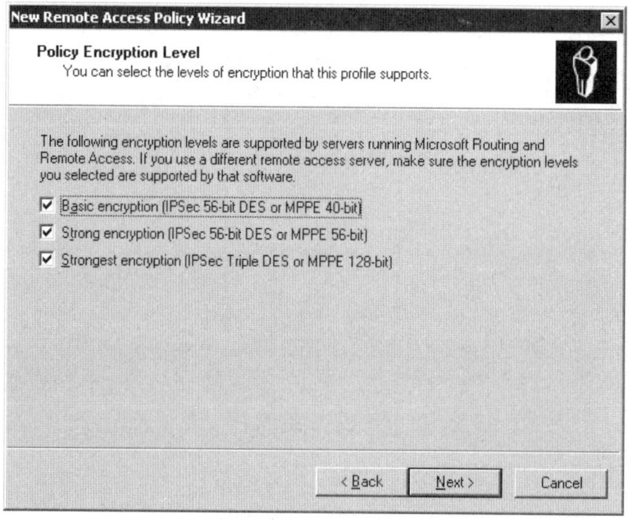

11. Click Next to accept the default settings.

The Completing The New Remote Access Policy Wizard page appears.

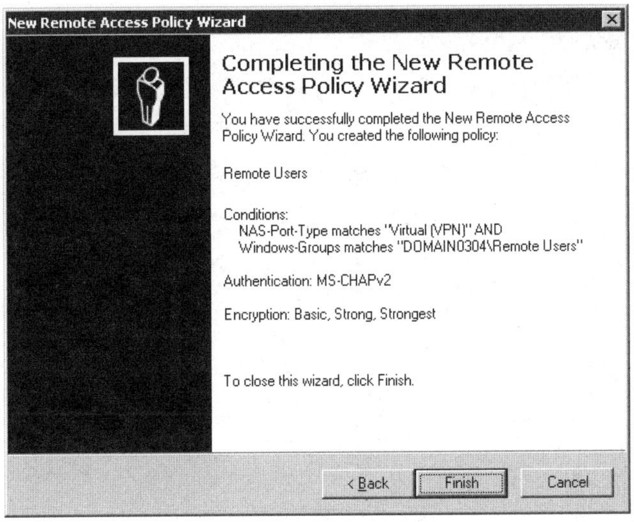

12. Click Finish to complete the wizard.

The New Remote Users RAP appears in the Routing and Remote Access console.

13. In the Active Directory Users and Computers console, open the Tina O'Dell Properties dialog box.

14. On the Dial-in tab, select the Control Access Through Remote Access Policy option and click OK.

15. On Computeryy, attempt to re-establish the connection to the remote access server.

QUESTION *Why is the client unable to connect to the remote access server?*

16. On Computer*xx*, in the Active Directory Users and Computers console, double-click the Remote Users group you created in Exercise 12-1 and, in the Remote Users Properties dialog box, click the Members tab.

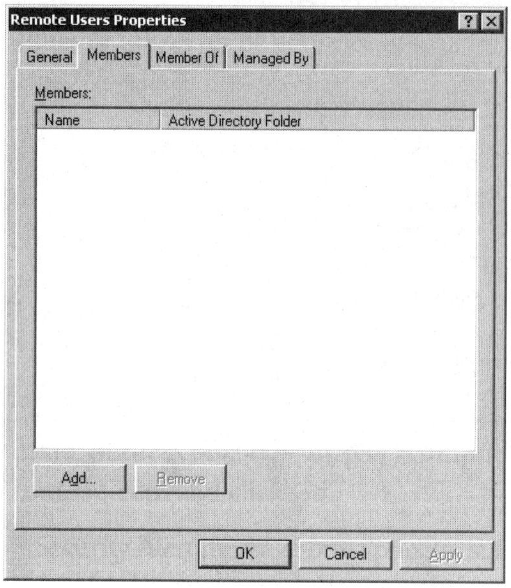

17. Click Add.

    The Select Users, Contacts, Computers, Or Groups dialog box appears.

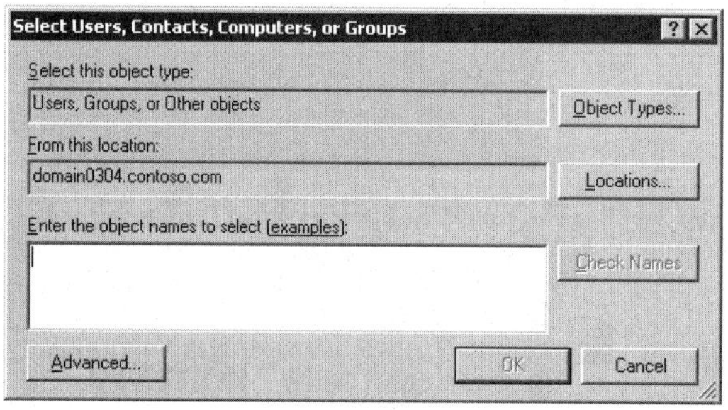

18. In the Enter The Object Names To Select box, type **tinao** and click OK.

    Tina O'Dell is added to the Members list.

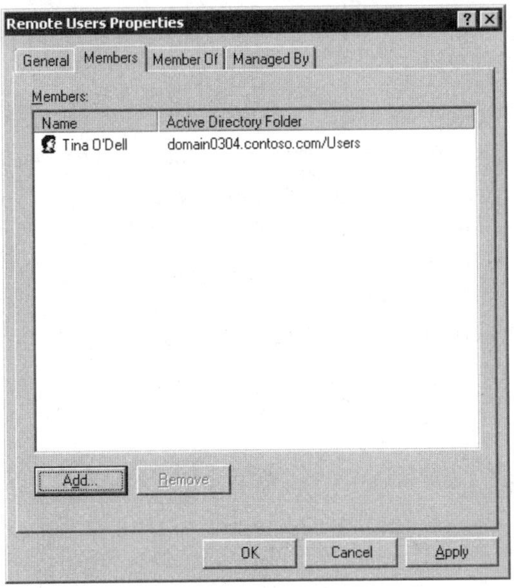

19. Click OK to close the Remote Users Properties dialog box.

20. On Computer*yy*, try again to re-establish the connection to the remote access server.

QUESTION What is the result?

21. In the Network Connections window, right-click the Computer*xx* icon and click Disconnect on the context menu.

22. The client disconnects from the server.

23. Close all windows and log off both computers.

LAB REVIEW QUESTIONS

Estimated completion time: 15 minutes

1. In Exercise 12-2, which tunneling protocol did the VPN client on Computer*yy* use to establish a connection to the remote access server? How can you tell?
2. In Exercise 12-3, what would be the result if you also selected the Use Extensible Authentication Protocol (EAP) in the Advanced Security Settings dialog box on the client computer?
3. In Exercise 12-4, what would be the result if you used the Administrator account to connect to the remote access server instead of the Tina O'Dell account?

LAB CHALLENGE 12-1: CAPTURING REMOTE ACCESS TRAFFIC

Estimated completion time: 30 minutes

The Routing and Remote Access service included with Windows Server 2003 and the remote access client included with all current versions of Windows both support VPN connections using PPTP or L2TP. The object of this challenge is to capture a sample of the network traffic generated when a remote access client connects to a RRAS server using each of these two protocols. To complete the challenge, use Network Monitor on Computer*xx* to capture traffic as you as you connect to RRAS on Computer*xx* with the client on Computer*yy*, using the Tina O'Dell account you created earlier in this lab. Save the captured traffic sample as a file with the name Domain*xxyy*Lab12-4.cap. Then reconfigure the client and the server to use L2TP instead of PPTP and capture a second traffic sample in the same way, giving it the name Domain*xxyy*Lab12-5.cap. Submit the two captured traffic samples to your instructor, along with a write-up of the procedure you used to reconfigure the client and the server.

TROUBLESHOOTING LAB B: IPSEC

Troubleshooting Lab B is a practical application of the knowledge you have acquired from Labs 7 through 12. Your instructor or lab assistant has changed your computer's configuration, causing it to "break." Your task in this lab will be to apply your acquired skills to troubleshoot and resolve the break. Two scenarios are presented that lay out the parameters of the breaks and the conditions that must be met for the scenarios to be resolved. The first break scenario involves IPSec encryption problems and the second break scenario involves IPSec communication problems.

> **NOTE** In this lab you will see the characters *xx* and *yy*. These directions assume that you are working on computers configured in pairs and that each computer has a number. When you see *xx*, substitute the unique number assigned to the lower-numbered computer of the pair. When you see *yy*, substitute the unique number assigned to the higher-numbered computer of the pair. For example, if you are using computers named Computer01 and Computer02:
>
> Computer*xx* = Computer01 = lower-numbered computer
>
> Computer*yy* = Computer02 = higher-numbered computer

> **CAUTION** ***Do not proceed with this lab until you receive guidance from your instructor.*** Your instructor will inform you which break scenario you will be performing (Break Scenario 1 or Break Scenario 2) and which computer to use. Your instructor or lab assistant may also have special instructions. Consult with your instructor before proceeding.

Break Scenario 1

Colin, a colleague of yours in the IP department at Contoso, Ltd., gives you a call because he has a problem with his IPSec systems that has him stumped. Colin has a Microsoft Windows Server 2003 computer on his network that functions as an intranet Web server; the human resources department uses it to provide company employees with information about their health insurance claims that must be kept confidential. The Web server computer is called Computer*yy*, and Computer*xx* is the domain controller for Colin's domain, which is called domain*xxyy*. Colin created an IP security policy designed to encrypt all of the HTTP traffic running to and from the Web server and deployed it throughout his domain. When testing his IPSec deployment by connecting to the Web server on Computer*yy* using Microsoft Internet Explorer on Computer*xx*, Colin can see that the IP security policy was successfully deployed both to the Web server computer and his test client computer. However, when he captures a sample of the traffic on the network, the HTTP packets are not encrypted. Colin would like you to take a look at his IPSec deployment and try to determine what has gone wrong.

As you resolve the problem, fill out the worksheet in the Lab Manual\TroubleshootingLabB folder and include the following information:

- Description of the problem.
- A list of all steps taken to diagnose the problem, even the ones that did not work.
- Description of the exact issue and solution.
- A list of the tools and resources you used to help solve this problem.

Break Scenario 2

Connie is attempting to protect the intranet Web traffic on her local subnet using IPSec. Her Web server is running on a Windows Server 2003 computer called Computer*yy*. Connie has created an IP security policy called Intranet Web Security and deployed it to the entire domain (domain*xxyy*) using the Default Domain Security Settings console on Computer*xx*. However, the filter list for the policy calls for only the traffic running between the Web server and the rest of the local subnet to be protected. Upon testing her configuration by connecting to the Web server from another computer (Computer*xx*), Connie discovered that although communications with the Web server occur, they are not protected by IPSec. Connie would like you to examine her IPSec configuration and help her determine why her Web traffic is not being protected.

As you resolve the problem, fill out the worksheet in the Lab Manual\TroubleshootingLabB folder and include the following information:

- Description of the problem.
- A list of all steps taken to diagnose the problem, even the ones that did not work.
- Description of the exact issue and solution.
- A list the tools and resources you used to help solve this problem.